THE KING'S PLEASURE

The King's Pleasure

NORAH LOFTS

DOUBLEDAY & COMPANY, INC.
GARDEN CITY, NEW YORK

Lines from "A Ballad for Katherine of Aragon" from UNION STREET, by Charles Causley. Reprinted by permission of Houghton Mifflin Company and David Higham Associates, Ltd.

For
JULIET O'HEA
who shares Katharine's faith,
kindliness, and determination.

THE KING'S PLEASURE

A BALLAD FOR KATHARINE OF ARAGON

(From UNION STREET by Charles Causley)

The Queen of Castile has a daughter
Who won't come home again
She lies in the grey cathedral
Under the arms of Spain
O the Queen of Castile has a daughter
Torn out by the roots
Her lovely breast in a cold stone chest
Under the farmers' boots.

1

Mules, everybody agreed, were more sure-footed, so Isabella of Spain rode on a mule, her heavily pregnant body wrapped in a rain-repellent leather cloak, on her head a hood of the same material, her feet encased in a pair of boots similar to those worn by foot soldiers. The winter rains had set in and the roads which through the long hot summer had been ankle-deep in dust were now over hoof deep in mud, sticky as glue. Every time the mule put a foot down there was a squelching sound, every time it lifted one there was a plop. Sometimes, under the smooth shining surface of the mud, there was a dip; then the mule stumbled, recovered itself with a jerk and a heave and plodded on: sometimes, under a mere skim of mud there was a boulder, thrown in to fill a hole visible last summer; striking one of these the mule stumbled again; recovered and plodded on. Each time this happened Isabella felt like a woman holding a basketful of eggs riding on a seesaw; after each jolt the question, All right? All well? Yes, thanks be to God, no harm done. The child, so soon to be born, would be her tenth; four were alive, thank God; few mothers had been so blessed; but with every stumble and jolt she knew a small fear—not here, please God, not in the open, in the rain. Alcalá de Henares is not so far away; the road is bad, the going slow, but please, I beseech thee, let me arrive, settle into the place prepared for me and there let the child be born.

She was Queen; she could have ridden comfortably in a litter slung between two mules, or carried on the shoulders of willing men, but to do so would have been a concession to female weakness, and she scorned it. God had called her to take a man's place in the world, and handicapped as she had been by her female body, she had taken that place, filled it adequately, done as much as, or more than, any man could have done—all by the help of God. She must not weaken now.

In everything Isabella could see the hand of God, working slowly, sometimes obscurely but to a sure end. Because there was no male heir she had become Queen of Castile, and she had married Ferdinand of Aragon, thus uniting the two kingdoms and making them strong enough to attempt to drive out the Moors who had occupied the south of the Iberian peninsula for six hundred years. She did not deceive herself; Ferdinand might look upon the campaign, now in its fifth year, as a means to increase his own power; for her it was a Crusade, Christian against infidel, as urgent and important as any Crusade waged centuries earlier to free the Holy Land. For Isabella, Spain was holy land and to wage the war of freedom she had ridden, slept, eaten, suffered and endured alongside her army, showing fortitude in the face of hardship and in defeat a certain grim cheerfulness which communicated itself to the men.

The army, with one of its hardest and most successful campaigns behind it, was moving into winter quarters, making on this drear day for the bleak upland town of Alcalá de Henares, where there was a palace of a sort. It was a comfortless place, ancient, ill-heated and in poor repair; its owner, the Bishop of Toledo, used it only once a year when he made his visitation, and he took good care that this should be neither in winter nor in summer, but in late spring or early autumn when, for a brief period the weather was tolerable. He was always preceded by a baggage train, laden with hangings and cushions and soft feather bedding, silverware and little luxuries in the way of food. The Queen of Castile could have taken similar precautions, but she never did. The horses, mules and donkeys in her train were laden enough without carting a lot of useless gear from place to place. Even her personal luggage was kept to the minimum; with her always were her suit of armour, her riding clothes, three changes of linen and two dresses, one plain and simple made of Flemish cloth, the other very fine, a rich reddish purple silk, so boned and padded and embroidered that it was almost as stiff as armour. Both were old; she had other things to do with her money than to buy fripperies. Yet she was an elegant woman, with narrow feet and delicate hands, white and well kept; her hair, once golden, now silver-gilt, was washed every other Monday, even when, as often happened, Monday had seen fighting renewed. She had a fastidious nose and in her youth had used and liked a perfume distilled from roses; but the trick of making it was a secret, brought to Spain by the Moors when they came out of the east and as soon as she knew her destiny she had abandoned its use, making do with the simpler preparation made from crushed lavender, native to Spain.

On this day her few clothes, her few toilet necessities were all contained in a brassbound hide box, which also held everything that a baby might need. The enforced parsimony was evident there, too. For the new baby nothing new. The baby clothes had served many times already; for Isabella, Juan, Joanna and Maria and babies who had died young; well washed and bleached by the summer sun in the south, they would serve again for the child who would, God willing, be born in the Bishop's palace at Alcalá de Henares. Not in the rain and the mud, the birth precipitated by a fall.

Isabella hoped for another son. The one she had already, Juan, had survived the danger period of infancy and first youth and was now seven years old, healthy, intelligent, charming, God be thanked; but he was only one life, only one heir; life was so full of threats; another boy would be a kind of security; and if this child were a boy, and if Juan lived, the younger one could become a cleric—perhaps even Pope.

Jerking along, in increasing discomfort, the leather cloak growing heavier and then porous so that finally the wetness seeped through to her skin, Isabella cheered herself with thoughts of the future. Juan King of a united Spain, with not a Moor left alive in it; Carlos—for so she would name this child, should it be a boy, on the Papal throne, and all her daughters married to kings, linking Spain, so long isolated, to Europe, carrying their Spanish piety and good manners with them.

To her second son, if God so favoured her, she would say, "You were almost born in a saddle." She would not say that if this child were a girl. She had learned from a long, hard experience what turns of speech appealed to men and what to women. She had been compelled to speak both languages and could switch from one to the other without conscious thought. When her husband, Ferdinand, who had been at the rear of the long train, urging on the laggards, brought his horse alongside her mule and asked how she did, she said:

"Mules are somewhat overrated; but at least I am still in one piece."

He laughed. A woman would have been more sympathetic, would have said things like "Poor lady!" or "How courageous you are, madam." *Weakening* words. The sort that she had resisted for years.

Ferdinand said, "Not long now. That fellow who broke his ankle and was heaved up on top of one of the baggage wagons just told me that he could see the roofs. Then the road dipped and he lost sight of them again, but in less than an hour we should be there."

They were there in less than an hour. The Bishop's palace was as stark, as bare as she remembered it; but it was a suitable place for the birth of a child who, if a boy, would be obliged to subjugate the flesh, at least for a time, and if a girl would be the fourth daughter, with all the really advantageous marriages made before it was her turn, and might become a nun.

Freed of the mule's movement and relieved of her sodden clothes and heavy boots, the Queen felt better and derided herself for her fears of a somewhat premature delivery. She proceeded in her usual, orderly way, moving slowly but purposely. First a visit to the little chapel, ill-lit and cold as a tomb, where she knelt and thanked God that the journey had been completed without mishap save for a broken ankle and one wagon wheel smashed; she prayed that God would forgive her for the lack of complete faith that had made her fears possible.

Then to more mundane matters. First of all—before the children, even, the need to make certain that every man would sleep under cover in this night of wind and rain.

The Bishop's palace, like every other place where Isabella had stayed in the last four years, was virtually a barracks, only a few private rooms reserved for the Royal Family and its immediate entourage; but even so, and with every outbuilding brought into service, it was still necessary to find outside billets for a great number of soldiers, and a senior officer had been sent on ahead to make arrangements. The Queen knew how ordinary people felt about having soldiers thrust upon them, but it was a necessity in winter and it was the turn of the people up here in the northwest to assume their part of the burden; the towns and villages to the south, near the fighting front, had stripped themselves to keep the army fed during spring and summer; that was what made these long winter journeys an essential part of the year's routine. Isabella had done her best to instil a crusading spirit into her army; men were forbidden to loot or to meddle with respectable females; they knew that their Queen disapproved of drunkenness and of the use of foul language. On the whole her rules and her wishes were regarded, but there were exceptions which distressed her less than might have been supposed; it was an army of men, not of monks, that she had gathered and she was shrewd enough to realise that the men who sometimes broke rules were not necessarily the worst soldiers.

"Every man has a roof over his head?" she asked.

"Yes, your Grace." The officer added—for unless the queen was in childbed tomorrow, she would be out and about, inspecting and criticising, and he did not want his efforts underrated: "Of a sort. It was not easy. Since last year a dozen houses at least have become untenanted and have fallen into total disrepair; and at the lower end of the town there is a sickness."

"Plague?" Isabella asked sharply, prepared to move on tomorrow if this were so. Of all diseases the plague was most to be dreaded; even the bodies of the dead emitted a fatal contagion.

"No, madam. I was not myself sure, but the surgeon-in-chief whom I consulted as soon as he arrived, assures me that it is not. The sick are fevered, restless and raving, but they show no sign of plague. I ordered the area to be cordoned off and placed out of bounds. It contains several wineshops and . . . other places."

"You did well," she said. She knew what he meant by other places. Again regrettable, but what could one do? Take an ordinary man away from his family, deprive him of most of life's comfort, expose him to the constant danger of death, and could you blame him for snatching at a passing pleasure? You could not. Nor were the women themselves, the rather pathetic camp followers or the homebound ones who welcomed an army's arrival in their town, much to be blamed. They were so *poor*. The poverty of her people was a matter of great concern to Isabella; she could distinguish between poverty accepted as a way of life, for the glory of God, by certain religious orders, and poverty inflicted by circumstance. Over the greater part of Castile, and of Aragon, the soil was poor and the climate inclement, veering between too-cold winters and too-hot-and-dry summers. North of the Pyrénées was France, very fertile and rich, and farther north still England where green grass was plentiful all the year round and there were—it was said—more sheep than people. The wool of these sheep was shipped to Flanders where it was made into cloth, a saleable commodity. In this lucrative two-way trade Spain could take no part. It was a pity, but it was a situation which would not last forever. Next year, please God, the rich Moorish provinces would be restored to Spain; minerals, vineyards, orange and lemon groves . . . And at the very back of her mind there was another thought.

There was a Genoese sailor, a man called Christopher Columbus, wandering about the courts of Europe, searching for a patron who would fit out an expedition to enable him to prove his contention that the world was a globe, not a flat surface and that by travelling towards the west he could reach the rich, fabulous world of the Indies whence came by slow, expensive, overland route or by Portuguese caravel things like sugar and cloves and cinnamon and ginger and precious stones. It sounded a fantastic idea, but no more fantastic than that a woman should be Queen of Castile in her own right and called to wage the last Crusade. And win it. She meant to, if she lived. She visualised the last Moorish King driven out of Granada, fleeing back to Africa, where the Moors belonged; she visualised herself just able to afford this westward voyage which might conceivably end in the East and bring the wealth of the Indies, where even kitchen utensils were—they said—made of silver and gold, under the control of Spain. To God nothing was impossible.

The matter of the soldiers' comfort dealt with—not without reason they regarded her as The Mother, and so referred to her—she turned her attention to those to whom she was actually mother. They were, so far as the building and its amenities allowed, comfortably installed. There was the Infanta Isabella, fifteen years old, very solemn and, even Isabella admitted, pompous; an admirable girl in a way, but once she had so exasperated her mother that Isabella had said, "You talk to me as though you were my mother-in-law!" The younger Isabella's destiny was settled; she would be Queen of Portugal, and her solemnity, pomposity and complete lack of humour would make her a most excellent queen; she had been reared and educated for the position. Isabella the Queen of Castile had always been aware of her own faulty education—she had become Queen through the premature death of her stepbrother and been obliged to learn Latin, the language in which all legal and diplomatic matters were phrased, in a hurried three weeks. As a result she had paid particular attention to her children's education.

Juan, as the heir, already had his own establishment, a separate little court for which Isabella had lain down the rules and which, even on journeys like this one, ran smoothly. All well, Isabella thought, and moved on to the more cramped quarters where her two younger daughters and their attendants were housed. Maria, the baby of the family until the new one came, was settling down to sleep, almost too drowsy to be aware of her mother's presence; Joanna, who was six, was giving trouble; not for the first time. She had rejected her supper and now refused to go to bed.

Isabella endeavoured to be an impartial mother and outwardly achieved this aim, but Joanna, so beautiful, so precocious and so strange, was her favourite daughter, almost as much loved as the only son. Deep concern and apprehension lay at the root of this preference. It was impossible for Isabella to look upon her second daughter and not remember that her own mother had been mad and had passed the last years of her life under restraint. But I am sane, she told herself whenever that memory struck; and then immediately she would think of things like left-handedness, stammering, a colouring of eyes or hair skipping one generation. To any of her other children, on this evening she would have administered a rebuke, an admonition; to Joanna she said:

"Come here and tell me what is the matter."

She sat herself on a hard wooden stool and would have taken Joanna on to her lap—but she had no lap these days, so instead she put her arm around the child and pulled her close, held her firmly, aware of vibrating tremor.

"We have all had a hard day," she said in her calm, low voice. "It is unkind of you, Joanna, to make things more difficult."

"I know. I am sorry."

"Then why do you do it?"

"It is a bad place, Mother. Not a place to eat and sleep in. A place to go away from. Could we not go away? Now."

"It is cold, and not very comfortable," Isabella said. "But it is better than being out in the night and the rain. I think it is a good place, Joanna. I was very glad to arrive here. I shall eat my supper and go to my bed and be grateful to God for the food and the resting place. You should do the same. Come along now, eat just a little and then go to bed like my good, sensible little girl."

"I can't," Joanna said with a violent shudder. "Not here."

"Why not?"

"Because of the coffin."

"What coffin?"

"The brown one."

Despite all her faith, despite her practical and rational mind, Isabella felt a little superstitious shiver. She had long ago, before she bore her first child, given orders that no money should be wasted on her funeral, should she die. Masses for her soul, yes, they must be asked for, paid for, but no mummers, no black plumes; and a simple wooden casket, such as every peasant somehow managed to afford. It would be brown.

More to herself than to Joanna she said:

"This is nonsense! You were so tired that you fell asleep on your feet and dreamed. Making such a fuss about nothing, about a dream! And if you are not hungry, I am," she said, fighting off fear as she had done so many times before: she was thirty-four years old; women who did not die in their early child-bearing years often did later on, in their thirties; and the last months had been strenuous, the last ride not one that a woman so far advanced in pregnancy should have attempted. But if she died, she died; God ruled; it might not be His wish that she should live and drive the Moors from Granada and send the Genoese sailor on his westward voyage. It was all in God's hands and she must leave it there. What was left to her own mere human agency was to see that this distressed child ate something and went to bed.

"Come," she said, heaving her laden body up; "you can share my supper if you promise, afterwards, to go straight to bed."

Always the same, the lady governess thought sourly; the normal child, sound in mind and wind and limb was taken for granted, the less normal one pampered and spoiled.

Isabella, watching the child eat and become restored, even merry, thought about life and death, soldiers, children, the vast responsibility which lay upon a woman called upon to play a man's part in the world without owning a man's impregnable body. Tonight, tomorrow or perhaps the next day, she and the task she had to set herself, might end in the bloody and painful business of giving birth. But if so—the brown coffin—all the will of God, not be questioned or disputed.

2

The baby was born on December 16th and was a girl. Isabella was disappointed that the dynasty had not been reinforced by the birth of another prince, but since God in His infinite wisdom had given a daughter instead of a son, she accepted His decision with cheerfulness.

Her moment's superstitious fear, which Joanna's mention of a brown coffin had evoked, was not in the least justified; it was a comparatively easy birth; the baby throve and in a short time Isabella was on her feet again, resuming the duties of Queen, army commandant and mother. But while she lay in bed, recovering, she had time to think and some of her thoughts centred about Joanna who, at six, should now be outgrowing childish fancies. Princesses were born to a definite destiny, that of making marriages which bolstered political alliances and their characters must be trained for the purpose; to allow a king's daughter to grow up fanciful, wilful and unpredictable could make trouble in the future and was certainly not kind. Princesses must be stolid, placid, adaptable. Joanna might be steadied by responsibility; so, from the first, Isabella placed upon her some of the duties of caring for the new baby. "If she cries, you must try to soothe her. When she is older you must amuse her. You must always think of her welfare and comfort before your own." She intended the duties to be merely nominal, a means of occupying Joanna's attention, but Joanna, in whom there was a capacity for boundless, blind devotion, took them seriously and sometimes annoyed both ladies-in-waiting and nursemaids by her officiousness; sometimes there were complaints and appeals to the Queen who could always point out that in general Joanna's behaviour had greatly improved and that while she was fussing around the baby nobody else needed to.

Isabella had had an English grandmother, Katharine of Lancaster, and for her she named her fourth daughter; an act of sentiment rather than policy; England and connections with England—except in the way of trade—were worthless now. The Wars of the Roses had ravaged the country and decimated its nobility, and since August the country had been ruled by an upstart Welshman whose only claim to the throne was through his great-grandfather, a bastard later legitimised but excluded from inheriting the crown. There were men with better claims, there were pretenders and it seemed highly unlikely that Henry Tudor would be King of England for long. When Isabella, taking her brief rest, looked at her fourth daughter and speculated about her future she never once visualised her as Queen of turbulent England; there were steadier thrones. And in her heart Isabella still felt that this child, born in the very middle of a Catholic Crusade, might show a vocation for the religious life. Such things must be left to God; what must not be left to God, since He must not be bothered with such petty details, was the matter of rehousing twenty men lodged in a barn that had lost its roof in a recent storm; dealing with a soldier accused of rape, the non-delivery of a consignment of grain, promised from nearby Aragon, Ferdinand's own Kingdom. Tact must be exercised there; Ferdinand was still very Aragonese in his thinking; Castile was his because he had married her, Queen of Castile, but Aragon was not hers, even to criticise. Perhaps, when she was up and about again and capable of looking into the matter closely she could find, somewhere involved, a Jew who could be made culpable. Jews had no nationality; they could be blamed with impunity . . . There were dozens of such things to be seen to.

Katharine, as she emerged from baby to identifiable child, was, Isabella rejoiced to see, going to be pretty; not beautiful like Joanna who had the fragile, vulnerable loveliness of a flower, but pretty; she had clear large eyes, grey, tinged with

green, her eyebrows were thin and arched, her hair, darkening
from childish silver-gilt became brown, with a russet red shade
in it, her complexion was fair and unblemished and she had
inherited her mother's grace, an ability to look elegant without
extraneous trimmings. Her temperament was as satisfactory as
her appearance; less stolid than the Infanta's or Maria's, less
volatile than Joanna's.

For Katharine, making every day another step out of baby-
hood into ordinary life, the centre and pivot of her life was, for
years, Joanna, slavishly devoted so far as physical matters were
concerned; she would change plates if her portion of any dish
seemed preferable to that given to Katharine; for Katharine
always the rosiest apple, the juiciest orange. From Joanna,
Katharine received her first lessons, plodding away to learn
things which Joanna had mastered in an hour. "You are *slow*,"
Joanna sometimes said impatiently and Katharine came to realise that, compared with Joanna whose acceptance or rejectance
of everything was instant, she was indeed slow. "But I never
forget anything," she said, not defensively, but humbly—offering her good memory as a sop.

The lessons, the lives, the food they ate, the beds they slept
in were all subjected to the progress of the war. Isabella, intent
to do her duty by everyone, to oversee everything, dragged her
family along behind the army. The war went on; there were
tedious journeys, uncomfortable lodgings, scanty meals. Always
Joanna was there, presiding over Katharine's destiny not like a
mother—Mother was waging war on the Moors—but like the
good fairy in the stories which Joanna would tell on the long
jogging journeys. Joanna was a wonderful storyteller, though
sometimes her tales had a frightening element in them that
would have scratched Katharine's nerves and made her afraid
of the dark, of thunder and several other things but for the fact
that Joanna herself seemed so fearless, and Joanna was always
there.

The shocking fact that Joanna would not always be there
broke upon Katharine on what was, apart from this revelation,
a gay and glorious occasion, their sister Isabella's betrothal to

Alfonso of Portugal. Isabella was so much their senior, and so
sedate that she had played little part in their lives; but she had
always been there, and soon she would not be; she would go to
live in Portugal.

"You won't ever get married and go away, will you?"
Katharine asked anxiously.

"Of course I shall," Joanna said with a rapt look. "I shall live
in Burgundy, and in Brussels and Vienna. I'm looking . . ." she
broke off, seeing Katharine's face. "Not yet," she said hastily.
"Years and years . . ." But Katharine was facing for the first
time in her life the truth that no human relationship is permanent; she was already, in her mind, bereaved; so she wept with
the noisy abandon of a five-year-old. Doña Elvira said sternly,
"What behaviour! Tears on such a day bring ill luck to the
bride." Katharine choked and blinked.

"Joanna, will you have me to live with you whenever you
go?"

"I couldn't. You'll be married yourself. You'll have to live in
England. In London." That sounded somewhat meagre after
Burgundy, Brussels and Vienna, so Joanna ferreted about in
her mind and produced another place name. "And Windsor, I
think."

"Oh. Oh dear. What a pity."

"Yes, it is," said Joanna, worldly wise at eleven years old.
"But, you see, there are four of us and you are the youngest . . ." That again sounded condescending, so she added,
"Your husband has a nice name though—Arthur; like the King
in the book; the one with the Round Table and all the brave
knights." She had read the story in a battered manuscript from
her mother's library and retold the tales, much simplified. Not
that this English Arthur would be much like the one in the
legend; for one thing he was a year younger than Katharine
and said to be delicate and he had no breeding. Joanna had a
sharp ear for gossip and had mastered the art of being un-
obtrusive if she chose; things had been said in her presence
because she was not noticed or because she was regarded as too
young to comprehend. She knew that the King, her father, had

not much wanted a marriage alliance with England, and had rejected the first advances; then for some reason that she did not understand, all political, to do with France and Italy, he had changed his mind. It seemed that the King of England had been offended by the rebuffs and now demanded, with Katharine, a dowry that Mother said was extortionate, but admitted must be paid. It could be afforded once Granada was conquered and the war over. It could be the more easily afforded because Joanna herself needed no dowry at all. The Emperor Maximilian planned to marry his daughter Margaret to Juan, at the same time as he married his son, Philip, to Joanna. So there had been a mutual abandonment of dowries. Joanna knew that hers would be the most splendid match of them all and she felt sorry for Katharine who would have to live in a small island where, when it was not raining it was foggy.

"And you'll be rich," she said, still intent upon comforting Katharine. "The King of England is very rich and very, very mean. When he dies Arthur will inherit a great fortune."

She had no very clear idea of what a great fortune meant, and Katharine who was never to have any financial sense at all, understood even less. But it sounded nice, and young as they were, both little girls—like everyone else closely connected with Queen Isabella—knew what it meant to be poor. War was a costly business; cannon and cannon balls and chain shot, and gunpowder and scaling ladders and a hundred other things must come before new dresses or shoes.

"If I am to be rich," Katharine said, "I shall buy some horses, and come to visit you."

"I will visit you, too. Though I shall not be rich. My father-in-law squanders and borrows and does not repay. Mother said so. But if I can get a horse I will come."

It was typical of their upbringing that horses should be almost a standard of currency. They had spent more than one night in a wagon from which the horses had been unhitched in order to be harnessed to a gun carriage; they had seen knights in armour made temporarily as useless as tortoises because their horses had been killed. They had heard it said of a beleaguered city— And now they are eating their horses! A good sign; soon that city would yield.

War with its privations, its horrid sights, its occasional glories, its setbacks, was for years their natural environment because Isabella was conscious of her duty as warrior and as mother. She never willingly allowed them to be in danger; she had them housed and fed as well as she could and gave them as much attention as possible. But she was engaged in what she regarded as a Holy War and that came first.

Lodged behind the lines, in places to which any man who might be expected to survive in order to fight on another day was brought and roughly cared for, the children became accustomed to the sight of maimed men, and dying men. The Moors had devices as yet unknown to the west. One of them was a thing no bigger than a pear, with a fuse of tow; this when thrown exploded and stuck to the object against which it exploded. A knight in armour, hit by one of these things, could be roasted alive; or, hacked out in time, be horribly scarred. And there were men with hands and arms lopped off, men holding their bowels in their hands against the gaping stomach wounds. There were dead men too.

Katharine was still a child when she realised what a dead man meant. She had never seen Alfonso of Portugal, but he died, and Isabella came back to Spain, all muffled in black, pale and weeping.

Mother said, "You must all be kind to Isabella; she has suffered a great loss."

Joanna said, "To lose a husband must be the worst thing . . ."

Katharine thought: And every dead man we have seen carried past meant as much to some woman . . .

It was a thought to put away, prickling and uncomfortable and not to be shared. Who would understand?

There was another thought, running alongside, more personal and immediate.

"Joanna, I cried that day in Seville and Doña Elvira said tears brought ill luck to the bride. Am I responsible for this?"

"How could you be, stupid one? Doña Elvira has a sharp tongue. Had you laughed she might have said the same. Men die when God wills. And you need not grieve for Isabella. I will tell you, but it is secret. You must not say a word. Promise. She is to have another husband. Alfonso's cousin, Manoel, who is now King of Portugal. *She* says she would sooner be a nun, but Mother thinks that by the time the arrangements are completed, she will have come to her senses."

But what about all the other dead men and the women who wept?

There was little time for such thought. Granada fell, and Katharine stood, in her best dress, holding Joanna's hand and watched the last Moors ride, defeated, out of the palace-fortress of the Alhambra. And when the Te Deum had been sung in the building, only this day snatched back from Allah and Mohomet, they had the whole, fabulous fairy tale place to explore. Flowers and fountains, marble floors, terraces. A different and very wonderful world.

And then, in no time at all, another wonderful and amazing thing; a visit to Barcelona to welcome home the Genoese sailor, Christopher Columbus, whom Mother, despite all her other commitments had furnished out with three little ships so that he could go out and test his theory that the world was a globe and that by going west he could reach the east, the Indies.

"Nobody else in the whole of Europe," Joanna said, gripping Katharine's hand hard, "would give him a hearing, leave alone a ducat. Mother did. And she was right."

So it seemed; the swaggering little Admiral believed that he had proved his theory; he had brought back specimens of strange birds and beasts, most of them stuffed, but monkeys and parrots still alive, and six wild brown Indians, painted and clad in feathers. Of the great wealth in gold and silver of the East he brought on this trip only sample quantities; but it was there. Spain would one day be as rich as Portugal; and since Spanish ships would sail to the west, while the Portuguese held to the old sea road around the tip of Africa, the friendliness between the countries would not be impaired.

Now that the main war was over—though the conquered province was far from completely subdued—a more settled and normal way of life was possible and Isabella brought attention to bear upon her daughters' education. They were more thoroughly instructed in academic subjects than most princesses of the time, and they must also learn domestic skills, spinning, weaving, plain sewing. Then there were the social arts, singing, dancing, playing the lute, doing fine embroidery, mastering the rules of precedence and etiquette, learning how to behave with grace and dignity even in trying circumstances. Joanna would be Empress one day, and Katharine Queen of England. They must be fitted for their high positions. For Maria no definite plans had yet been made, but she, too, must be ready for the position to which God would undoubtedly call her.

3

With so much to learn and so much happening, time went all too fast and the thing which Katharine so dreaded, the parting with Joanna, came about. Joanna sailed away to Flanders to marry Philip. She went gladly, already romantically in love with the young man so well-favoured that he was called Philip the Handsome.

Katharine said gloomily, "You are glad to go. Leaving me does not make you sad at all. The thought of parting from you breaks my heart."

"Only because you are too young to understand. You will, in time. When you are fourteen, fifteen. Sisters love each other and hold one another dear, but that is not enough. Men and women belong together. Besides, there will be the visits to look forward to. Where is that map? Look, when I am in Flanders and you are in England, we shall be close." She pointed to the seemingly negligible stretch of water.

"Mother never has time to go visiting."

"Mother is different."

Mother was now busy with the expulsion of all Jews from Spain; with preparations for Juan's wedding to Margaret of Flanders who was to set out at about that same time as Joanna left; and with arrangements for the widowed Isabella to marry Manoel of Portugal. But she had time to notice Katharine's glum looks, and as for everything, a remedy to suggest.

"There is no need to go about with that melancholy air. You will still have Maria." The very close association between Joanna and Katharine had left Maria somewhat isolated, a fact which, when Isabella had time to notice it, had drawn admonitions. It was true that Maria was a self-contained child, inclined to be dull, but being always left out of things did not improve matters. "What is more, you will soon have another sister, Margaret. She may be homesick at first and our ways may seem strange to her. You must behave to her as you wish Margaret Tudor to behave to you when you go to England."

It was sound, sensible advice and kindly meant but Katharine spurned it. It simply showed how little grown-ups understood. For one thing nobody could ever take Joanna's place; and for another, if she made a close bond with Margaret there would be another wrench when she herself went to England. She would try to be kind to Margaret, to take a little more notice of Maria, and naturally she would continue to love her mother. But when she thought the matter over she decided that she would never wholeheartedly love anyone again until she was married. Men and women, as Joanna said, belonged together, and the husband-and-wife relationship seemed the only safe and durable one.

There was evidence of this before her eyes. Few people could be less fundamentally alike than her father and mother and sharp disputes between them were frequent. Partly this was the result of circumstance; it was all too easy for Father to accuse Mother of favouring Castile and all things Castilian and Mother to retort that she could say the same about him and his Aragonese. Yet all differences seemed to blow over; they continued to work together and plan together and as far as their various duties allowed, to be together. That was the kind of link with another human being which she craved; and she hoped that she would find it with Arthur Tudor.

Margaret arrived; she was pretty enough and gay—Mother said giddy—but with a gaiety quite different from Joanna's. She had not, by Spanish standards, been well-brought up and seemed not to mind; she made no secret of the fact that she thought the Spanish Court old-fashioned and dull and pompous. She decried even the Spanish dresses, complaining that they made it impossible to move one's arms. "And is it necessary to move one's arms? One is not expected to go hay-making in a satin gown," Isabella said coldly.

"When I am Queen I shall alter everything," Margaret said to Katharine. That sounded rather shocking. And on another day, Margaret said something even worse. "The Queen, your mother, can afford to behave as though she had no legs. She can throw off these pompous rules whenever she is tired of them. She has only to start a war and she can dress like a man and enjoy a man's freedom."

"The Queen, my mother, has never started a war in her life," Katharine said fiercely. "But, once involved she has never lost one."

Since that could not be said of Margaret's father, the Emperor, the argument ended there. Yet, despite the fact that there was no great fondness between them, Margaret, indirectly, influenced Katharine in a way that possibly shaped her whole life.

The young couple had been married only a short time when preparations were made for the journey to Alcantara where Isabella was for the second time, to cross the border into Portugal. Katharine was to go with her father and mother, and two days before they were due to start she developed a rash. Smallpox, everybody said, except Mother, who, taking a look said, "Nonsense. She has eaten something that disagreed with her." Then, because everyone else seemed dubious and frightened, Katharine was wrapped in a blanket and carried into Isabella's bedroom and put on a couch, given a long drink of goat's milk, and presently fell asleep.

She woke to the sound of voices; Father and Mother in argument; one almost always knew because in dispute Father's voice grew shrill and sharp, Mother's deep and gruff.

"Don't say nonsense to me," Father said. "It is fact. Look at peasants, scraping and saving to get married at thirty, or soldiers who have to weather four or five campaigns. What they do in bed never hurts them; the young of the rich often die within a year or two."

"Give me one example."

"I could give a dozen. They're said to die of other ills; but the truth is they've spent their vital forces and so fall easy prey. You'd be well advised to bring the girl to Alcantara and give him a rest."

"They would not agree to be parted."

"They'd obey a direct order. You could say you wanted Margaret as part of Isabella's train. Promise her half a dozen new dresses."

"Whom God hath joined let no man put asunder."

"Give me patience! Who spoke of sundering them? All I say is, give him a rest. They're young and she's an insatiable bitch. He's thinner and paler and his cough is worse."

"Then the doctors must examine him. And also give their opinion upon the other matter."

"Is that not what I began by saying? Sometimes . . . You are supposed to be an intelligent woman . . . I said, did I not, that Dr. de La Sa told me that in his opinion the marriage should not have been consummated for a year."

"In less than a year I hope there will be a child."

"There may well be. A child without a father."

"Nonsense."

"Will you not say nonsense to me? I am not one of your mercenaries. I am your husband."

"You should remember that more often."

Even inside the sheltering blanket Katharine felt the sense of danger threatening, something violent about to happen. But nothing did.

"Will you order Margaret to come with us to Alcantara?"

"No. And if you do I shall countermand the order. This is Castile."

"Then if the boy kills himself . . ." Father said. She heard the rapid footsteps, the slammed door. There was a silence so deep that for a moment or two Katharine thought both her parents had gone. Mother could move almost soundlessly. Then there were hands, gentle about the blanket. Katharine pretended to be newly awakened. Such pretence she knew was the equivalent of a lie; it must be confessed and she would do penance.

"And how is the smallpox?" Isabella asked, peering closely. The rash had vanished. Mother, as always, had been right. But not about Juan.

That was the terrible fact which left its indelible stamp on Katharine's mind.

They were still making merry on the frontier; even the younger Isabella seemed happy again and restored, when word was brought that Juan, in Salamanca, was very ill, dying, dead.

"If the boy kills himself . . ."

After that things were never quite the same. Juan's death was, Katharine admitted to herself, to her a lesser matter than Joanna's departure because their lives had been less closely intertwined; but he was her brother, handsome, amiable whenever they met, and to think that anyone should die so young was sad.

It was sad, too, to see the effect upon Mother, the lightly silvered hair growing white almost perceptibly from day to day, the step heavier, the shoulders a little bowed.

For Spain, plunged into grief as it was, there was still a dynastic hope. Margaret was pregnant. Mother's wish for a child within a year seemed likely to be fulfilled. But the child was born prematurely, dead. Spain had no heir.

Then, in Portugal, Isabella gave birth to a son who was named Miguel. That she died in childbed nobody seemed to notice much. Women, especially Princesses, were, Katharine reflected, like soldiers, expendable. Miguel lived for two years, heir apparent to Portugal and Spain. Then he fell ill of a childish ailment and died. Fortunately for everybody's peace of mind, just before he did so, Joanna, in faraway Ghent, had borne a son who was named Charles and who, if he lived, would inherit more territory than any other man in the modern world. Flanders, Burgundy, Austria, Spain and the expanding colonies in the west, in what people were beginning to recognise as a new world.

A new world was opening out, new ideas, some of them very strange, were spreading; but the old ideas still had power. One was that Spain and Portugal must be linked by marriage. The period of mourning for Isabella was hardly over before plans were afoot for Maria to take her place. Could Manoel marry his deceased wife's sister? Yes, if the Pope made a special dispensation. Couriers began to hurry between Spain and Rome and presently the necessary permission arrived. With the same solemn pomp as had twice accompanied Isabella to the border, Maria went to marriage and Queendom.

Katharine and her mother spent the next winter alone in Granada. Ferdinand had combatted his grief at Juan's death by an increased activity and could usually contrive some good reason for being wherever Isabella was not. He blamed her for the boy's death and then, when his own sorrow eased, was displeased by her continued melancholy which he considered excessive. She never abandoned her mourning clothes, and now wore, under the black, the rough habit of a Franciscan nun.

In December 1500 Katharine was fifteen and it had been arranged that she was to leave for England as soon after her fifteenth birthday as the weather made travel possible and when the new year came she found herself looking forward to the prospect of getting away and at the same time accusing herself of heartlessness. When she was gone her mother would be lonely indeed.

Nobody who was not forced to it would set out on such a journey in January or February and the March gales were notorious; but April came and May and Isabella's only mention of plans was a negative one; there was plague in the north and travel would be unwise at present.

"Would it not be possible for me to leave from Huelva? Or even cross into Portugal and sail from Lisbon?"

"You are so eager to be gone?"

"I am not anxious to leave *you*, or Spain. I dread the parting. But the Prince of Wales writes more and more impatiently." Arthur wrote in Latin, good enough but less perfect than her own—a fact that she found touching—and he wrote how much he looked forward to her coming; he said he already looked upon her as his wife; he hoped that the gales would not be prolonged this year.

Isabella's Ambassador to England, Dr. Puebla, had also written, urging that the Princess should leave for England soon: the King of England mentioned the matter at every interview and seemed to be growing suspicious.

"I have been betrothed for twelve years," Katharine said, as Isabella sat silent. "And I must go, sooner or later."

"Not unless you wish," Isabella said, to Katharine's astonishment. "I have been thinking. I want what is best for you."

Katharine's heart gave a little jerk. A change of plan—which meant a change in political attitudes—at this late hour! And she so accustomed to regarding herself as Princess of Wales; so ready to love Arthur who was young, and sounded friendly. But there was nothing she could do. Princesses had as little say in their own destinies as hounds and horses. She waited for her mother's next words with breathless trepidation, remembering something that now seemed to have an ominous significance— amongst all the things she had learned English was not included. Had this withdrawal been planned all along?

Isabella stood up and began to walk about in a characteristic attitude, her fingers linked, tips upward, her head bent, her shoulders hunched. Katharine rose immediately.

"Sit down, child. Sit down. Words come to me more easily when I am on my feet. The truth is, and I see it more and more clearly as time goes by, this is a false, hollow world and any woman is well out of it. I suppose that on the face of it I have been luckier than most. But I can say frankly that had I my time over again I should do differently. I should go into a convent and devote myself entirely to the worship of God. Would you prefer that to marriage?"

"Become a nun? Mother, I should hate it!" Too violent, too vehement. "I have no vocation. I am not good enough. I try to be good, to love God and please Him, to obey the laws of the Church . . . But to take the veil . . . I never once thought about it."

"Then think about it now . . . I am not trying to persuade

you; I am offering you a choice that I think no girl in your situation has ever been offered before. An opportunity to abandon the world before it betrays you. As it will . . . it will . . . I know. I speak of what I know. Win a war and prepare for another! Here we are in the Alhambra but Granada is not subdued. Bear children, they die, or are sold away like calves. And men—I'll warrant that your father is now in some hunting lodge, with a fat peasant girl whose name he may know tonight but will not remember tomorrow."

It was like seeing a great fortress crumble and collapse under the fire of culverins. Mother, a woman who had managed so well in a world made for and by men. Mother, indomitable, resourceful, proud.

But she is growing old, and I am young. I want to be married and have children. I love fine clothes and jewels, and music and dancing and gay company.

"Think about it," Isabella said again. "Of all my children you are most like me and for that reason I wish to spare you. I bore ten children, three are now alive. I sent Columbus out and what did it profit me? The whole thing ended in a sordid little quarrel over who should govern in a place that is not the India he thought to find. Child, there is nothing, nothing in *this* world that once taken in the hand is worth handling."

Katharine was too young and uninformed to know that her mother was suffering from the menopause and singularly unfortunate in that it had coincided with the loss of a son, the death of a daughter and a grandchild and presently with a husband's infidelity.

She said, very gently, "Mother, I think that those God chooses for a religious life, He calls. Had He called you the Infidel would still rule here. And I do not feel any desire to be a nun."

"Then I pity you. You will have the world to deal with," Isabella said.

Next day it seemed that this dispirited conversation had never taken place. Activity began; stuff for dresses, ladies and maids in waiting to be chosen, the silver plate and jewels that were part of the dowry to be selected and packed, the escort to ride with her to Corunna picked. Isabella, who wished that she had abandoned the world before it had a chance to betray her, saw to it that Katharine, going out to face the world, went well provided.

She took with her, in coin and goods the worth of half her dowry, the other half was to follow; she took a household of sixty people including Doña Elvira who had been chosen as her duenna. She took twelve huge chests containing her clothes and linen.

She also took what she had been born with and what fifteen years had taught her. She was deeply, but not fanatically pious; she had a fixed aversion to war; she had the born Spaniard's Francophobia; she had a longing for a relationship that would be permanent; she knew that for a future Queen to bear sons was a matter of paramount importance. She went with hope and goodwill. She was healthy, pretty, accomplished and affectionate.

In bright summer weather the Queen of Castile's daughter set sail for England, and all the auguries were good.

4

Henry Tudor rode towards Dogmersfield, a palace belonging to the Bishop of Bath, some forty-five miles out of London, at which, at last, *at last*, the Princess of Spain who was to be his daughter-in-law, had arrived.

It was now the second week in November, the weather was foul, the road deep in mire. Henry's mood matched the road and the weather. He was deeply suspicious about this whole business; it had been too long coming to the boil. The girl had been supposed to set out as soon as travel was feasible after her fifteenth birthday—that was eleven months ago; she had left Granada in May, sailed from Corunna in August, met with bad weather and needed the services of an English pilot from Devon to get her on her way again. She had landed in Plymouth in early October and been met, there, and at each stage of her journey, by the local officials and gentry whom Henry ordered to show her hospitality and every possible civility. The fact remained that no one had yet seen her, close to and face to face. There was a female official known as a duenna, a veritable tiger, who had so far managed to stand between the Princess and even the lords under whose roofs she had lodged; and when Henry had demanded of his own household steward, Lord Willoughby de Broke, sent to meet the girl at Exeter, "Well, what is she like?" the answer had been, "Your Grace, it would be difficult for me to say. She was so shrouded and beveiled, in Spanish fashion. About so high."

Henry knew that Ferdinand of Aragon was not to be trusted; in his mind he always thought of him as "that fox beyond the Pyrénées," and he hated him because in those early, unsure days, Ferdinand had shown, by his rejection of the first marriage offers that he thought little of England and had no confidence in Henry's ability to keep his throne. He'd changed his mind—but only because it suited him, and he had paid, or would pay, in good hard cash for that earlier hesitation; but it did occur to Henry as delay followed delay that Ferdinand might have outwitted him after all and sold him what he called "a pig in a poke." This Katharine was, after all the eleventh child, and any family of more than three was likely to produce one member in some way defective; since the betrothal was made this girl's brother had died, somewhat mysteriously; a sister had died in childbed and there were some very curious stories going the rounds about the sister who had married Philip of Burgundy, wrong in the head they said.

Whom to believe; what to believe? His own emissaries to Spain had reported favourably about the Princess. Deluded? Bribed? Well, he intended to see for himself; and if the girl had, as he rather thought she might, a hare lip, a squint, one shoulder or one hip higher than the other he'd turn her, her duenna, the vast expensive household which Spanish dignity demanded, back to Plymouth and though it was November that clever Devon pilot, what was his name? Stephen Brett—who'd brought her into Plymouth, could take her back. England was no longer in need of a Spanish alliance. It had been arranged, and he, busy with a thousand other things, involved with the complete reconstruction of a country broken by civil war, had let the thing ride. It was still a good match and the dowry he had demanded was something to be considered; but the keeping at a distance, the mention of veils and such flummery, alerted him. So despite the rheumatism which was beginning to trouble his bones, he rode out to see for himself; to interpose his judgement between Arthur and any kind of disillusionment. Arthur was already romantically and imaginatively in love with his Spanish princess and Arthur was so constituted that if he saw her and she was maimed or infirm he would simply love her more than ever. Arthur was—his father admitted it—given to the most costly extravagance of all, pity. For Arthur always the lame dog.

If the delay, which Henry believed to be a bit of Ferdinand's cagey policy, meant, as he suspected, that Ferdinand had hesitated to put his goods on the counter, it was better that Arthur never saw the merchandise. Send Arthur, who was, after all, Prince of Wales, on an official errand that would take two days, and ride out to see for himself.

He swung himself, stiff and chilled, out of the saddle in the courtyard at Dogmersfield and was met by Doña Elvira and the Archbishop of Santiago, rigid as statues. He realised that his arrival, unannounced, unheralded, was no surprise to them; it should have been; but by now he was accustomed to the way that news could be spread. Let a tax assessor set foot in a village anywhere in England and the word was out, silver was whipped off sideboards and dropped into wells, pigs and cattle driven into the woods; a plodding peasant ploughing a field, tending sheep, or indoors nursing a broken leg could still, in some mysterious way, communicate with others of his kind and issue the signal, "Danger." He was not astonished to be met and greeted, very correctly; but he was annoyed, and his suspicions were deepened, when he was told that he could not see the Princess. Doña Elvira, in French—which he understood, having spent much of his youth in exile in Brittany—explained the rigid Spanish rule. Until the wedding, nobody, not even the prospective bridegroom, could see the bride unveiled. The Archbishop, in sonorous Latin, confirmed this.

Henry's mood splintered; despite himself he was impressed by Doña Elvira who did not look like a woman who would lend herself to a shifty trick; but then, wouldn't Ferdinand know that and select her purposely? And he was aware of being a parvenue, ruling with a firm hand and sound good sense over a Court where such niceties of etiquette played little part; the stateliness of the English Court had vanished with the Plantagenets; he himself had no time for such rubbish, but confronted with it felt reluctantly that it was the product of an older and more dignified régime than his own. There was another thing too—the Archbishop spoke Latin as though he had been born to it; Henry's, like Isabella's, had been acquired for practical use only. Henry felt inferior, but only for a moment; he had come up the hard way and was a hard man. And he was King of England. He said it, addressing himself to the duenna,

"Madam, I am King of England. The only rules observed here are those I make myself. I wish to see the Princess."

Doña Elvira turned to the Archbishop and spoke a few words in Spanish; he answered in the same tongue. Then she said:

"Your Grace, I deeply regret that it is impossible. The Princess is weary from her journey and has retired."

"Then I'll see her in her nightshift," Henry said. The best way, really; there were ways of padding clothes to disguise deformities.

They looked shocked and stunned. Then the duenna said:

"It will take a few minutes," and rustled away. Henry moved to the fire where his wet clothes began to steam. He was on his own ground, the Archbishop, in a sense, his guest; he knew that he should make some attempt at conversation, but had no intention of exposing his faulty Latin any more than was absolutely necessary. For a second he regretted not having brought some of *his* clerics with him; Cardinal Morton, Archbishop of Canterbury, was a match for any of his kind in the world.

Doña Elvira opened the door of the adjoining room, and made a sign, curtseyed as Henry passed her in the doorway, and stood aside.

Katharine curtseyed, too. Henry, without speaking looked at her, closely and calculatingly as though she were a horse he had been offered in sale. The gauzy, voluminous veil which had so far defeated curious English eyes, was thrown back away from her face; her shoulders and hips were level, in fact she stood well, holding her head high; there was no blemish on her face, not even the sallowness associated with Spanish blood, her complexion was fair, a clear pink and white; her eyes were grey, shy yet quite steady under his deliberate, assessing stare. For a girl not yet sixteen she was very well grown, somewhat taller than de Broke had indicated.

Relief and delight swept through him; a proper, royal Princess; if he'd had her made to his own specifications, she couldn't have been more satisfied. In the English fashion he leaned forward, kissed her cheek and said, "Welcome to England."

He saw that the phrase was meaningless to her. You'd have thought that in twelve years, knowing she was destined for England, they'd have seen that she learned English. He repeated his welcome in French: and that she appeared to understand, for her face lighted with a smile and she inclined her head a little; but she said nothing and the horrible suspicion struck him that there might lie the truth; poor girl, she was dumb! That would never do; such afflictions ran in families; imagine the next heir to England being dumb, unable to hold his own in a Council Chamber.

He half-turned and shot a question at Doña Elvira: "Can she speak at all?"

"The Princess of Wales," the duenna said frigidly, "is taken by surprise at your insistence to see her . . ." Her black eyes raked Henry from top to toe, his filthy, muddy riding clothes, still faintly steaming, the ancient battered hat awkwardly snatched off under his arm. The words *and by your appearance* hung on the air.

"My French deserted me, your Grace," Katharine said, recovering it. She had learned it from her sister-in-law. "It is most kind of your Grace to ride so far and in such bad weather in order to welcome me in person." She smiled again and Henry smiled back at her. The smile changed his face entirely, rearranging the harsh lines which determination, anxiety and self-discipline had engraved on his weathered skin. They took, in that moment, an odd liking to one another.

Henry was no sentimentalist and his imagination in some respects was limited, but he realised that the girl would wish to see her bridegroom, not her father-in-law.

"Arthur may arrive this evening," he said. "Or he may not. He had a longer journey and the going is foul. But he is eager to see you—as I was—and will ride hard."

"I look forward to our meeting," she said, and smiled again. As with Henry the smile made a difference. In repose her face inclined towards the solemn and the effort of recalling her French made it rather more solemn, just as it stiffened her diction. But smiles were interchangeable currency. Smiling, Henry said:

"I'm hungry. You must be too. I'll clean up a bit and then we'll eat roast beef together, eh?"

"That will be most pleasant, your Grace," she said.

Roast beef was the national dish; it could only be eaten in a country where there was so much rain that there was enough grass to nourish cattle all through the summer, so that they could grow to maturity. In places where pastures were dry and scorched by mid-May calves must be either slaughtered, or starve to death and were brought to the table as veal. The English obviously thought very highly of roast beef; it had been served at every place where she had stayed since her arrival in Plymouth.

But this evening the roast beef had a different flavour because of the company in which it was eaten.

Arthur arrived within the hour. It disturbed Henry to realise that had his worst suspicions been well-founded, he would have only an hour to work in; he'd counted on twenty-four hours at least. As it was, all was well. He was able to take the hand of his son, the hand of the Princess from Spain and bring them together with complete satisfaction. In Arthur the Yorkist and Lancastrian blood ran side by side, unifying England; in his bride ran the blood of ancient royalty; brought together they would found a dynasty the like of which England, the like of which no country in the world had ever seen.

In their rather stiff little letters to one another Katharine and Arthur had made vows of love and each was in love with the idea of being in love; now, brought face to face, they felt a mutual disappointment. Katharine thought: Oh, but he's a mere child; Arthur noted with dismay that she was at least five inches taller than he was. He had known that she was a year older, but on the whole females were smaller than males and he had hoped for a tiny bride. He consoled himself by the thought that she was very pretty, in all but those extra inches, the princess of every boy's dreams; and perhaps she had finished growing while he might any day begin to shoot up. It was not the first time that he had been made aware of his lack of stature; his brother Henry, four years his junior, was almost as tall as he was, and a great deal more sturdy.

Both of them, inwardly ashamed of their disappointment, took great pains to be pleasing, and paid one another compliments in Latin, and made little jokes and laughed, all under the King's pleased, benevolent eye. Arthur was both intelligent and well-educated and Henry felt a self-made man's pride in his son's accomplishments, was pleased to think that the boy's upbringing had been so different from his own. And the fact that Arthur was small and slight and took small interest in weapons and their use did not matter much; he would never be obliged to fight for his crown. The turbulent era was over; the boy would inherit a united England, at peace from border to border. Nevertheless, the thought occurred to the father, as it had occurred before: it was a pity that *physically* his two sons could not have changed places; Arthur, who would be King, had the physique of the churchman, Harry, destined for the Church, was plainly built for kingship. "That great boy," as his father called him in the frequent moments of annoyance, was as much too large for his age as his brother was too small; not over-grown, a word that suggested lankiness or awkwardness, Harry was beautifully proportioned, was already an excellent horseman and a useful performer in the tiltyard as well as in the tennis court. Arthur was mild-tempered; Harry in a rage was something to see. Now and again Henry felt that his second son would find his priest's vows of continence hard to keep, but this was all part of the plan. The whole business of the Wars of the Roses went back to the fact that Edward III had had several sons, who had most of them had sons, a too great a proliferation of putative heirs in any emergency. Henry did not intend to have his Tudor dynasty go by that road. Arthur was heir; Harry would be Archbishop of Canterbury and any child he sired—some clerics did have children—would be smuggled away into obscurity.

After supper Katharine—without consulting Doña Elvira—asked Arthur if he would like to see some Spanish dances. He said eagerly that he would. Dancing was not a pastime that he enjoyed, but he liked watching it. So the room was cleared and some musicians found and Katharine danced, in Spanish fashion, with one of her ladies, Maria de Rojas, as once she had danced with Joanna. Henry, watching and applauding and approving thought— And they said she was so weary she had gone to bed; one cannot believe a word they say.

Doña Elvira, supervising Katharine's disrobing, apologised for the intrusion upon Katharine's privacy, using the apology as an opening for the expression of her displeasure.

"One has always been given to understand that the English were without manners. That their King should be such a boor I did not expect. Coming into this room in a state that no mere courier in Spain would dare to present himself."

"I think it was because he already looks upon me as one of his family," Katharine said. Rallying from her disappointment she had enjoyed herself that evening, had basked in Henry's approval and in Arthur's admiration, had felt curiously free and gay for the first time in years.

"If that is so," Doña Elvira said sternly, "he is wrong. Until the final benediction upon your marriage has been pronounced neither he, nor his son, should have seen you unveiled; and certainly they should not have been invited to watch you dance."

"That was my fault," Katharine admitted; but something had taken possession of her; the result of the air, the rain, the roast beef? "They came to welcome me and I wished to please them. And I did."

She had pleased them, and she was glad. She could, she felt, afford to ignore Doña Elvira's carping and criticism. In a few days she would be a married woman; she would not need a duenna . . .

In a few days she was married, in circumstances of such pomp and splendour and lavish expenditure as London had not seen for many years. The King of England knew that he was regarded as parsimonious, and if that was the word applied to a man who disliked waste of money, very well, he was parsimonious and to hell with those who used the word deridingly. But, like many miserly people, when he wished to spend he spent with élan. Delighted with the prize which his son had drawn in the royal-marriage lottery, he hurried back to London, issued orders, opened his purse. Katharine walked to her wedding in St. Paul's along a great platform, hung with fine red worsted cloth, so that she was in full view of all the throng. Leading her along by the hand was Arthur's brother, the Duke of York, called Harry in the family to distinguish him from his father.

He was ten years old; six years younger than she was, four and a half years younger than Arthur of whom, at first meeting, she had thought: Oh, but he's a mere child; but although Harry was maybe an inch shorter than Arthur, he bulked larger in his white satin suit, trimmed with gold; and he had an astonishing confidence of manner. Ten years old, a child, performing one of his first public official duties and doing it as though he had done it twenty times, fifty times before.

He took her hand in his. With that attention to some irrelevant detail that is possible in moments of nervous tension, she noticed that he had well-shaped hands, with square palms and long fingers. The one that held hers gave signs of rough usage, the skin peeling away from what had recently been blisters in two places and one knuckle badly grazed.

They stood for a moment, alone at the end of the elevated platform, with the eyes of the massed congregation upon them. The space they must walk to reach the end, where another, transverse platform bore the King and the Queen, the Lord Mayor of London and the priests who would officiate, looked endless.

"Your hand is very cold," Harry said in his excellent Latin. "Are you afraid?"

"A little," she confessed.

"There is no need to be. They are only people." The hard brown hand tightened on hers reassuringly. "All we have to do is to keep in step. Now, left foot first . . ."

It occurred to her that he enjoyed being looked at and admired; but the calm ease of his manner and the clasp of his hand restored her confidence. At the end of the platform he released her hand, made a low bow and stood back, watching with bitter, unchildlike envy while his brother Arthur and the pretty Princess were made man and wife.

Why had he not been the first-born? He knew—it was impossible that he should not know—that he was in every way more suitable to be King one day than Arthur was, or ever could be. Arthur was shy with people, whereas he, disdaining most of them, got on well with everybody; Arthur was always tired, his own energy was boundless: Arthur was inept at games and sports, he was good, and intended to be better: Arthur was so retiring that even now, on his wedding day, he cut no figure at all; the one whom all these people would remember, and talk about afterwards was the Duke of York who would never have a wedding of his own. The second son, destined for the Church.

He bore no grudge against Arthur, of whom he was fond and towards whom he often extended a somewhat condescending protectiveness; his resentment was against Fate; Arthur should have been the second son, or a girl—he'd have made a splendid girl. Harry had been obliged to comfort him over this night's business, which Arthur confessed to dreading. "That public putting to bed, all those lewd jokes . . ."

"You need only to laugh. And then . . . think of afterwards. It is said to be . . . not unpleasant."

Arthur, dreading the preliminaries, dreaded the afterwards even more. He was in love with his pretty, amiable bride, but, in the secrecy of his heart, he admitted, not in that way. To talk to, walk with, sing with, confide in, spoil a little, a special kind of sister who would belong to him and never be given away in marriage. Still, he realised that he was caught in the dynastic mill and must just do his best as occasion rose.

After the long and exhausting ceremony, there was the ride to Baynard's Castle, properly cleansed and aired, and with a great bed with fine new hangings set in a chamber spread with rushes brought all the way from Suffolk and unique in that when trodden upon they emitted a pleasant odour. The bedding procedure was preceded by a feast, interrupted by music and singing and the antics of dwarfs and jugglers. Most people, by the end of it were a little tipsy: in the maelstrom of noisy merriment the Prince and Princess of Wales sat in a small patch of quietude and Katharine saw Arthur begin to wilt. The flush was still on his smooth cheeks, but it had contracted into patches, almost circular, on each cheekbone; the rest of his face was chalky white except for smudges of fatigue below the eyes.

She said, "It will not be long now, Arthur," and realised that this would-be comforting statement was open to misinterpretation. "I have seldom been so tired in my life," she said, exaggerating. She knew then that had it been her fortune to have for a husband a man, full grown, strong and tough, the Arthur of the stories, she would now be entertaining very different feelings; a little fear perhaps, but a pleasurable fear, a looking forward to the culmination of a wedding day, the great day in a woman's life. As it was she knew that towards Arthur her feelings were maternal; she, the mother, merely wished to get this bone-weary child to bed and see him fall into a recuperative sleep.

The moment came at last; the bawdy jokes, the hearty good wishes all done, the curtains drawn round the great bed, the room silent and the well-trampled rushes giving up their scent. Katharine remembered how sometimes, towards the end of one of those long journeys across Spain, Joanna, playing the mother, would put out her arm and pull the sleepy head on to her shoulder. How comfortable it had been.

She did the same thing; putting her arm around the slight, tense, too-hot body, cradling the golden head on her shoulder, kissing the brow—a little alarmed to find it so damp.

"Sleep," she said. "Sleep well, my dear one."

He said, "Just for a little. The crowds and the noise . . . I revive as quickly as I tire; I have great recuperative power. If I close my eyes and lie still for a few moments . . . all will be as it should be."

"All is," she assured him. She felt him go limp.

She lay awake long enough to think how like, in build and colouring, Arthur was to her brother Juan—though Juan, being older than she was, had never seemed like a child to her. And Juan had exhausted his strength, killed himself, over the business of getting Margaret with child. Father himself had said so, accusing Mother, anxious to blame in his first grief. That, she made up her mind, there and then, was *not* going to happen to Arthur. They would wait. With this decision made, being young and healthy and tired, she fell asleep herself.

They both slept until morning. Arthur, conscious of having failed in his duty, apologised, thus endearing himself to her even more. Poor child! She told him—and there was apology in her voice, too, of her overnight thoughts; she pleaded the case of Juan and Margaret: "We are married," she said, "nothing could make us more so. Nothing. But we should wait."

Nothing could have suited him better; the warm intimacy of the shared bed, the scent of her hair; the status of being a married man . . . and all without the thing which he did not yet want to do, did not yet feel able to do. A sister who was more than a sister.

"But they will know," he said, "and mock me."

"This is between ourselves; who could possibly know?"

"Those who make the bed," he said miserably, aware that this comfortable, shrouded place was not the whole of the world. "I think . . . I have been told . . . they will look . . . there should be a little blood."

Nobody had told her that. How astonishing!

"Yours? Or mine?"

"Yours."

"Those who come looking shall find what they seek," she said. She pushed back the bedcurtains and reached for the knife which lay beside the dish, piled high with apples and pears on the side table. Not her hand, that would show; her foot. She jabbed at her heel, judging that to be the less sensitive part.

The first bedmaker to witness this proof of deflowering thought: "What a lot! But they're different to us, them Spaniards!"

Arthur, completely reassured because his pretty princess

understood him so well and was the other self he had always
longed for, moved a farther step away from the reality of life,
his position and his duty and threw himself into the part. When
the first gentlemen, a bit thick-headed and bleary-eyed, cautiously opened the door of the marriage chamber, he called to
them, before they did anything else, to bring him something
to drink. "Marriage is thirsty work," he said.

The Prince of Wales was expected to keep Christmas at
Ludlow. Katharine had not been alone in remembering her
brother Juan and Margaret. There was a suggestion that she
should remain with her father- and mother-in-law and that
Arthur should go to Ludlow alone. But that seemed a cruel
decision to make; the two young people were so plainly in love;
Arthur seemed no worse for his marital exertions. So they left
for the west together and Arthur enjoyed showing Katharine
the romantic, still almost untamed country whose title they
bore, and she told him about Granada, Madrid, Corunna. He
promised, with the wild west wind howling about Ludlow, to
build her, one day, a palace the equal of the Alhambra, the
tender plants, the orange and lemon trees all under glass.

Then, late in March, coming back from a meeting of the
Council—a thing of pretence, a sop to Welsh pride, all major
decisions being taken at Westminster—Arthur said that his
head ached and that his throat was sore. It was nothing, he said,
he would be better in the morning, but he allowed himself to
be persuaded to go to bed, with a cup of hot, well-spiced wine
to drink and a hot brick at his feet. He had a restless night,
alternately shivering and sweating: in the morning his fever
was high and his doctor bled him in the left foot and advised
that he should have nothing to drink since liquid encouraged
the sweating. Denied so much as a sip of water, Arthur still
sweated and burned and shivered, and through an endless day
Katharine sat by the bed, holding his hand, stroking his head,
replacing the covers his tossing disarranged. The doctor padded
in and out with a pill to be swallowed, a plaster to be applied;
he bled the patient from his right arm; he was aware of his
heavy responsibility, this sick boy was the King's son; no effort

must be spared. He wished that this had happened in London, where he could have called upon colleagues to share the burden—and if things went wrong, the blame. There was a doctor in Ludlow, but he himself had the sweating sickness, which had been rife in the town for some time.

In the evening Arthur asserted himself, perhaps for the first time in his life.

"I will not die of thirst," he said in a low croaking voice. "I want some water, cold, straight from the well."

"My lord, you must not . . ."

The Tudor temper flashed. "It is not for you to tell me what I must or must not. I want cold water and I want it *now!*"

Katharine herself held the cup for him, urging him to sip slowly, now and then moving the cup away, "Enough, darling, enough," but his hot damp fingers closed on her wrist, "More. I could drink a gallon."

When, two days later, the heir to the throne lay dead, the doctor attributed his death to the drinking of cold well water and if asked to give the *true* reason for the Prince's demise, would have said, "his own wilfulness." But such things could not be said to Kings, about the sons of Kings. He dismissed the whole business of the sweating sickness and the gulping of ice-cold water from his mind; the courier who set out on the 3rd of April to carry the news to London, was instructed to tell the bereaved father and mother that their son had died "of a consumption."

Katharine was in no position to dispute the verdict; smitten down by the same sickness—her head had been aching and her throat very sore when she held the water to Arthur—but in a different form because she had more vitality and made a series of recoveries, suffered a series of relapses. She was still in bed and very weak when Arthur's coffin, so light that it seemed to confirm the verdict of a consumption, a disease which wasted, was carried out of Ludlow and by easy stages to burial at Worcester. It was May, warm and sunny, when in her widow's garb she set out for London and the world where the death of a boy had changed everything.

5

The King of England said, "Surely, the most preposterous suggestion ever made. It would take that fox, Ferdinand, to put forth such a proposal of bare-faced robbery. Is he mad? Send her home with that half of her dowry that has been paid; *and* pay her her dower rights as Dowager Princess of Wales; that is a third of the revenues of Wales, Chester and Cornwall. And what the wedding cost me . . ." He thought furiously of the fountains spouting wine, the food for all comers, the prizes for the jousting, the complete refurbishing of Baynard's Castle. And all for what? A marriage that had lasted four months. "To this," he said, slapping his hand on the paper, "I shall never agree."

Cardinal Morton, whose financial genius had made his King the richest monarch in Europe, said:

"I am inclined to think, Your Grace, that this proposition was not intended to be taken seriously. When Dr. Puebla took it from his pouch there was another paper—you know how they interfold—which he stuffed back hastily. And he looked very sly."

"His eyes are so set that facing a loaf of bread he would look sly. If this is not a serious proposition, what is it? Apart from being something any brigand would blush at?"

"I can only think, Sire, that the intention was to shock so that another proposal, perhaps equally shocking, but in a different way, might seem acceptable. That is my guess. I cannot know."

"If anything could be as shocking as this, but different, I should be interested, very interested, to see it. Have him in."

Dr. Puebla came in. He had been the Spanish Ambassador to

England for many years; he had negotiated the betrothal between Arthur and Katharine. He was a Jew and though it might seem strange to other people that Isabella, busy driving the Jews from Spain, should maintain one as her chosen representative in a country of growing importance, Dr. Puebla did not find it strange at all. When, because money was needed for other purposes, his salary was not paid, he never whined or grumbled; in a free busy town like London, any man who was conversant with law, could stand on his two feet and had the use of his tongue, could make a living. In lean times he had supported himself and his staff; and he had a modest little fortune, every penny of it honestly made, safely tucked away. And he was clever.

He came in, bowed very low to the King, less low but low enough to the Cardinal.

"This, Dr. Puebla," Henry said, tapping the paper again, "is a ridiculous proposal."

With a nice mingling of surprise and reproach in his tone, Puebla said:

"I am grieved that Your Grace should think so. It is in exact accord with the terms of the marriage settlement."

"We then visualised a long marriage and the Princess's revenue being spent in England, to the benefit of the country from which it derived."

"The circumstances are sad indeed. But—if I may say so— it was not the fault of Princess Katharine that her married life should be of such short duration."

"She is now sixteen years old. She could be drawing this vast income for the next fifty years!" The thought agitated him.

"The purpose of all marriage settlements is to provide for the female, whatever circumstances may arise."

"She is a pretty girl; still young; very amiable. She will marry again," Henry said brusquely. "You may inform your master that I—more generous than he—will excuse him the payment of the other half of her dowry. With that in her hand she will make some man a very desirable wife. And that is my last word on the subject."

Dr. Puebla took a swift, almost imperceptible glance at Cardinal Morton's face. The Cardinal gave a slight nod of the head. It is the last word.

"Men set such ridiculous store by virginity," Dr. Puebla said plaintively. "The Princess is all that you say . . . but to put it coarsely, she is now secondhand. However, I will inform my master, and Queen Isabella, of Your Grace's decision."

He hurried away to the large, ancient, draughty house in the Strand where Katharine and her suite were now installed. It was called Durham House because it belonged to the Bishop of Durham who never used it, having other and more comfortable residences. Puebla hoped to avoid any meeting with Doña Elvira whom he disliked as much as she disliked him, and who was now back in full charge of the Princess and her household, and this he managed and made for the apartment of Father Alessandra, Katharine's confessor who had been with her at Ludlow.

"It is," he said, after a few preliminaries, "a question of Her Highness's future. I suppose there could be no doubt that the marriage was consummated?"

"That surely is a question that should be put to her duenna. Once the Sacrament of Marriage has been performed marital acts are not subject to the confessional—and even if they were they would be under the seal."

"But you know, as well as I do, that Doña Elvira would not tell me the time of day correctly."

"Nor me. She has such a jealous and domineering disposition that she wishes to be Her Highness's duenna, controller of her household, her confessor and Spanish Ambassador, all in one."

The mutual enmity made for a feeling of fellowship between them.

"You cannot help me then? The question is of some importance." The second paper in his pouch, unread by anyone but himself, was concerned with the importance.

"Naturally, I have heard things, in the ordinary way," Father

Alessandra said. "I do not go about with my eyes and ears shut. You may take it from me that the marriage *was* consummated."

"Oh dear."

"You sound displeased, Dr. Puebla."

"It makes things a trifle more difficult. And the poor boy was so young, so frail."

"He was married. He would recognise his duty. And so would the Princess."

"Yes, yes, of course. Naturally."

Dr. Puebla hurried away to write a letter to Spain, telling Ferdinand and Isabella that their first suggestion had been rejected out of hand; and that he had it on the best authority that the marriage between Katharine and Arthur had been consummated.

He had slightly exceeded his duty. Queen Isabella, like Father Alessandra, felt that such a question should be left to Doña Elvira.

Katharine had been glad enough to escape from the strict, sharp-tongued woman with her insistence upon strict Spanish etiquette. After the exceptionally free life at Ludlow as a married woman, it was hard to be obliged to return to tutelage and supervision. But Isabella in a letter expressing sympathy— though sorrow came to all—after urging her daughter to be brave and resigned to the will of God, had added that she was to place herself entirely in Doña Elvira's hands and never to forget that a young widow must be even more discreet in her behaviour than an unmarried girl.

"Your Highness," Doña Elvira said one day. "There is something which I should know. Are you with child?"

Blushing, Katharine said, "No. Would that I were." Sometimes it seemed to her that restraint had been mistaken; poor Arthur with so short a time to live; and a baby would have been something . . . "I know what you think, Doña Elvira . . ." The blush deepened. "Remember, I was ill. I was bled every day, sometimes twice. The rhythm was disturbed. I am sure that this month . . ."

"Did you and the late Prince of Wales live together as husband and wife?"

"How can you ask that? You know that we were hardly apart for an hour from the moment we were married until . . . he died." She was still in a weak, morbid state and her eyes filled with tears as she thought: Oh, poor little boy, poor little boy; he promised to build me a palace like the Alhambra; he had so many plans for the future.

"Then how can you be so sure that this disturbance of rhythm is due to your indisposition," Doña Elvira asked, pressing her point home.

Katharine was now crying.

"He was so young; and not sturdy. I remembered my brother and what was said when he died. So . . . so we agreed to wait. It was his wish, as well as mine. We said a year . . . And now, notwithstanding, he is dead. And he was so kind and clever and amiable, the child would have been . . . like him . . ."

It would also have been heir to England and you as his mother, would have had status; your future would have been assured, Doña Elvira thought, almost annoyed by Katharine's ignoring of the *real* situation. Unworldliness in others always affronted her. Still the information which she had extracted, was satisfactory; men set such a ridiculous value on virginity. She hastened to write to Queen Isabella. She wrote in good faith; after all virginity was a physical state, capable of investigation and proof or disproof and when Doña Elvira wrote, "She shared a bed with a sick boy and is still as virgin as when she came from the womb," she was certain that she was writing the truth.

Katharine, immured behind the double screen of mourning and etiquette, almost her only visitor her mother-in-law, Queen Elizabeth, ailing and prematurely aged and heartbroken over Arthur's death, totally ignorant or oblivious to what was going on in the wider world, was spared all knowledge of what was going on outside the walls of Durham House. She knew that her confessor, Father Alessandra, had been recalled but she did not know that he was recalled in disgrace because he was the originator of the story that she and Arthur had been man and wife in fact as well as name. Dr. Puebla—to Doña Elvira's immense disgust—was not recalled; he was far too useful.

Nobody told Katharine anything; she lived in a muted world. Even to stand by the window and look into the Strand where life went on, busy, avid, noisy and colourful was, by Doña Elvira's decree, ill-advised; a widow should show no interest in the outer world; or play cards; make or listen to any cheerful tune or even to seem to enjoy her food.

On the farther side of the double screen arrangements, the ultimate result of which none of the arrangers in their wildest dreams could have envisaged, were going on. The day came when Dr. Puebla produced, for the inspection of Henry and Cardinal Morton, Ferdinand's and Isabella's alternative suggestion—a marriage between Katharine and the boy who was now Prince of Wales.

"Agreed to," Dr. Puebla said, touching the King in his most vulnerable spot, "this would ensure that the half-dowry, already paid, remained in England and also the revenues to which, by law, the Princess is entitled."

"It would also involve a vast amount of legislation," Henry said, tempted, but cautious. "She was Arthur's wife. A Papal dispensation would be necessary."

"Such a dispensation was obtained, Your Grace, when Princess Maria of Spain married the King of Portugal, formerly wedded to her sister who died."

"She is almost seventeen years old. My boy is twelve. In view of what happened to my elder son I could not consent to any marriage for Harry until he is sixteen. Dr. Puebla, the ages are too disparate."

"The Prince of Wales—the late Prince of Wales—did not die of overmuch exertion in the marital bed, Your Grace. Nor of the consumption often associated with such activities. I beg you to forgive me if I speak frankly. I have gone into this matter. He died of drinking water, cold from the well, when the sweating sickness was on him. And the marriage was never consummated. I admit that once I thought otherwise, but I was misled. The Princess is a virgin. She is by law entitled to the half-dowry, already paid; and to her revenues under the marriage settlement. A most enviable match for any man. Even —permit me to say it—for the Prince of Wales, so different from his brother, at twelve almost a man."

He had hit Henry in his next most vulnerable spot. The King, who was also a father, had been almost ashamed of the pride he had felt, since poor Arthur's death, in presenting Harry to the people. This boy never tired, was never upset by what he ate, was never shy or reticent; was able, it seemed, to endear himself without effort to great nobles, sober tradesmen and humble peasants alike. It was sad about Arthur, but he was safe in the keeping of God and perhaps it was as well that he was out of a world in which he had never seemed really at home; Harry was better equipped to assume the burden of monarchy which Henry nowadays sometimes felt to be heavy.

"The fact remains that he is only twelve," Henry said curtly. He was not disposed to take this second proposal too willingly; the terms of the first had been too harsh. "I will agree that a dispensation be applied for. It may not be granted. In the interim I think that the Princess should renounce her revenue rights. I shall allow her . . ." he hesitated, reckoning swiftly; she had a ridiculously large suite, "a hundred pounds a month. That should pay her household expenses and anything over she can spend on fripperies."

Not ungenerous, Dr. Puebla reflected; though the value of money was rapidly depreciating. It was paradoxical; the Spanish galleons now beat their way from the New World which Columbus had discovered almost by mistake, and they carried much silver, some gold, some precious stones; the wealth of the world appeared to have increased, but a pound bought less than it did even a year ago, and there were times when he thought: If this goes on what I have gathered and hoarded against my old age will barely suffice. Perhaps Henry, King of England, felt the same about his stored-up fortune.

"I will inform my master, Your Grace. A moratorium upon

the dower revenues, in return for an allowance of a hundred pounds a month. And, if the Pope grants the dispensation, a betrothal between the Prince of Wales and the Princess."

The two people most nearly concerned in this bargaining were not consulted or informed directly; but the knowledge seeped in. Katharine thought: Another child; more waiting; even if Julius gives the dispensation, I shall be over twenty when I hold my first child in my arms; twenty was, by Spanish standards, old. But it was her mother's and father's wish that she should remain in England and wait, and she recognised their authority.

The Prince of Wales, still very busy adjusting himself to the change in his future, saw himself as peculiarly blessed. Even the beautiful Princess from Spain, the possession of whom, God forgive him, he had once envied poor Arthur, would one day be his. One day . . .

The waiting time was not, even for Katharine, completely dull. Once her period of mourning was over she was welcome at Court and went to Greenwich, Richmond and Windsor, to take her place as third lady in the realm in brave style, even though her dresses had to be furbished up and her attendants were growing shabby. Her allowance did not permit any expenditure on fripperies and the table at Durham House was often sparsely set.

The position of first lady was Elizabeth's, that was indisputable, she was Queen of England; in next order of precedence Katharine should have held place; but there was the old—and now hideous, though people said that in her day she had been beautiful—Countess of Richmond, the King's mother; jabbing the stick upon which she leaned to relieve her lameness into the floor as though she were piercing an enemy, she always forced herself forward.

"It is entirely wrong," Doña Elvira said. "Your Highness should assert yourself more positively. That old woman was never Queen, or Princess of Wales. It is against all the rules that she should precede you as she does."

Katharine said, "But she *is* old and to her it matters. Whether

I go second or third makes no difference to me. I enjoy the occasions." To a more sympathetic hearer she would have mentioned the items that she had enjoyed; but Doña Elvira would have said again, as she once had, "I fear that Your Highness has a frivolous mind." The remark had been wounding: to herself Katharine admitted that she liked the massed candles, the gay music, the brightly coloured clothes and sparkling jewels, enjoyed the food, especially after a spell of short commons in Durham House. Am I frivolous? We made merry at Ludlow and there was no rebuke. Is it wrong to be happy for an hour? To be happy for an hour in a world where—let it be faced—happiness was a rare commodity and misery abounded; the blind and crippled begging at every street corner; unwanted babies flung out to die—nuns of the Franciscan Order set out regularly between nine o'clock and midnight to collect the abandoned from rubbish heaps. In such a world was it wrong to snatch an hour's joy?

And it was not that one lacked personal cause for grief. On Candlemas Day in the year 1503, Queen Elizabeth bore the child about whom she had, throughout her pregnancy, spoken to Katharine. "I had two sons; one for the Throne, one for the Church. Arthur died and Harry's future was changed. I hope that this child will be a boy and live to take what was Harry's place."

"I hope so, too. And I will pray . . ." Katharine said.

But the child was a girl, hurriedly christened Catherine, the English version of Katharine's name, which was a compliment. Nine days later Elizabeth and the girl child she had borne were dead. Elizabeth died on her birthday; she was thirty-seven.

The Court was plunged into mourning; and from this mourning the King never truly emerged; there were no more festivities which Doña Elvira could deem frivolous; and within a month or two Katharine realised that the King's demeanour towards herself had changed. He could no longer afford to support her in a separate establishment, he said. In future she must regard herself as part of his Court; and since accommodation was everywhere limited, her suite must be much reduced.

It astonished her to learn how many of her Spaniards had been homesick, staying on this alien land, this abominable climate out of loyalty to herself. She tried to push the thought aside, but it would intrude, that a few of them had come with her in the hope of position and power, and instead of receiving the rich pickings which a Princess of Wales could be expected to have in her gift, they had been relegated to live meagrely, to be ill-clad and to shiver in ill-heated rooms. She was not sorry to say goodbye to her duenna.

With the King so low in spirits and his parsimony growing, life had few glittering occasions; an exception was the ceremony of her betrothal to the Prince of Wales. The necessary dispensation for their marriage was to be granted—though it would take months to arrive.

She felt that the occasion justified a new dress, and chose blue velvet, the low cut, square neckline and the sleeves edged with embroidery in silver thread and studded with pearls. She was eighteen years old and absurdly anxious not to look old to the eyes of her bridegroom-to-be, or to the eyes of the beholders; she was glad to think that since her arrival in England she had not grown in height; Harry had grown enormously, so much so that this time when he took her hand and they stood side by side, their two heads, so similarly russet, were almost level. And the fashion of the day made the boy, bulky as he was, seem even more full-grown. Tunics were padded, especially about the shoulders and sleeves, and then slashed, as though they were at bursting point, the insets of a contrasting colour. Harry on this day wore white satin, slashed over gold, and his confidence, his curious facility for attracting attention, to woo and at the same time appear to be unconscious of the crowd—as he had said, "they are only people"—made him the focus for all eyes.

His hand was broader and harder, but still warm and steadying and this time the touch of it held a possessiveness. This is ridiculous, she told herself, a boy of twelve! But something that had never moved in her before woke and stirred. She crushed it down; later, at the banqueting table, where they were seated side by side, it reared again, when he said:

"I beg you—forgive my lack of years. No man can choose his date of birth. Could I have chosen mine I should now be twenty; and ready to take you to bed forthwith."

She blushed hotly and he laughed; the blue of his eyes hard and brilliant as enamel between lashes that were thick, but short and bristly. On his upper lip, cheek and chin, there was a reddish golden fuzz.

"They say four years," he went on, "but if I can persuade the King, my father, it will be less."

He was a little beside himself. There was something heady in the thought that the will of God and the will of Harry Tudor were in such accord.

After this satisfactory if rather disturbing meeting, they saw each other seldom. The Prince was often out of London, entertaining, or being entertained. The King grew grumpier and more miserly. More than once Katharine was made painfully aware that the second half of her dowry had never been paid and that this was resented. Two of her ladies-in-waiting, who had remained in England because marriages loomed, needed the dowries which they had every right to expect, even from a Dowager Princess of Wales. Where was the money to come from? Katharine suggested selling or pawning some of her silver plate and jewels, but Dr. Puebla said that that would be unwise since they constituted part of the half-dowry that had been paid. She wrote to her mother, not a letter of complaint, but a statement of her situation, and added the comment that it was a long time since she had a letter from her. Weeks later when news came that Isabella was dead, some remorseful tears mingled with those of grief. In retrospect the calm, dispassionate letter looked like one long grumble.

Isabella of Castile had died worn out by worry and work. She had achieved much, but not enough. She had known for some time that her days were numbered—and when she died

Spain would be divided again. Joanna would inherit Castile, and some very disquieting stories had reached her concerning her eldest surviving daughter. Joanna's passion for her husband, Philip the Handsome, seemed to amount to mania. His infidelities maddened her; she had attacked one of his mistresses with a pair of scissors and would have killed her if not prevented. A dog of which he was particularly fond she had killed, because he caressed it. What kind of Queen of Castile would she make? Isabella was concerned, too, for Katharine. On what was to be her deathbed she was shown a copy of the Papal dispensation, legalising the marriage between Katharine and the young Prince of Wales. Satisfactory? It was what had been requested; His Holiness had granted the request and it was not for a good Catholic to question. Yet she did. Had too much attention been paid to material things; to financial arrangements? to the trade treaty that was part of the marriage contract? She had always been obliged to be practical; in her earlier years had delighted in managing, contriving, outwitting, out-bargaining. And now it all seemed a waste of energy . . .

Isabella died and, far away in England, Katharine felt her death, first as a grief and then, in its repercussions, as a damage.

The nub of the matter was that Ferdinand did not propose to hand over Castile to Joanna and her husband without a struggle and since he must prepare for war he could not afford to pay the now long overdue half of Katharine's dowry; this displeased Henry; so did the fact that the privileges and concessions granted to English traders in Spain were withdrawn without warning; so that a crowd of English sailors and merchants came back from Seville declaring that they were "all lost and ruined."

At the same time, the Emperor Maximilian, seeing that his son Philip and his daughter-in-law might have to fight for Castile, began looking around for friends, and making advances to Henry of England. Philip and Joanna had a daughter, Eleanor, nearer in age to the Prince of Wales. How would it be if a marriage were arranged between them?

Henry studied this from all angles; there was the matter of age; the fact that a dispensation had been necessary for the betrothal between Katharine and Harry; the fact that Eleanor's father would inherit the widest territory in Europe—and probably be elected as Emperor, as well. As a father-in-law far more desirable and useful than foxy Ferdinand.

The result of his deliberations was a deterioration in his treatment of Katharine; she was still attached to the Court but no longer part of it and in every place to which it moved, her accommodation became worse and less suitable to her rank. She was seldom invited to take part in any ceremony or share any festivity and she never saw the Prince of Wales at all. She was even poorer than she had been at Durham House, and but for the fact that Dr. Puebla liked her and considered her badly used, so that he spent his own money on comforts, she would have had no wine on her table, and sometimes no fuel for her hearth.

On a cold evening in December 1505 as they rose from the supper table, Henry said to Harry, "I wish to talk to you."

"Now, Sire? We were about to dance."

The question was just one more small sign of the not-completely filial behaviour which Henry had observed lately. The boy now fourteen and a half, almost full grown, was beginning to have a will of his own; and of course he was spoilt, everywhere deferred to because of his rank, his good looks and his accomplishments. In the old days boys of his age would have commanded their own armies, Henry remembered; Harry could not be ruled like a schoolboy much longer. Tonight he must be.

Henry said, "You can dance later," and led the way into a small room where a great fire burned. The close warm atmosphere was suitable to the aging man with his thinning blood, oppressive to the young man who, given permission to sit, unbuttoned his tunic and loosened his collar, revealing his thick muscular neck.

"Philip of Burgundy and his wife are coming here next month," Henry began.

Harry imagined that he knew why. His marriage to Katharine was to be brought forward and they were coming to attend it.

Henry's next words were a shock. "They are coming to discuss the possibility of your betrothal to their daughter, Eleanor."

"But I am betrothed already. To Katharine."

"That can be got round. I no longer regard it as a suitable match for you."

"In God's name, why not?"

"If you ask properly, you may be answered," Henry said crushingly.

"May I ask why not?"

"Ferdinand is no longer of importance. If he tries to keep Castile he will have to fight for it. When he dies Joanna will inherit Aragon, too. A firm link with Philip will be advantageous."

"How? May I ask in what way?"

"A useful ally."

"England needs none," Harry said proudly. "It is they who need us." And would do, more and more, when he came into his own and could spend some of that hoarded treasure on fitting out armies and restoring the navy, now a pitiable affair of rotting old hulks.

"And it would be good for trade."

The intensely blue eyes blazed. Harry said contemptuously: "Huckster talk! And where does it lead? Katharine and I joined hands, and there was a trade treaty. Broken immediately. The marriages of Kings should not be concerned with the sale of a few ells of cloth! To my eye the best cloth—the best chamberpot for that matter—will find its own market, regardless of who marries whom."

Yes, Henry thought—but not altogether without pride— there speaks the boy who has never lacked; never gone without his supper in order to have his horse shod, or his sword tuned, or a hinge in his armour mended. We work and plan and set them up and then they look down from the place where we have put them and call us huckster.

"You throw my one bad bargain in my face. Think of the

dozen good ones I have made. For England. For you. Think of this. The most powerful ruler in Europe will be your father-in-law; you will have a *young*, and I believe beautiful, bride, and a marriage whose legitimacy can never be questioned."

"Who would dare to question this one? His Holiness gave permission for Katharine and me . . ."

There was something about the way in which he said her name.

"A betrothal can be cancelled. Now listen to me. You will stand up before witnesses and solemnly declare that your present betrothal was made when you were too young to know what it was about; and that now that you do know, you refuse to ratify it."

The moment of outright defiance, foreseen by the father, had come.

"I will not do it," Harry said. "I knew what I was doing when I gave Katharine my hand and plighted my troth. And I stand by it."

The King rose, went to the hearth and kicked a log into place and then stood, back to the fire, his shoulders hunched.

"Katharine," he said, very slowly and distinctly, "is my widowed daughter-in-law. Her dowry was never fully paid; she is my ward and my pensioner. *Mine to dispose of.* Must I wear the crown day and night to remind you that I am King of England? If you are going to talk and behave like some lovesick shepherd boy, dispose of her I will. I'll marry her myself if needs be."

Old, almost fifty, round-shouldered, shrivelled and with a cough! In bed with, married to, the pretty Princess from Spain. Revolting.

But have a care. He is King of England.

"I should hardly have thought that, unfit as a bride for me, she would be fit for Your Grace. And another dispensation would be needed."

"They are easily come by, these days."

"And what must I do to prove that I am not a lovesick shepherd boy?"

"Stand up and renounce your betrothal. Privately. No need to inform the world as yet. And look and act agreeably when Philip and I discuss the possibility of marriage between you and his daughter. That at present is all that is required—except a little more awareness, Harry, that I am your father and anxious, in all respects, to do my best for you."

To capitulate too easily, having said, "I will not do it," might give rise to suspicion. And worse than that it might reveal what was in one's mind. And his mind was set like stone.

"I know," he said, giving his most charming smile. "And I suppose I have much to learn about betrothals and treaties and the political game in which they are used as cards. I am learning now what heirs from birth learn while they are still lisping."

Disarmed and reassured, Henry said, "Go to your dancing, boy."

Harry went, away from the music, towards his own apartments; loitering and scowling.

Then, holding his right wrist with his left hand, he went into a room where a yawning page waited.

"Tom, can you handle a pen at all?"

"I am reckoned to write a good clear hand, Your Highness."

"I strained my wrist at tennis this afternoon. Sit down and write, and make it plain. Begin: Matthew, my good friend . . ." It was a letter such as any young man might write to another; news of himself and of London; mention of the fact that Philip of Burgundy and the Queen of Castile, sister to the Princess of Wales, were coming to England; unwisely choosing January for the Channel crossing. "Now," he said, "take a new line. Write—You may in the next few weeks, hear some strange tales. Take nothing to heart. Between you and me all is well and ever shall be, as I hope shortly to show." He paused.

"Thank you, Tom; that is all."

"Is it writ to Your Highness's satisfaction?" Who knew? A page who could write might become a scribe, a secretary.

"Very well done. I can make shift to sign and seal it. You may go."

Left alone he took his knife and cut off the part of the paper that held the genuine message; then he cut from the rest the four words of Katharine's title. He folded the half letter and applied the wax lavishly, pressing the slip that bore her name into the wax and testing that it held. It was a very necessary communication, but it must be anonymous. Women tended to hoard and cherish things; to show letters to other women; or leave them lying about. He wished Katharine to be reassured; but he had no intention of provoking his father into keeping that truly shocking threat. He had a feeling that she would understand; she might even—and he smiled at the thought— finding the message where he intended to place it—think that it had fallen by some miracle.

Katharine found the letter in her place in chapel next morning. She did not open it. Before you approached God or put yourself into a position in which God could approach you, you must empty your mind of all distractions and mundane matters. Her mind was already distracted by the news, heard overnight, that Joanna was coming to England. The girlish promise, given long ago, was, after all, to be kept.

To Arthur she had described Joanna and spoken of her desire to make a visit to her sister and to be visited by her. Arthur had understood, as he understood everything, and planning for the future he was never to know, had included the visits in his plans. All his plans had gone with him to the grave.

Katharine, a widow, with no assured position and little money could not go visiting, or extend invitations. But now Joanna was coming. At last there would be someone to talk to without any reserve. Katharine had two very devoted ladies, still, but it had always seemed to her to be lacking in dignity to discuss with them the petty humiliations to which she was subjected, or her shortage of funds, or even the fact that she was never allowed to see the Prince of Wales, to whom she was, after all, betrothed. To Joanna she could tell all these things; Joanna was older, cleverer, might be able to advise her; might even lend her some money.

When she opened the letter she was puzzled. There was no signature; the writing resembled none she had ever seen. She recognised the good-will in the message; someone wished to reassure her; there was also a hint that soon she would hear something calculated to disturb her. She did not connect this with the coming visit, for it was common knowledge that Philip and Joanna had been negotiating with Henry about the marriage of their son, Charles, to his daughter, Mary Tudor. They were coming to complete the talks in person, and to discuss the accompanying trade treaty. And how could that affect Katharine? "Between you and me all is well . . ." The only person between whom and herself there was anything that she could think of was the Prince of Wales; it was not his writing and he would have signed his name.

The Court, including Katharine, moved to Windsor and waited. Philip had chosen one of the worst months of the year for a Channel crossing and the voyage had been hideous. Some of the escorting vessels were wrecked, and when the royal couple finally landed at Melcombe Regis Philip was certain that he had been spared from drowning only because at a crucial moment he had vowed that if he lived he would give his own weight in silver to two religious houses.

He arrived at Windsor alone; Joanna he said was so ill and exhausted that she was unable to travel. Actually they had had one of their most virulent quarrels and she had refused to accompany him.

Katharine, admitted to the ceremony of welcome, waited for a moment and then approached Henry:

"Your Grace, I ask permission to go to Melcombe Regis, to see my sister and help to tend her."

Before Henry could answer, Philip said:

"That would be *most* inadvisable," with so much emphasis that both the King and Katharine looked at him with startled inquiry.

"She may already be on her way. She is not seriously indisposed." Nothing wrong with her except bad temper! "She has great recuperative power. And it would be a pity if you missed one another on the road."

With a tenacity towards her own ends that she hardly ever displayed, Katharine addressed herself to Henry.

"I should need only two horses. I would take my own man, Francisco Filipez." Expense need cause him no concern. But Henry had heard the emphasis in Philip's voice and said:

"No, no. It would be better for you to wait here in readiness to greet her."

There was no more to be said.

Katharine waited. Joanna did not come; nor did she send any message. Worried by the silence Katharine repeated her request to be allowed to set out, and this time Henry could plead, with some truth, the inclement weather and the state of the roads. He had now learned from Philip how *most* inadvisable it would be to allow the two sisters to meet before Joanna had come to her senses and given in.

"And," Henry said to Katharine, "I could ill spare you. On an occasion like this a Court needs a chief lady."

There was some truth in that. Henry had thrown off his melancholy and, once again, his parsimony. For ten days Philip was royally entertained. Outside the great grey pile of Windsor, snowstorms obliterated the daylight, substantiating Henry's argument that Joanna was weatherbound somewhere and that if Katharine set out she would be weatherbound too; but inside great fires and thousands of candles blazed and there were feasts and games and dancing. Young Mary Tudor showed her skill with the lute—a skill largely acquired from Katharine; and for the first time in many months Katharine found herself in the company of the Prince of Wales whose manner to her was polite but exceedingly formal—except on one occasion when, commanded by the King, she and Maria de Moreto had given a display of dancing in the Spanish style; the same dance that she had performed, years ago, with lighter feet and a lighter heart, at Dogmersfield, under Doña Elvira's cold and disapproving eye.

Harry jumped up and said, "I would like to try it. Show me."

Philip and Henry, who in the intervals had had long, entirely satisfactory talks, could well afford to sit and laugh.

The true style of Spanish dancing could not be acquired in ten minutes and Harry seemed to be out of his element; clumsy. It involved the minimum of physical contact and for that reason woman could dance with woman and man with man. But under cover of the music Harry said, "Believe nothing that you hear . . . old men sit in corners and plot." And then, having set everybody laughing, he called to the musicians:

"Enough. This is no dance for me." He stood still and held out his hand.

"I thank you for your patience with me. One day I shall do better."

The same warm, reassuring clasp and a glance, no more, from the intensely blue eyes.

"My Lord of Burgundy, I yield place to you," Henry said. Philip of Burgundy stood up and came forward. Henry went and sat by his father.

Old men sit in corners and plot. Perhaps to the Prince of Wales Philip of Burgundy seemed old; but he was only twenty-seven, handsome and vigorous; and ten days of jollity, out of his wife's ambience, with everything going well, had given a patina of happiness and self-confidence to his physical attractions. Katharine thought, dispassionately, that if Charles, offspring of Philip and Joanna, inherited a tenth of his parents' charm and good looks, Mary Tudor could count herself fortunate.

On the tenth day, coincident with an improvement in the weather and exactly twenty-four hours before Philip was due to leave, Joanna arrived.

Any other woman, so pared to the bone, would have been hideous; there were hollows in her cheeks and at her temples and her hands, held to the fire, looked transparent; she contrived to be breath-takingly beautiful. Her eyes, greener than Katharine's, had a feverish brilliance; her skin was like cream satin, her mouth as red as rosehips. Even the King of England who at fifty seemed to be an old man, stared at her with admiration and responded to her animated chatter with smiles.

Her husband watched this display of charm with some apprehension; Joanna's moods were unpredictable and could change more swiftly than the wind. In the tossing ship she was the one person who had shown no panic at all; she had crouched at his feet, her arms around his knees, saying that she did not mind drowning so long as they drowned together: a few hours afterwards she was screaming abuse at him and refusing to set out for Windsor. However, ten days' separation had been as much as she could bear and that she had come at all seemed to hint that she had changed her mind on the subject over which they had quarrelled. He could only hope that she would not let slip something indiscreet.

"And is this," Joanna said, looking around with a shiver, "the best that that old goat can do for you?"

Katharine, accustomed to inferior accommodation, looked around as though seeing her bedroom for the first time.

"This is not so bad as some of my lodgings. At least it has a hearth. Sit here, close to the fire. Oh, I have so longed to see you; and now the time together is so short. I wanted to come to where you were, but for some reason the idea found no favour."

Joanna's eyes glinted.

"And I suppose Philip said, every day, that I should arrive tomorrow. Running after him like a bitch cringing on its belly; begging to be forgiven. I always have, in the past. But this time I stayed away ten whole days; to show him that I could live without him."

"Then you were not . . . not really ill?"

"I am never ill; at least not in the ordinary way. I suffer from one mortal complaint—its name is Philip of Burgundy. I longed to see you, Katharine, of course I counted every wasted day . . . but we had such a quarrel." She put up one delicate hand and pushed back her hair and looked distraught. "Did you

and . . ." For a horrified second she had forgotten the name of
the boy Katharine had married ". . . Arthur ever quarrel?"

"I thank God, no. Never an unkind word."

"No time," Joanna said. "Philip and I had a year, a wonderful
year. Then he ceased to love me and began to torment me.
Deliberately. He is a fiend, Katharine, a fiend."

To Katharine he had seemed to be a handsome, good-
humoured, rather bovine young man, anxious to please and
easily pleased.

"And lately I have had to be so careful," Joanna went on,
lifting her hair again. "Because now he is trying to get rid of me.
He is so clever. He thinks I am blind. But I know. I see through
him. He wishes to drive me mad; he would like me to be shut
up in one of those houses where nuns act as gaolers to the de-
mented. Then he would have Castile, a new mistress every week
and his damned hounds. So you see, I have to be very careful.
At that place with the strange name—Melcombe Regis?—he
took me by surprise and put me in a rage. But I held out ten
days. That should balance things." She laughed: and again
pushed her hair back; the gesture was as regular and as meaningless as the twitch that affected some people's eyes and made
them seem to be winking. And the laughter, like the accusations,
had a hollow sound. This was not the Joanna to whom Katharine had planned to talk, of whom she meant to ask advice,
and perhaps borrow money. When she was not speaking or
smiling or laughing, Joanna wore a look of settled melancholy.
She had always tended, Katharine remembered, to extremes,
too easily exhilarated, too easily downcast.

It was difficult to know what to say; yet something must be
said.

"Are you in such good health, Joanna? You are very thin.
When one ails one tends to take to heart things that are not
important. This notion that Philip is ill-intentioned. . . . I
thought he greeted you with great affection."

The green eyes narrowed and glinted.

"He was relieved to see me. He knew that this time he had
gone too far. Also he was anxious to placate me." That gesture

again. "Listen; I will tell you what happened at Melcombe Regis. Then you can judge of his intentions. I will name no names. There is a person of whom I am very fond, but we have not met for years and my life has been very full and to be honest the person had become a name, little more. Some time ago, in the midst of many other plans and arrangements—you can have little idea of what one is called upon to deal with and consider, Philip mentioned, quite casually, something which would affect . . . this person, in a most damaging way. I made no protest; I may even have agreed; it is sometimes difficult to remember." The hand went to the hair. "It was not, in any case a plan likely to come to anything. Then . . . we had, as you will have heard, a terrible voyage. I forced myself to calm, but I expected to drown at any moment and at such times one looks back over life and remembers. I realised that this person was very dear to me. While I was feeling thus—we were no sooner on land and our clothes changed—Philip spoke again of his plan and his determination to carry it out. I did protest then; I said I would not be a party to it. *And* I saw what he was trying to do—so to upset and torment me that I should behave like a lunatic in England, in front of English witnesses. He has often said that I am mad and should be locked up—but those who know me well do not agree with him. I have friends . . . but not in England . . . You see in these quarrels he speaks soberly, he says *terrible* things in a soft voice, with a smile sometimes. In itself that is maddening."

And so, did you but know it, is that regular movement of hand to hair.

"I cried, I went on my knees and beseeched him not to do this thing. He took no notice—he never does. Then I said that I would prevent it. I am Queen of Castile *now*, he as yet is only Duke of Burgundy. And then he said that if I moved a finger or said a word he would never sleep with me again. Knowing how I love him, he said that to me. And I said I would not come with him to Windsor. To love someone who does not care a fig for you is a very terrible thing, Katharine. I pray you may be spared it. But—there again; Philip says only the Devil would heed any prayers of mine . . ." Abruptly she began to cry, as unrestrainedly as a child, but bitterly.

So beautiful, so lively; so rich in worldly goods; and so unhappy. For whether Philip were actually unkind or not she believed him to be, which was almost as bad.

Katharine dragged her stool near to Joanna's chair and put her arm around the frail, sob-shaken figure.

"Cry on my shoulder," she said. "Perhaps things will look better now that you have told somebody." Perhaps Joanna also lacked somebody in whom to confide completely. *I* meant to tell her things which I could tell no one else; but what have I to tell? Little slights, lack of money, a sense of having been relegated. Nothing.

Presently she said, "You have your children, darling."

"They are *his* too. To dispose of as he likes." Joanna lifted her head and gave Katharine a peculiar look. "I am never allowed . . . not even over Charles' riding. His pony was far too fat—in Flanders they are—and his legs grew more and more bowed. I said he should not ride for a year; or have a less fat pony. Philip just laughed and took him riding for hours every day. Now he will be bow-legged all his life—and none too tall to begin with. And of course, Charles thinks that I tried to interfere with his pleasure and when Philip says that Eleanor is the most beautiful girl in the world and I say that it is not a thing to be said to a child, vain enough already, she thinks I am decrying her. So they love their father and hate me, and would be glad to see me shut away."

More than the report of the quarrel at Melcombe Regis—a nameless person whom Philip planned to damage and Joanna tried to protect, just possibly someone of whom Philip had cause to be jealous?—this telling of domestic bickering showed just how unhappy this seemingly promising marriage had proved to be. After thinking it over, Katharine said:

"Perhaps it ill becomes me to say so because what I have been called upon to bear is by comparison nothing; but if you could be calmer, Joanna. To become excited; to laugh and cry too readily, to show rage . . . it never serves. I have found . . .

I know that my experience has been different . . . but with the little humiliations over the dowry and other things, I always say to myself: You *are* Princess of Wales, behave with dignity. You are so much more. You are Queen of Castile and if you could cultivate calm even Philip, if his intentions are as bad as you suspect, would pause. He would have no ground . . . do you see what I mean?"

"Calm," Joanna said using the word as though it were the name of some vice. "You speak to me of calm!" The last tears had vanished from her eyes which gleamed with positive malice. "Now, show me. Let me see how calm you can be when I tell you that you were the person over whom Philip and I quarrelled ten days ago at Melcombe Regis."

She jumped up and went to the far side of the hearth, hugging herself with her arms and looking dangerous, and desperate and mad.

"But you said, just now, that Philip planned to damage . . ."

"And is it not damage to propose that your betrothal to the Prince of Wales should be ignored and that he should marry our daughter, Eleanor?"

Katharine remained calm, so calm and still and so deathly pale that Joanna thought: I have killed her; she will fall from the stool. Fright banished hysteria and she ran forward and knelt, holding Katharine by the shoulders.

"I should not have said it. Katharine, forgive me. I was against it, I begged and implored . . ."

"You were right to tell me," Katharine said.

"But not like that. Not as a taunt. You see. You said calm and I thought . . . There are times when I think I am mad."

Her hands were very hot. Katharine shrugged herself away from their clutch.

"Sit in the chair, Joanna. I need no support. I am not even much surprised." Her voice was firm, though her lips were white. "I have felt, for some time, something wrong. The way I have been treated. This explains . . ."

It explained the unsigned letter in an anonymous hand; it explained that warm, reassuring handclasp. Harry was young, in no position to defy his father; but he had wanted her to know: "Between you and me all is well and ever shall be." "I thank you for your patience with me. One day I shall do better."

"There will be," Joanna said eagerly, "another match for you and you can trust me to see that it is a good one . . . someone suitable and agreeable. And Katharine, I do beg you, I beg you urgently, say nothing of this. He said that if I made a sign or breathed a word he would never sleep with me again. And that I could not bear. The last ten days . . ."

"Trust me. I shall say nothing. I shall wait."

Joanna, with another lightning change of mood, said:

"You spoke of calm and assuredly you have set me an example."

It was one by which she had little opportunity to profit. Within a few months Philip the Handsome was dead and the brown coffin was a reality. It was of bronze.

Their last months had been spent in Castile, where, because Joanna was rightful Queen, and beautiful and capable—if she set her mind to it—of charming all comers, Philip had deferred to her, and stayed close, not flaunting his infidelities and not taunting her. The brief time of revived happiness made her grief the worse. She refused to have the coffin lid fastened down. Wherever she went it went, in a litter carried by horses all draped in black and with black feathers on their heads; about it monks, in relays, chanted. And at each stopping place, all over Castile, where the rightful heiress had come to show herself to the people, the lid of the coffin must be lifted and Joanna, who should have been asserting her rights, wooing partisans and reminding everyone that she was Isabella's daughter, knelt, sometimes weeping, sometimes praying, but more often staring in a kind of wild ecstasy upon the great handsome man, now a corpse, embalmed but deteriorating, the husband who was now hers, and hers alone.

It was Ferdinand, her father, who finally, not without cause, had her put away into a house where nuns acted as gaolers for the insane.

6

Katharine waited. Nothing happened and nothing was said. In June 1507 Harry had his sixteenth birthday and the time for their marriage had arrived, if the contract were going to be honoured. After that hope dwindled; there seemed no reason why she should not spend the rest of her days as Henry's unwelcome pensioner, poorly housed, shabbily dressed, sometimes so short of food for her household that finally she was obliged to pawn the plate and the jewels that were supposed to be part of her dowry. The other half was never paid. She wrote repeatedly to her father, who never answered. An ambassador who espoused her cause and told Ferdinand that his daughter's circumstances did little credit to Spain, was sharply told that it was Castile's duty to pay the rest of the dowry, Aragon could not be held responsible.

Sometimes she thought that honour was a virtue that had vanished from the earth; her own betrothal had been ignored; there was now talk of Charles' betrothal to Mary being broken so that he could marry a French princess whose dowry was Brittany; and Henry VII, prematurely old and in failing health, had professed himself willing to marry poor Joanna, "mad or not." It was a wrong-headed world and perhaps she was as well out of it; often left behind now when the Court moved. She sewed a great deal, read, observed her religious duties scrupulously, made music and played cards with the members of her small household.

The spring of 1509, coming in with the early flowers and the young leaves on the trees and the cuckoo calling, found her at Greenwich. The Court had moved to Richmond.

Only the King knew that he had gone to Richmond, his

favourite palace, the place with which he had once shared a name, to die. Everybody knew that he was in ill health and had a troublesome cough and little appetite; what else was wrong with him he kept to himself having lost faith in physicians who, for all their nostrums, purgings and bleedings, had not cured his cough. He intended to die if he could arrange it, without their troublesome attentions.

From Richmond he unobtrusively made preparations for death. Throughout the length and breadth of England there were religious houses, once flourishing, now fallen into decay, with three or four old monks or nuns controlling and mismanaging hundreds of acres, potentially valuable, or drawing the revenues of country markets, levying tolls on bridges. The wealth could be better employed and in a few days the King, aided by Wolsey, his Almoner, and watched by his son, gave the order for the funds of several to be diverted and used to build a great hospital in Bath and to provide daily alms for the poor in chosen places. There was a touch of miserliness, as well as good commonsense about even these final charities. But he said, privately to Wolsey, that he wished ten thousand Masses to be said for his soul, and paid for out of his personal money; and in order that other prayers, freely offered from gratitude and goodwill should be said on his behalf, he ordered a general gaol deliverance, a pardon for all those who had broken his laws.

And even so, Death caught him unawares. April the 21st was a beautiful day, warm as June and dry; his cough was alleviated, his heart laboured less; even his secret symptom which he had taken such pains to conceal, seemed slightly abated. He told himself that this morning he felt well enough to have the serious talk with Harry which he had been deferring from day to day. So, having despatched the morning's business from his bed, he was helped into his old robe and slippers and sent for his son. As usual his eyes brightened at the sight of him.

"Lend me your arm, Harry, and I can make shift to walk in the garden. It is such a fair morning. And I feel better."

"I am glad to hear it," Harry said; but he offered his arm with reluctance. His father's arm had grown thin as a stick, and though he frequently complained of feeling cold, his skin held an unnatural heat. His coughing fits were distressing—but disgusting too, producing quantities of mucus. And lately there had gathered about him a curious odour, the smell of age and decay. Harry had an inordinate hatred of anything less than perfect health, perfect form. Many men of position had dwarfs and freaks about them constantly and seemed to find them amusing, he was revolted by them; and if, as often happened, amongst the crowds which he loved—and who loved him—there was at the forefront a blind man, or a cripple, or a man lacking a limb, he would, after a glance, look away. "Give him a shilling and tell him to stand back." Decrepitude repulsed him too. He had a poet's susceptibility linked to a vast egoism; brought face to face with any proof that a man could not be strong and healthy, handsome and young forever, the one cried, "No! No!"; the other whimpered, "Me too? One day? God forfend!"

But he offered Henry his arm and suffered a whiff of what he privately called the smell of old dog. Through his own padded sleeve and the sleeve of the robe he could feel the contact of the sharp bone, and soon the heat, against his own healthy flesh. Old, sick men, he thought, should be content to stay in bed. And then, instantly, he was penitent. Poor old man!

"In which direction, Sire?"

"The seat under the yew. I have something to say—for your ear alone."

The river sparkled and flashed in the sun; the daffodils had broken and in the grass under the trees just beyond the formality of the laid-out garden the bluebells were in bud, a deeper blue than the open flowers would be.

"It is as warm as June," Harry said.

"In June you will be eighteen; that is what I want to talk . . ."

He seemed to stagger, sagged for a second very heavily against Harry's arm and then fell away, and would have fallen to the ground had Harry not quickly changed position, caught and held him.

Dead. Here in my arms. And no one within sight. He is my father; he is King of England. I cannot lay him down, here on the path. I must hold, I must carry . . . He lifted his father—heavier weight than one would have expected from his emaciated state—and stumbled towards the palace, and as he went he shouted in a voice that seemed too loud to be used in the presence of death.

Help came, and the founder of the Tudor dynasty was carried to his bed. He was not dead, yet.

For hours, through a noonday and an afternoon phenomenally warm, the next King of England stood or sat, generally in the window embrasure, while the physicians and the priests came and went. Now and again he wept, remembering how his father, confirmed miser that he was, had never been mean to him: thinking of the young man who had fought his way to the throne, made a marriage that linked red rose to white and healed the sores of the Civil War; loved his wife, begotten children. Reduced to this! Me too? One day?

He knew that death was not the end. The soul, its fleshly envelope cast off, lived on. There was the Judgement; Purgatory, Heaven, Hell. There would be the resurrection of the body, the communion of saints and the life everlasting. All men must die; on the day of one's birth the death warrant was signed. One knew that, but, aged not yet eighteen, on an April day, it was a thing hard to accept.

From the bed, suddenly the King, whom the physicians had given up and the priests regarded as a soul properly despatched on its journey, said, "Harry!"

"I am here," Harry said, hurrying forward. The dying man had spoken his son's name in a loud, clear voice but his next words were so weak and blurred that the boy, leaning over the bed, could hardly hear.

"Mistake, Harry . . . the Spanish girl . . . a bad thing. Free . . . let her go . . . Arthur . . . Choose . . . choose . . ." He made a noise like the beginning of coughing fit, but no cough came. Henry, King of England, was dead.

The room stank of death and there was no purpose in staying in it. The body could be left to those whose business it was. Tomorrow they would be crying, "The King is dead; long live the King," and he would be Henry VIII of England, a figure in two overlapping pageants, one mourning the dead, the other acclaiming the living.

Outside was the April light, tender, lingering. A little time to himself, who could grudge it? And, if they did . . . he was King now. And he needed to take the taste of death out of his mouth, to plunge without a moment's delay into something that was an assurance of life, death's opposite.

Katharine and Maria de Moreto had taken their sewing into the garden, the fine warm day having coincided with the day when the stables were raked out. The work they had been doing was not interesting; they both loved embroidery—stoles, altar cloths, vestments, bold, glowing colours mixed with gold and silver threads, but such materials were costly. This had been a mending day and both were secretly relieved when the light began to fail and the first chill of sunset set a term to it. They pushed their needles into the little pad stuffed with sawdust which absorbed moisture and prevented rusting, and wound the unused thread on the spools. They folded the shifts and petticoats.

"It is a pile," Katharine said, "we have been busy." Mended up, patched and darned, frayed edges cut off and rehemmed. "I will carry some."

"It is not right," Maria de Moreto said. A Princess should not act as porter; and whatever was said or not said, done or not done, one thing was sure; the Princess Katharine was the Princess Katharine and Maria de Moreto her waiting lady— since the marriage and departure of Maria de Salinas, her favourite lady and closest companion.

"By what ruling?" Katharine asked and took up half the pile of mended linen.

They were halfway along the avenue of pleached limes whose leaves, in the one warm day, had expanded into a translucent greenness when Harry entered it, walking swiftly with great strides. Katharine stopped, her heart jolting.

"The Prince of Wales," she said. "Here take these." She turned and pushed the mended things—evidence of poverty and makeshift—on top of the pile Maria was already carrying. She wished that she had been wearing her better dress, and her golden collar—her mother's last gift from which she would never be parted, no matter what the necessity. For, if ever dignity were needed, it was now. She was certain that within the next few minutes her fortitude would meet its final test. She was about to be discarded . . . Everything pointed that way. The fragile little hope, based on a cryptic message and a few words and a handclasp, had long since died. He was too young in a world where old men were powerful, with their schemes and their plots. And Joanna had warned her.

She advanced slowly, holding her head high; he came on quickly. When they were face to face she made him the most elaborate curtsey, holding her skirts, faded and shabby, into the prescribed fanlike shape, bowing her head. He took her by the elbows, pulled her up and kissed her; on the brow, knocking her headdress back. He said, very simply, "My lady," slipped his hands down her arms and took hers and stood looking at her with admiration, with love, with possessive greed, with curiosity. Under the stare she coloured. In him the life force, life-giving, life-begetting, sprang violently, defying death and the misery of the last few hours. He was able to say, almost casually:

"My father, the King, is dead."

She remembered, not the unkindnesses and neglect of recent years, but her welcome to England and the early approval and kindness.

"I am very sorry, my lord."

Answering something in his own mind, he said:

"He was fifty-five. And old before his time."

Me too? No! No! I shall not be old at fifty-five. I shall not ruin my eyes or hunch my shoulders brooding over figures in a countinghouse. At fifty-five I shall still be in my prime; aye and at sixty-five. What was that story some Venetian merchants told, vowing it true; some Turk had lived to be a hundred and ten.

"I have not come to speak of sad things. Or of the past. We must speak of the future."

He was making little of his grief, but she saw that his eyes were reddened and his cheekbones glazed by tears shed earlier. Wine heartened and comforted; she was glad to think that she had a little left of Dr. Puebla's last gift.

"Will you come and take a little wine with me, my lord?"

"Gladly. And except when you must, do not call me that. You are my lady. I am your servant. Your humble, loving servant; soon to be your husband."

Her blush deepened and he knew how right he had been to leave Richmond where death presided to come here, where a look, a word could make a girl change colour.

He had heard and understood his father's last words but he had decided to ignore them; they ran counter to his will. He had been patient, very cautious in his behaviour, wily in his evasions of other betrothals; he did not intend to forego his reward.

He let go one of her hands and holding the other fell in beside her and they walked to the end of the lime walk as once, years ago, they had walked along the raised platform of St. Paul's; a precocious, envious ten-year-old and a fairy princess from Spain.

At the end of the walk she made to go in the direction of her humble apartments.

"This way," he said. "As I came through I rattled the lazybones, and told them to make ready."

The Queen's apartments had not been used since his mother died. There was a musty smell in the air. But the servants left in charge, prepared to doze their time away for months, perhaps for the whole summer, had stirred themselves. The thickest dust had been swept from the surfaces of tables and chests and a newly lighted fire crackled on the hearth. Henry looked round and was satisfied that his order had been obeyed. He was King of England. For the next fifty years, God willing, his word would be law.

"We must wait six weeks, for decency. And then a wedding without display. Where would you wish it to be?"

"Here. If that would suit you . . ."

"Anything that you wish suits me—except the waiting. We have waited long enough."

"Then in the little Oratory of the Observant Friars on the palace wall."

"So it shall be. And to make up for the humble wedding, we will have a coronation of the utmost magnificence," he said. "On . . . on Midsummer Day."

The April evening lingered and darkened; the cuckoo called for the last time but the doves mourned on a little longer. At Richmond those whose duty it was prepared the corpse for burial. Couriers rode hard carrying news of the death. Wolsey made one of his rapid, conservative reckonings and came to the conclusion that with his throne Henry VIII would inherit a fortune of two million pounds in cash money, as well as all the other assets. *Together with his brother's wife,* thought the statesman-cleric, who would have wished things otherwise. In the room which smelt of the past the two young people looked to the future. Six weeks was nothing to those who had learned to wait. They had waited. Both of them believed that the outcome of their waiting was the will of God.

7

"White satin," Henry said. "All white; no colour, even in your jewels—that can come after. There is a coronet called the Orient Crown, all of pearls. The palfreys of your litter must be all white and maids in white dresses shall line the streets. You shall go to your coronation as a bride."

He had learned—or perhaps had been born knowing—that what the ordinary man saw with his eyes made more impact than that which he heard with his ears. He was anxious that all beholders on the Coronation Day should see Katharine as a virgin. There were still a few, old-fashioned people, his grandmother, Countess of Richmond, among them, who chose to believe that Katharine had been Arthur's wife in truth; that Doña Elvira and Father Alessandra between them had muddled things and that Pope Julius had been misled. These people, in the short time allowed them, counselled delay, spoke of the difference in age, calling it six years, spoke of indecent haste, spoke of other, better alliances, even spoke of the yet unfully paid dowry.

They all strengthened his determination. It pleased him to think that England had no need to make an alliance by marriage, that he had no need to bother about a dowry. He had no inkling of it but the pattern of his life was set—he the giver, rich and powerful, conferring favour with a flick of the finger, altering everything with a word. Before he died he was to have, after Katharine, five other wives and not one of them either important in her own right, or rich, four of them his own subjects. But Katharine was his first love and she offered him his first chance to play King Cophetua; it delighted him to take her from poor apartments and set her on the throne; to load her with jewels and replace her worn shabby gowns with the richest and most gorgeous apparel obtainable. Those who directly or indirectly decried her thwarted their own purpose.

"And your hair must hang loose; though I shall be jealous of every man who eyes it. Beautiful hair, wonderful hair." He took a handful of it and wound it about his throat.

She was so dazzled with it all—it was like being let out of a dark prison into the sunshine—that his object in presenting her on her first public appearance as Queen, decked in the symbols of virginity, escaped her. Had he suggested that she wear sackcloth and wooden shoes, she would not have questioned his whim. She was completely subjugated by him and so much in love that she felt wicked. Was it right sometimes to forget even God? To be so carnally inclined?

When the old Countess of Richmond and the Princess Mary, both of whom had avoided her for months, came with offers of friendship she found herself looking at the old woman and thinking: Did you ever know such joy? and at the young one: Will you ever know it? The answer was no. There never had been, was not, and never would be, a lover like Henry.

By the ordinary people the marriage had been welcomed. With them Katharine enjoyed a mysterious popularity. The English did not take kindly to foreigners, and there were times —especially when the trade treaty with Spain was dishonoured —when it was not safe for a Spaniard to walk the streets of London; but Katharine was pretty, in un-Spanish fashion; she had been widowed tragically early; and of late years she had been ill-done-by. English sympathy for the underdog was awakened. And there were all the elements of a romantic tale in the handsome prince honouring his betrothal as soon as his old father—obviously the obstacle—was dead. It was right, and it was also symbolic, part of all the new reign promised, youth in the ascendant, less taxes and restrictions, more splendour.

So the crowds roared themselves hoarse as the pretty Princess dressed like a bride rode to her coronation through streets hung with bright cloth and tapestries and cloth of gold. She was even more beautiful than she had been eight years earlier, and looked, they said, not a day over eighteen.

Katharine was aware that in half a year she would be twenty-four. She also knew that in return for all this adulation, she owed the crowd something—an heir to the throne. Please God, this would be a fruitful marriage and that she would be pregnant soon.

The celebrations were hardly over before she was with child and able to say to Henry—as soon as she was certain: "Dearest, you must not play any more tricks on me . . ." He loved dressing up and bursting into her apartments, followed by a group of young men, all disguised, as Moors, as Saracens, as Robin Hood and his merry men. She was never surprised or deceived, but she delighted in the pretence of being and receiving them as the occasion seemed to demand. Frivolity had played so small a part in her life.

"Sweetheart, *when?*"

"I think in *our* month. April."

Joanna's married happiness had ended when Philip turned from her when she was pregnant: Katharine, seeing her figure grow bulky and her face puffy, knew some anxiety. But Henry never veered. He could have been a middle-aged father watching over a pregnant daughter. When she could no longer dance he would sit beside her and watch until she urged him to join in; then he would dance, never more than once with any lady, and at the end of each measure, come back to her side with a question, was she comfortable, tiring, too hot, too cold? The musicians were instructed not to play too loudly; and never any sad songs; the ballad mongers were to bring no story that would hurt a lady's tender heart. No woman, Katharine was sure, ever had a more cherished, peaceful pregnancy.

They kept Christmas at Richmond, and on the seventh day of the festivities, she was at table when the pain struck. Nothing; I have been overeating. Again; and it is not in my stomach. Akin to, but worse than, the pains I used to have each month,

the pains love cured. July; and this is the first of January. Do
I imagine? No!

"I must retire," she said.

No real cause for panic; I was premature; Joanna once told
me that I was almost born on muleback; and I lived. He will
live.

She said, "Heap up the fire, warm blankets." Born untimely
into a winter world he would need comfort and great care.

But what the last violent wrench of pain brought into the
world needed no warmth, no cossetting. A female, stillborn.

Katharine bowed to the will of God. He ruled all and had
chosen, for some reason that it would be heresy even to question, to bring this pregnancy to nothing. But she was disappointed and feared that Henry would be.

Henry proved that he was unique among men.

"I am sorry. But we are young. There will be others. It is a
pity that you have nothing to show for your pains. Poor Kate,
all to do again." He held her hand, he kissed her and when she
was up and about again, planned things to divert and amuse
her. In after years when she heard him called "cruel," her mind
might accept the word; her heart never did; she had seen him
kind and cheerful in circumstances in which many a man—not
a King awaiting the birth of his heir—would have been gloomy,
reproachful or merely indifferent.

The ordinary people stood by her too. The few, very few,
women who could write, sent letters, all on the one theme. "I
lost three before I bore one living, a great boy I have now."
Most of the messages were verbal, "Tell Her Grace not to
worry. I lost my first . . . my second . . . my third." "I was
hard on forty when I bore my John, after three slips."

The seemingly boundless goodwill—actually proof of the fact
that once the English, from titled lady to fishwife, had taken
up an attitude, were loath to let it go—cheered and heartened
her. February; March; and the Court very gay, full of visitors,

attracted as though by a magnet; a Renaissance Court, but at the same time safe and orderly.

In April—our month—she was pregnant again. This time . . . God, God, please . . .

A year to the very day; on the first of January in the year of our Lord, 1511, this time properly prepared, in a room with new hangings, all embroidered with the initials H and K, she was brought to bed, properly attended, and delivered of a living child, a boy.

"A boy, thanks be to God," the midwife said, as much satisfaction in her voice as if she had begotten and borne him.

The child's first wailing cry was that of dynasty, sounding through Richmond, beyond and beyond. Bell-ringers leaned on their ropes and rocked ancient steeples; bonfires were lighted; people danced in the streets. A prince, a prince; one day to be Henry the Ninth. All England—not yet emerged from the celebration of Christmas into the workaday world—went mad.

And once again Henry showed himself to be unique. From the congratulations, the feastings, the planning for the most splendid christening any child had ever had, he removed himself to go, in midwinter, to a most inclement region of his realm; to stay in what he called "my little palace of Barsham," which was indeed a small and inconvenient if beautiful house; to cast off his shoes in the Slipper Chapel and walk, barefoot, to the Shrine of Our Lady at Walsingham, in order to give thanks to God for this great blessing.

"I wish I could go with you," Katharine said. "Lay my eternal gratitude, and my gift, with your own, at her feet."

"I will."

"I shall go myself, as soon as I am well enough."

"To be well, you must eat well," he said solicitously. "Dish after dish you pick at and send away. Is there nothing of which you could eat heartily?"

"Salad," she said. "With a dish of salad I could outeat you."

Some Spanish dish, he supposed. Bearing the word carefully in the forefront of his mind he went and found Wolsey who knew a little about everything.

"Thomas, what is salad?"

"A dish, Your Grace."

"I know. What made of? How cooked? The Queen has expressed a desire for it."

"A desire which cannot, alas, be gratified. Not in England nowadays."

"Why not *nowadays?*"

"Once," Wolsey said, "there were salad gardens all along the banks of the Thames. They ran to ruin, or so I understand, during the late wars. And sheep are more profitable."

"It grows then?" Henry asked with interest. "Order me a salad garden at each palace and manor."

"Even so—in mid-winter. Though I believe that in Flanders they grow lettuces and carrots and such things all the year round, under glass to save them from the frost."

"Then we, too, will have glass. Meantime order what is needed from Flanders."

"But Your Grace it would be withered and dead . . ."

"Why? A great tree can be transplanted if the roots are dug out wide enough. I want a salad garden dug up, entire, and shipped here with all possible speed. I want some Flemings who understand such things. We will have a whole house of glass if necessary. You see to it. I am on my way to Walsingham. I hope to find a dish of this stuff on my table when I come back."

Katharine must have whatever she wanted: but there was more to it than that. Wolsey's words about the late wars underlined a fact—the later Plantagenet kings had enjoyed a standard of luxury never since attained. During those wars England had dropped behind a little, and not yet caught up because his father cared nothing for such things. He would alter all that. Imagine a King of England obliged to send to Flanders for a dish of salad!

Thomas Wolsey, humbly born, the son of a butcher and grazier at Ipswich, had reached his present position, King's Almoner, by industry and attention to duty. The post in itself was not important; but even in the elder Henry's time he had begun to twist it to his own ends. No former Almoner had been so often consulted, taken into such confidence. The younger Henry had inherited him, relied upon him, had already made him a member of his Council; said to others, "Wolsey will see to it," to Wolsey, "I leave it to you." Wolsey, in the service of his King, and in the interests of his own inordinate ambition, was prepared to work twenty hours a day and to achieve the impossible without breathing hard or allowing the sweat to show. Promotion would come.

By the twentieth of February the Court was at Westminster. All the royal residences were a little too small for the number of people who must be accommodated and each in turn must be used, then vacated and cleaned and aired; regular movement was the habit. But because it was winter it had been decided to leave the baby Prince of Wales with his household, his wet nurses and his paraphernalia at Richmond.

To leave him was a wrench and for the first time Katharine understood why her mother had dragged tired, hungry children from battle front to winter quarters and back again. Poor Mother, she had tried to compound her duty as parent with her duty as Queen. Her own was by comparison a small problem; the baby was in good hands and it was necessary that she should take her place as Queen of England at the great—the most resplendent tournament—planned to take place at Westminster in honour of her son's birth.

The tournament had been splendid. Henry—disguise again—had ridden in the lists as Sir Loyal Heart, wearing her sleeve. Sleeves had now become of such importance that they were garments in themselves, detachable and interchangeable. Ladies, prewarned, had three made so that one could be given to the favoured knight without leaving one of their own arms bared.

She sat in the ladies' gallery overlooking the tourney ground and saw Sir Loyal Heart, wearing her sleeve, white slashed with rose, challenge and defeat all comers.

Later she sat at the table, on the dais of the great hall, and watched what anyone who was not conversant with the English would have thought to be a dangerous riot. Dozens of young men, most of them apprentices, broke into the hall, snatched food from the lower tables, drained wine cups, twitched away gold lace and even jewels from women, and buttons from men.

"It is their way of showing their pleasure," Henry said, and jumped down to join in the melée. They stripped him too. The fun might have lasted another hour had he not remembered the dish of salad; when he did, he called the guard, his Beefeaters, and had the hall cleared.

He came back to the table, in his shirt, all aglow.

"My doublet has gone for honour and largess," he said, laughing. Then Francisco Filipez, her own server, one of those who had lived through the lean days with her, set a great dish of crisp young lettuce, carrots the size of a little finger, sliced cucumber, tiny radishes like rubies, all gleaming with oil, between her and Henry.

At the same time the Duke of Buckingham, whose turn to take the honour it was, moved into position behind Henry with a bowl and a towel. It was a dish that called for the washing of hands.

"So," Henry said. "Now let me see you outeat me."

There was a little commotion behind the screen at the door. Henry said, "If it is the mob returned, tell the yeomen to lay about with intent."

Buckingham jumped down, made his way to the door, vanished behind the screen.

Somebody said, "Holy Mother of God!" and from the lower end of the hall a stunned silence spread like an incoming tide.

Buckingham, making his way through those who had heard, through those who were passing the word, had a face bleached white as bone. When he reached the dais, standing at a lower level, looking up, his face contorted; tears sprang from his eyes.

"The prince is dead," he said.

There were many princes in the world; but only one over whose demise Lord Buckingham would weep.

8

This time she was stunned by grief, bewilderment and remorse. She knew that everything that happened in the world happened because it was God's will, and being the will of God the child would have died had she leaned over his cradle. Yet the thought was unavoidable: There was I, making merry at Westminster while my child drew his last breath at Richmond.

Henry was grieved but still stout-hearted; the child had lived for fifty-two days, that gave hope for the future. There was still no hint of reproach in his manner towards her; nothing but kindness and the desire to comfort.

"Grieving," he said sensibly, "will not bring the boy back; and too much misery could undermine your health, upon which the next child depends."

He thought she spent too long on her knees in cold chapels, fasted too often and too severely. He was himself conscientious about his religious duties and attended Mass every day; but he did not kneel for hours as Katharine did, praying for and hoping for enlightenment as to where she had been at fault to deserve such punishment.

His response to his loss was to think about it as little as possible; to look towards the future, surround himself with good company and allow himself no time for brooding. He was a man, he needed an heir; but his whole life was not centred, as Katharine's was, on a lunar cycle: Am I? Am I not? Perhaps next time.

Also the future into which he looked was different; this year he would have his twentieth birthday; she her twenty-sixth.

The year passed, and the next, without any sign of what she

hoped for; otherwise they were full and happy; and in 1513 Henry paid her the highest compliment which a King could pay his Queen.

War against France had long been talked of. Louis XII had encroached in Italy and Henry and Ferdinand could persuade themselves that in attacking him they were defending the Pope. Both had other motives; Ferdinand his own interests and ambitions in Italy, Henry the ancient claim of the Kings of England to the throne of France. Also war, he felt, would be as exhilarating as any tournament.

"When I go to France," he told Katharine, "I shall leave you as Regent."

"I hope that war may be avoided," she said. He was disappointed.

"No Queen has been Regent since Edward the Third appointed Philippa to be his Regent when he went to France."

She had by this time acquired some knowledge of English history.

"The Scots attacked then. The Battle of Neville's Cross?"

"They are unlikely to do so this time. James of Scotland is my brother-in-law; we have a treaty. Is it fear of the Scots that makes you look so grave?"

"No. If I look grave it is at the thought of your absence; and of the dangers that you will face."

He laughed.

"Danger? From whom? Old Louis of France? One of his knights? When no man in England has yet unhorsed me."

"There are other dangers. I have seen war. For every man who falls on the field three die of disease—sickness flourishes where men live close, and another dies of privation."

The mention of disease woke his horror of it.

"I shall not live close. As for the rest, there will be no privation in this war. Wolsey is ordering the provender; biscuits, cheese, dried fish; twenty-five thousand oxen, all prime beasts, will be slaughtered and salted down. And no man of my thirty thousand will spend a night under a hedge or a haystack. There will be tents for all. And what is more, we take the Twelve Apostles with us."

"In what form?"

"Twelve great guns, now being cast; each bears the name and the image of an Apostle." The knight's sword, the yeoman's bow still had their part to play, but a modern King, planning a modern war, must have modern weapons. Henry spoke with childish pride about his cannon, and indeed he and his friends wore, all that spring, the air of boys planning an outing; they were a generation too young to have known war and when they thought of it they thought in terms of glory; there'd be some blood shed, mostly French, and exciting opportunities to show off skill and courage.

"This, you will see, will be my glorious year," Henry said. "And before I leave, I hope to get you with child again." He could still make her blush.

She hoped that she was pregnant—too early to speak of it, too soon to be quite sure—when she rode down to Dover to see Henry and his host embark. The fleet was the largest ever to leave England; four hundred ships waited in the June sunshine to carry the men, the armour, the horses, the pavilions of the nobles, the tents, the cannon, the provisions. It was a momentous occasion; it was a splendid show; but as she stood for a little while on the beach after Henry had gone aboard, she felt the onset of loneliness—they had been much together in the last four years, far closer than most couples of any rank; fear for his safety—she knew what war was; and a heavy sense of responsibility—for even Wolsey had gone with his King and here she was, in charge of England with two old men, Sir Thomas Lovell, left behind to advise her, and the Earl of Surrey, who was to take charge of the northern border in case the Scots should attack despite the treaty.

She withheld her tears until she was riding, between them, on the way back to London. Then the thought—the wind carries him in one direction, this horse carries me in another and who knows what may happen before we meet again—brought the tears.

She said, "Forgive me, my lords. I know . . . a great occasion . . . not to be marred by weeping . . ." There was a faint echo there, from the past; tears on a wedding day, ill luck to the bride . . . Tears at embarkation. Bad luck to those who sailed? God forbid.

Neither of the old men answered her and she thought that their silence was evidence of disapproval; she looked at each apologetically. They were both weeping too.

"To be left behind, with cripples and dotards," the old Earl said. "I am seventy years old, but I can still ride as hard and fight as well as any youngster. I need no tent to lie in, or beef in a cask. In my day a soldier had the sky for roof and lived on what he could find." Scorn quenched his tears. "Pretty popinjays. I could outlive any three of them and I take it amiss that my very experience should disqualify me."

"It did not," Katharine said vehemently. "It was because of your experience, because you could ride and fight with the best that His Grace chose you to guard the border. The rearguard must be the best—or so I have heard my mother say."

Sir Thomas Lovell said nothing. Her Grace might take amiss any complaint. But he felt in the same way; there'd be a victory to match or eclipse Agincourt, and here was he, left behind with cripples, dotards and *women*.

"The border is quiet as a graveyard," Surrey said.

And so let it stay, please God. Let nothing happen while Henry is absent. Let me sit at Greenwich and feel this child grow; and in March bear a boy, hardier than the other.

The old men wished otherwise. Let the King of Scots ignore that marriage link and the treaty; let the trumpets sound, let the warning beacons blaze; give us a chance to show that the years have toughened, not weakened us. *Let us show what old men can do?*

It was their wish, not Katharine's, which was fulfilled. As soon as the King of England and the pick of his nobility were safely engaged across the Channel, the Scots, following the old pattern, moved southwards. The border, that quiet graveyard, sprang into life again. Surrey halted the invasion which made mock of all marriage alliances and treaties, at Norham, and Katharine as Captain-General called out all available reserves. Men older than Surrey snatched down weapons that had hung on their walls, unused since the Battle of Bosworth Field, heaved themselves onto horses, relatively as old, pastured for years, and rode north. And with them went apprentices from every town and city, some armed only with the tools of their trade, yardsticks, butchers' knives.

To her own surprise Katharine found herself capable of making rousing, patriotic speeches; God's hand, she said, moved in support of those who fought to protect their homeland. She reminded them that the English had always been the most valorous of nations. The old men and the boys went to war with these heartening words in their ears. Those who survived remembered.

She was definitely pregnant now, nauseated at the most inconvenient and unexpected moments. When she said that she must go to York, a rallying point, Maria de Moreto protested.

"It is two hundred miles; five days at least in the saddle. Your Grace, in this state, it is impossible."

"My mother did longer journeys; on worse roads."

And lost several babies that way. Not a thing one could say forthright.

"His Grace, when he returns would wish to find you in good health, a child on its way . . ."

"I must go, Maria. I promised to lead them. They look to me."

Amidst it all she wrote to Henry, as she had done regularly, once a week since his departure; she sent him fresh linen and many admonitions about changing his clothes if he were caught in the rain or became overheated. Her worst fears for his safety were lulled; the French had avoided rather than courted a face-to-face conflict and the only engagement of any importance was called the Battle of the Spurs because the French knights had prodded their horses into headlong flight. To Katharine who knew what real war was, what was going on in France, the exchange of prisoners, the ransoms, Henry firing with his own hand one of the Twelve Apostles, seemed to be what he had imagined it, an exercise in chivalry. She was engaged in a real war.

Things her mother had said came into memory: "An army must have something to fall upon. Men run, but a wall or a fence will steady them and they will turn and fight again."

York, Katharine thought, must be what Surrey's men had to fall back upon. She would be there, with the cannon taken from the Tower.

Fresh recruits fell in at every market square and at every crossroads and by the time she reached Buckingham she had a sizeable army; the country men came armed with sickles, scythes and hay forks.

She held to another of Isabella's axioms—leader and men should be as little separated as possible—and lodged in the one inn of the town. She was hardly installed there when there was a commotion, first in the street, then in the yard. She thought: Quarrelling already! It was, she knew, the curse of armies such as this, seasoned soldiers reserved their spleen for the enemy. She went to the window that overlooked the yard and saw a horse with hanging head, heaving flanks and sweat-streaked hide standing just inside the gateway, while a young man thrust his way through the throng that gathered round him and shouted:

"Hinder me not. I must tell the Queen."

News from France! Her heart halted; the crowded yard swirled in a grey blur. She caught at the window sill to steady herself and called into the greyness:

"Tell me *quickly*."

"A great battle. A great victory, Your Grace."

"And the King?"

"Well, when last I heard. This battle was against the Scots."

Her sight cleared and there was the yard, full of men with their faces lifted up towards the window where she stood; country faces, bronzed from harvesting, paler townsmen's faces, and the face of the young man in tawny, all striped, paper white where the sweat had run freely, grey where the dust had gathered.

"Come up," she said, "and tell me all."

He was as nearly exhausted as the horse which had carried him on the last stage of his wild ride, but, unlike the horse, he knew the worth of the message he bore and the necessity of delivering it properly. On the six stairs that led to the Queen's room he wiped his face on his sleeve so that when he knelt before her he seemed to wear a mask, all greyish, with blazing pale eyes.

The news he brought was wonderful. Never in the long history of war between English and Scots had such a decisive victory been won by either side. The veteran Earl of Surrey had pushed the Scots back to the foothills of the Cheviot Hills and there, by a cunning deployment of his forces, surrounded them. James of Scotland was dead, cut almost to pieces, nine thousand lay dead on the field.

"They will remember Flodden, Madam."

And so shall I; that moment by the window . . .

"What is your name?"

"Harry Percy, Your Grace. I am son to the Earl of Northumberland. Too young for France, they said: but I was at Flodden." The grey mask twitched into a sardonic grin. "And because I ride so light, honoured to bring the news."

Well, wars were fought to be won; and one must think that decisive victories were less wasteful of men than long-drawn-out wars of attrition, skirmishes and sieges.

But how was Margaret of Scotland feeling at this moment? As I would feel at hearing that Henry was dead, cut almost to pieces . . . and for every one of those nine thousand dead men some woman weeps.

She was sickened; but she had learned lately that a resolute ignoring of bodily weakness helped. Fix the mind, the inward eye upon something extraneous, even a thing so trivial as a milestone, or the clink of a loose horseshoe, and the bad moment passed. She fixed her eye and her mind on the thing which the boy wore, knotted around his waist like a sash; a piece of cloth, crudely dyed, the colours at odds with the tawny doublet.

"What is that that you wear?"

"Oh, this? I took it from the Scot I killed, Your Grace. He wore things of more value—but I did not wish to profit . . . All Scots carry these, cloak, blanket, pillow, for most the only equipment, beside arms, that they have." As he spoke he unknotted the sash and shook it out, astonishingly wide.

"It is your trophy," she said, "but might I ask it of you? I could send it to His Grace. It would look well as a banner."

He began to smooth out the creases, "Had I known that it was to be so honoured, I would have carried it more carefully. Folded and wrapped."

"It does very well," she said.

"Oh," he said with a remembering look, "there was something I was to ask Your Grace. My lord of Surrey wished to know what to do with the body of the King of Scots."

Nausea again.

"It should be embalmed. The place and time of interment will be for His Grace to decide."

James had played false, but he was a King. He was also Henry's brother-in-law; he would be buried with due pomp.

And now the makeshift army could go home; some regretfully, some, already homesick, most gladly. She had no need to push on to York. She could sit down and write letters.

"I will write to the Earl of Surrey and despatch my letter tomorrow. Not by you. I think you should rest for a day."

He was affronted.

"Your Grace, I am not tired. A little sleep and a fresh horse . . ."

There was something immensely touching about boys of that age; fifteen? sixteen? So much touchy pride, such an anxiety to prove themselves the equal of men. Please God she would mother such a one.

She wrote to the old Earl of Surrey, jokingly reminding him about the importance of the rearguard and congratulating him upon the wonderful victory. Then she wrote to Henry, telling him the news, but careful not to make Flodden sound superior, or even the equal to the Battle of the Spurs. Of James IV she wrote: "It should have been better for him to have been at peace than to have this reward." And she told Henry that she was sending him a Scots coat—the only name that her tired mind could fix upon—to hang from his banner. And then she thought that, spared the further fighting and the ride to York or beyond, she would make her way back to London by way of Walsingham and she ended her letter, "And now I go to our Lady at Walsingham."

It was a woman's place. It was said that when the Saracens overran the Holy Land, the Virgin was grieved to see her little house at Nazareth fall into infidel hands and had appeared to a Norman lady in Norfolk and asked her to build a replica, giving specific instructions. Angelic hands had helped in the building and in the inmost sanctuary there was a little flask, filled with the milk from the breast that had nursed the Saviour of the world—still liquid after more than fifteen hundred years.

It was the season of pilgrimage; humble and unassuming she took her place with the rest and prayed for a child, a living boy, lusty . . . Holy Mother of God, not my need alone, England's need . . .

There were dozens, hundreds of them, helping with the last harvesting, brown-faced, barefoot little boys. And in and around Walsingham more of them, eager to hold a horse's head, eager to carry the shoes one must discard, eager to sell the crude, yet oddly pleasing images of clay or wood. The world that September seemed full of little boys.

It was still September when she miscarried.

One must not give way to despair; it ranked with gluttony, avarice and anger amongst the deadly sins. She knew that she must not dwell upon the loss of some part of her flesh, a little red lumpish thing, no bigger than a pear; but she had looked forward to greeting Henry with the news. Oh God, why? What have I done?

Henry came back, safe and well, full of his exploits; as loving as ever, and yet, she sometimes felt, subtly changed. Over two matters that autumn he surprised her by showing a ruthless streak. One was the disposal of the corpse of the King of Scots. She spoke of it, thought he had forgotten and reminded him. "Why bother about him? He stabbed me in the back. Let him rot." The embalmed body was bundled away into a lumber room. The other matter was the marriage that was to seal the peace between France and England; a marriage between Henry's sister, Mary, and Louis XII. Mary was eighteen, old enough to have a mind of her own, too old to be easily compliant; at the same time too young for an old, ailing man. She wept and protested, made what seemed to Katharine pitiable little attempts at defiance. Henry was adamant.

"Take her aside," he told Katharine, "and make her see sense."

"She is in love, Henry; that makes it harder."

"Unworldly, girlish nonsense about Charles Brandon. She is a princess not a lovesick . . ." He halted abruptly and his face took on a curious remembering look; but whatever he remembered seemed to make him more irascible. "This mopish atmosphere wearies me. Tell her, if she weeps again in my presence, I shall send her to Hatfield until she sails for France."

The reference to a mopish atmosphere was a little disturbing. It was true that since his return she had found it more and more difficult to match his exuberant high spirits; some of the pranks, once so amusing, seemed silly; the days of hunting, a pastime she had adopted eagerly because it meant being with him, she now found exhausting and every now and then, even when she was making merry, the thought would strike, like a cold draught —twenty-eight and I have no child. But, disturbed or not, she risked one more protest on Mary's behalf.

"She is eighteen; and at that age one's heart can be set. As we know." Surely that would move him. It did not.

"A different thing altogether," he said, "and you are not to encourage her."

Mary, without encouragement from Katharine, struck her own bargain. In every marriage ceremony there came a moment when the bride could say, "I do" or "I do not."

"And I will say I do not, loud and clear, in Notre Dame, unless you promise me that when the old man dies—I hope it may be soon—I can choose my second husband myself."

She made other conditions, too; she would have only English women and girls about her. Prospective candidates for the honour of accompanying the Princess Mary to France came to Court to be inspected and approved. One was Sir Thomas Boleyn's second daughter, Anne; among the fair, pink-cheeked young creatures, her colouring marked her out; darker than any Spaniard; not pretty, but with a certain grace. Katharine noticed her, a changeling child . . .

Mary left for France in October 1514. Two months later Katharine gave birth to a boy, born living, dead within a few hours. He had not even been christened; nameless he went to join other unbaptised infants in Limbo. The will of God? Yes, she must cling to that because beyond there was nothing but darkness and chaos; and a mind that might, all too easily, run distraught. Why? Why? She asked God and there was no answer; but when, mourning, she put the question, perhaps for the twentieth time, to Maria de Moreto, Maria said:

"The blame lies elsewhere, Madam. It is not *your* punishment; it is *his*. And well deserved."

Her voice was hard; she was a hard woman. She had been born, eighth child, fifth daughter into a family of the kind which only Spain could produce. Immensely proud, wretchedly poor. In such a family sons, handsome enough, might make advantageous marriages, or, clever enough, attain some official post; daughters without dower, but with some looks, might make marriages, not altogether mésalliances. But even the most determined and resourceful parents grew old and lost hope and energy. By the time that Maria was twelve she was acting as page to her brothers, even polishing armour at times, and as maid to her pretty sisters. Servants were plentiful enough in the unproductive countryside in which her father's crumbling castle stood, but they expected to be fed, and whenever there was a shortage the old man would go stamping and shouting through the kitchens and stables, driving them out. "Look to God to provide for you, not to me." They fled; and presently, finding God's rations even shorter than their master's, they drifted back. In the interim periods Maria did the menial work.

One of her brothers, who had attained not the hoped-for good marriage, but a minor appointment in Isabella's Court, remembered his little sister with gratitude, and when Katharine's suite was being gathered, had mentioned her name. So she had come to England. She was rather less than a year older than Katharine, but she was hard, sour and intolerant.

Katharine said, "And what has His Grace done to deserve such punishment? Missed a Mass? Eaten meat on a fast day?"

Too late, Maria realised what her outburst meant. *She*, if she answered the question, must cause distress to the mistress she adored. She said primly:

"I spoke inadvisedly. It is not for me to criticise His Grace."

"But you did! Now, you will sit on that stool and you will explain what you meant. If His Grace is at fault, there is a remedy. He is as anxious as I am."

In moments of emotion her voice always deepened, as her mother's did. It was like a man's, like the voice of the fearsome old father who had dominated Maria de Moreto's youth. It woke fear's memory. Maria turned pale, was glad to take the stool.

"One must be to blame. And it is not Your Grace; so pious, so charitable, wearing the rough habit under the silk and the velvet, going to Walsingham again, and to Canterbury. Therefore it must be His Grace. That was all . . ." She let her voice trail off and she managed to produce the smile, sick, sly, false which had been her defence in another time, another world.

"You meant more than that, Maria," Katharine said.

Well, Maria thought, better the knowledge than the whispers, the sly looks. Sooner or later someone will tell her.

"It gives me sorrow to say this, Your Grace. But I ask myself, what blessing can a man expect on his own marriage when he sins with another man's wife?"

Katharine turned pale, but she remained calm and her expression showed more astonishment than shock or anger or hurt. It was, quite simply, unbelievable. Men did often seek, in another woman's arms, something they failed to find in their wives'; but not Henry. It had been a consolation for her childlessness that the love between them had never ceased to be lively and fresh. After six years, no lessening of passion or pleasure. A perfect relationship, she would have said, in bed and out of it.

"Maria, are you *sure*? People spread such wicked . . ."

She saw by Maria's face that it was true.

"Who is she?"

"She was born Elizabeth Blount," Maria, born Maria de Moreto, said with contempt in her voice. "She married Sir Gilbert Taillebois and followed him to the war. At least to Calais where the King met her. Now she has a manor, called Jericho. In Essex."

That had the ring of truth. Henry often went in that direction, his destinations variable, Brentwood, Romford, Tilbury; and always he had had some reason for going alone.

"Calais. That was months ago. *Has she borne his child?*"

"Not yet."

"And everybody knew. Exept me."

"Know is too firm a word. Whispers. Rumours. Jokes about the walls of Jericho falling. I made it my business to find out. Your Grace wearing your knees to the bone . . . And it is true, I swear it. So you need no longer ask *why*. God has His ways of punishing men; and the innocent suffer with the guilty."

"One lapse, Maria," Katharine said defensively. "His Grace was absent almost four months. And in *France* . . ." A Spaniard, speaking to a Spaniard, had no need to complete the sentence. Of all peoples the French were the most easygoing in such matters.

A natural curiosity made itself felt.

"What is she like? Very pretty? Very young?"

"Fair, they say. Somewhat plump. And with a shrew's tongue. Sharp words, spoken with a smile, can pass for wit."

Was that the attraction? I am older than he? I have taken each loss to heart. Perhaps I have become too serious, even in my loving.

"Maria, I hope that you contradict this story whenever, wherever you may hear it. The old King was strict. His Grace had no opportunity to sow, as the English say, his wild oats. I shall make little of this, except to point out, as is my duty, that adultery is sin and imperils his soul."

And even for that, great strength was required. The happy, the seemingly perfect relationship . . . only last night . . . He would be angered. It was plain that he had done his best to keep her in ignorance. Some men flaunted their mistresses. Kings had been known to bring their paramours to Court, splendidly dressed, dripping with jewels and forced their Queens to accept and recognise. Henry had spared her that. Or God. God knew the inmost secrets of the heart and knew what each could bear.

"Come to bed, Kate," Henry said at last. She was overlong at her prayers and would take a chill. Katharine was praying for strength and courage, praying that Henry might not be angered and that he might take notice of what she had to say. But he could not be kept waiting forever. She rose from her knees and went to the bed. Henry threw the covers back. "Come and get warm." He pulled her close and, holding her, blew out the candle.

After a few seconds he asked:

"What is wrong with you tonight? So long at your prayers; and now . . . ?"

"I heard something today that made me sad."

"You sadden too easily," he said, handling her more pur-

posefully. It was some silly little thing, he thought; she had
heard of some woman giving birth to a child; or a nun dead;
or an orphan sick; or one of her many protégées turning out
badly. "Nobody can bear the woes of the world." For six years
she had found refuge from woe on his breast; tonight, clutching
and fondling, he felt the difference.

"Who or what made you sad today? Is it anything I can deal
with?" He had lightened her grief often; once even countermanding the death sentence passed on some silly—but dangerous—boys, because she had been sad, saying that they were
young, and how would their parents feel?

She said, "It is a hard thing to say. And I beg you not to be
angry."

"Have I ever been angry with you?" He could ask that with
a certain smug justification. Many a man, married for six years
and with no living child would have blamed his wife, said harsh
things. Many a man, let down as he had been by Ferdinand,
would have said spleenish things to the man's daughter. Henry
never had. He was a poet and to him more than to ordinary men,
love was a beautiful, shining whole, a climate, a country, not
of this world. Set apart.

Katharine said, "No. But darling, I have never yet spoken of
Elizabeth Taillebois. And now I must."

The convulsive movement he made shook the solid bed. She
waited for the rage. She knew Henry's temper. Into fury, as
into everything else he threw the whole of himself, strong body,
lively mind, ardent soul.

But now after what seemed a long silence, full of dread, he
spoke in a muted voice.

"I hoped you would never know. It is a thing no woman—
not even you—can understand. You must not even think . . ."
Usually so fluent with words, he spoke haltingly. "Unfaithful
in the act; never more, Kate. Never in my heart. No love concerned. Nothing that you and I . . ." He knew that he could
never hope to explain. Presently, in a more positive voice, he
said, "I am heartily sorry, sweetheart, for any pain I have caused

you. Forgive me." His hands added—And forget. It would have been easy to do; but it would be a failing in duty.

"I do. I have. But Henry, it is sin."

"As well I know. The penances lasted longer than . . . Five Masses one day. When I should have been hunting." He sounded plaintive; almost ill-done-by. She could imagine Dr. Langford, his confessor, growing sterner with each iteration.

"We are told," she said gently, "to avoid occasion for sin."

"I do. I have tried. Then something starts; a tune, a scent, a mere thought in the mind. No woman knows . . . See," he took her hand and guided it. "Here we are, talking of *my* wickedness and *he* is so unruly . . . Kate, my love!"

Afterwards she wondered, whether for the good of his soul, she should have been firmer; wept perhaps, made the most of her hurt and extracted promises. She examined herself sternly, too, in another direction. Had she been right to be so pleased to hear that Henry's heart was not concerned. She had believed it and been gratified, whereas, really, in the eyes of God, surely the heart's involvement was the only possible excuse.

Then she gave up thinking about it; for though Henry had made no promises and she had been too easily distracted, on that night or one soon after, what she had prayed for came about. In May, am I? In June, I think so. Then certainty.

This time she carried the child full term and on February 18, 1516, gave birth to a baby, very strong and lively; even the first cry was different; not a kittenish wail at being confronted with an alien world, but a lusty noise—Here I am! There was only one tiny flaw in the happiness; the baby was Henry's daughter, not his son.

Henry proved himself equal to the occasion. He was as pleased as though Mary had been a boy. No prince, not even the little boy who had died at Richmond, ever had a more ostentatious christening; no child ever had a more doting father. There were many men, indeed the majority of men, who would have turned away, saying, "After all this, a mere girl!" Henry spoke proudly of "my daughter," and would carry the baby about to take the air in the garden or to be presented to visiting notables and ambassadors who, if they valued his goodwill, were prompt and fulsome with their admiration. In his complex and sometimes contradictory character the paternal instinct was strong. Katharine was one day to learn that any child of his was an extension of himself. In addition, this little girl, solid and thriving, was a promise for the future. Next year she would have a brother.

When Henry spoke of the boy who was to come, Katharine said, "I hope so," or "God grant it may be," but as Mary survived the most dangerous period of early infancy and she herself did not become pregnant again, she sometimes wondered, in her inmost mind, whether it mattered so much. Her own mother had been a Queen, one without equal among Kings; could not this child, properly trained, well-educated, be to England what Isabella had been to Castile? The English, she realised, would have to be converted to the acceptance of a female ruler. Long ago, another Henry, dying without a son, had wished his daughter to become Queen, but the moment he was dead the young woman's male cousin had claimed the throne and there had been a civil war of such savagery that men had said that Christ and all the saints slept.

Still, things were different now; Henry I had died in 1135; this was the sixteenth century and in four hundred years fashions in thought and social attitudes underwent changes.

Whenever Katharine entertained such thoughts, sooner or later she was bound to think of Thomas More, Henry's closest *friend*. A King's society was, like an archery target, a thing of concentric circles, narrowing down. At the centre of Henry's wide ring of acquaintances, servants, jolly companions, men to be sparred with, using weapons or words, More was unique, the very centre. He was thirteen years older than Henry, but he seemed to have learned the trick of perpetual youth without missing the lessons taught by experience. He was, in intellect, one of the new men, a humanist, a disciple of Erasmus, a student of Greek—and in Greece, in classical times, women had not been despised. He was good-looking, a thing which counted enormously with Henry, and he was witty, which also counted. Katharine had realised, quite soon after her arrival in England, that verbal quips, the seemingly flippant yet telling comments that provoke first laughter and then thought, could only be made in the tongue to which one was born. To More's witticisms her own response was always just that perceptible second slow.

But she liked, admired and trusted him, and in planning her daughter's future, somewhat prematurely, she counted upon his support. He had a daughter of his own, Margaret, whom he was bringing up, so far as education went, exactly as though she had been his son. And when, leaning over the infant Mary she had said to Henry, "Children at an early age learn so easily; she must learn Latin and French as she learns English. And all the other things of which I am ignorant," Henry had said, "To what end? The time would be better spent in acquiring the graces."

One evening, at the little supper table, private and intimate, she asked a bold question: "Sir Thomas, have you found that your daughter's learning"—he had been boasting about it— "has interfered with her acquiring of the grace desirable in a woman?"

"How could it, Your Grace? God knows His job. Every woman is born with grace. Imagine a man making a curtsey or climbing a flight of stairs, cumbered with skirts! I often think: God tried His prentice hand on man and then improved, as apprentices do, and so made woman."

Henry said amiably, "Tom, that is near heresy!"

"Heresy, your Grace? *The adoption and maintaining of a belief contrary to authorised teaching.* Hardly. And what always struck me forcibly was that in Eden, whereas Adam turned about and blamed the woman whom God had made for tempting him, Eve was more moderate in her denunciation and simply said that the serpent beguiled her. She did not say: "The serpent *whom you made*, thus shifting the blame. Is it possible that when it comes to point, the female more willingly accepts responsibility? Is that a heretical question?"

"It does not answer mine, Sir Thomas," Katharine said mildly. "I am anxious to know because I want Mary to be thoroughly educated, but not at the expense of grace, charm, feminine accomplishments."

"A girl," Henry said, "should be able to read and write; to dance well and to ride, to make herself agreeable even to those whom she does not find compatible. And if she can sew a fine seam," he said, smiling at Katharine who had sewn so many for him, "all the better. My sweet Kate, you have only to look in your glass to see how Mary should be modelled."

She said, "I thank you. A pretty compliment! But the world has widened since I was schooled. I want Mary never to be at a disadvantage."

More's ear, always sensitive and sharpened by long hours in courtrooms where the downright lie was negligible, the half-truth, the insinuation important, informed him that between Henry and Katharine there was a difference of opinion which probably neither would have acknowledged. The Queen looked upon her daughter as heir to England; the King saw her as some man's wife.

He said, "Wait a little and let the child be your guide. We none of us ever learned anything we did not wish to learn; and no one ever will. Colet taught me Greek and I learned, because I wanted to read the stories; in his school at this moment there are a hundred and thirty boys, half of them have no wish to learn Greek and no amount of beating will inculcate that wish. To the child offer all things; give her what she reaches for."

It was the kind of halfway answer to which, in his dealings with Henry, More was driven with increasing frequency. He was an honest man—so honest that he was sometimes called the only honest lawyer in London, but tact was needed in conversation with the King who was responsible for all appointments and all promotions and More had a wife and family for whom he felt responsible. In addition he was genuinely fond of Henry, admired his qualities and enjoyed his company. Occasionally, when a matter was important and no tactful answer available, he would take refuge in silence. Then Henry would say, "Lost your tongue, Tom?" and More would say, "No. The line of your argument," or "my ability to agree on this subject."

This evening, on the subject of female education he had been honest, saying what he truly believed and in such a way as to displease neither hearer—or so he thought, but though Katharine was satisfied—offer everything was exactly what she intended to do, Henry's face took on a petulant look; he had expected more positive support. After all, he had made his *own* views plain. He cast about in his mind for a suitable way of expressing a mild displeasure and found it so easily that his face brightened into amiability again. He put down his knife and said, "It has come to my ears, Tom, that when someone congratulated you on being in high favour with me, you replied: 'Make no mistake; if my head would buy him a castle in France, he would have it.'"

Where did eavesdroppers hide? Where were such gleanings marketed? More wondered. He had spoken those words, in the privacy of his own house, to a man he trusted absolutely—the man he hoped to have as a son-in-law one day. What a dangerous world!

"Yes. Those were my words. You mislike them, Sire?"

"They show small faith in me, Tom."

"A tribute to your good sense and care for your subjects' lives. How many stout fellows' deaths would it take to capture a castle in France? Surely against them one head, even such a one as mine . . ." he laughed and spread his hands. "Incidentally a tribute to my own good sense too. Being in favour should not make a man think himself indispensable."

Whatever sting the reported remark had once held, it was gone. Henry said warmly, "Not regarding yourself as indispensable renders you so to me, Tom. I would not give your head for twenty French castles!"

Just for a moment another presence seemed to hover about the table as all three who sat by it thought of another indispensable man, Cardinal Wolsey, Archbishop of York, Bishop of Lincoln, holder of a dozen other clerical offices and the Pope's Legate in England.

Katharine thought of him with a certain dislike. Well as he had organised provisions for the army to invade France she suspected him of pro-French sympathies and of wishing that Henry had not married a Spaniard. This feeling was instinctive rather than reasonable, but it tended to make her critical of his ostentation, his extravagance and self-importance. Once the French war was over—with Flodden reckoned as part of its victory—Henry had showered favours upon Wolsey, given him three dioceses in a single year and practically ordered Pope Leo X to send the coveted Cardinal's hat to the man without whom he, King of England, could do nothing of importance. Wolsey had promptly abandoned the plain cassock which had been his wear, and the mule which had been his mount. Now, clad in scarlet satin, mounted like a prince, he outshone every noble in the land, and sometimes came near to rivalling Henry himself. His building schemes were inordinately ambitious, his hospitality royally lavish, nine hundred people were said to eat at his expense even on an ordinary day. It was possible for Isabella's daughter to think, tolerantly— The man is compensating himself for his humble birth. Possible to think— Only in England could a butcher's son rise so high. But under all such thoughts, under the personal distrust, was a more deeply rooted feeling. A man who had clambered so far by way of the Church, should be more attentive to his clerical duties. Dioceses and livings were not to be collected and held and exploited, like cattle or acres of land. Wolsey might be an administrator without equal, a diplomat of the utmost skill and cunning, a sound theologian, but he was not a good priest. Yet, whenever she reached this conclusion, a little self-distrust would round off the circle. Could it be, she wondered, that she misjudged him because she was jealous of him? Henry spent so much time with him, held him in such high esteem. . . .

Henry thought of his faithful servant with complacency. It was right that the greatest King on earth should be served by the most splendid minister. He admired Wolsey's taste and style, and if he ever remembered his humble origin it was only to underline the thought that a King could make so lordly a creature out of a butcher's son. Even Wolsey's extravagances reflected glory on himself. And that a man should be able to employ his remarkable talents in a sphere so far removed from that into which he was born reflected credit on England, so different from France and Spain where all high office was the prerogative of the aristocracy. Added to all this was his complete certainty that Wolsey was utterly devoted to himself; in Wolsey there were no reserves at all. If Wolsey ever hesitated when confronted by a suggestion, or spoke a word of unpalatable advice it was not from scruple or principle but because he had the King's good at heart. There lay the difference between the two Thomases. It was possible for Henry to imagine a situation in which More would put a moral or religious consideration first. Just possible. Not that this detracted from Henry's esteem of More; in a paradoxical way it enhanced it. Henry admired integrity. As he thought his complacency grew; he was a fortunate man; an amiable wife of his own choosing—and how many monarchs could claim as much? One true Thomas to use and another to enjoy. Only one thing lacking—and that would be granted in time.

Thomas More thought of Thomas Wolsey with admiration and a certain pity. It was impossible not to admire the tenacity and industry of a man who could sit down to a job at four in the morning and stay there for twelve hours, not eating, ignoring the needs of nature. Impossible not to admire a mind, so acutely intelligent, so widely informed, and gifted with such power of memory. At meetings of the Privy Council it was noticeable how when some matter was mentioned—even a matter presumably outside the man's immediate range—he could, without reference to book or paper, produce some relevant facts or what appeared to be a considered judgement. More, whose own tastes were simple, also admired the way in which Wolsey had taken to grandeur; ostentatious perhaps but always within context; never vulgar. Even his enemies—and he did not lack them, though they might snarl enviously behind his back, face to face with him, never failed to be impressed by his personal dignity. But More, who missed very little, had seen Wolsey's single weakness—a too great dependence upon the King: he had, to a dangerous degree, made Henry Tudor his god. And if for any reason his god should cease to smile, should turn away his face, or frown, what would the poor fellow have left?

Wolsey, the indispensable man, brushed against all their minds and was gone and Henry reverted to his baby daughter, and again in terms which showed Katharine that when he looked towards the future he did not visualise Mary succeeding him.

"We may pick and choose what the child shall learn," he said; "when it comes to whom she shall marry there is no choice. I've given this some thought of late and there is only one man fit to mate with my daughter—her cousin Charles."

"But he is far too old," Katharine said. "By the time she is marriageable he will be thirty and more."

"In his prime," Henry said, ignoring, as usual, anything which did not exactly fit his wish. "He is now King of Spain, when Maximilian dies he will have the Netherlands and Austria; and he is certain to be elected Emperor. Mary will be Empress."

To both his hearers there was a touching naïveté in this confident plan-making.

"It would hardly do to count upon it," Katharine said. "Before Mary is half-grown Charles will be under pressure to marry and . . ." She realised what she was about to say, faltered a second and then finished the sentence, controlling her voice, "beget an heir." Once one admitted that a subject was too sore to be touched upon it was sore indeed.

"Mary will be worth waiting for," Henry said. "And if Charles should need advice as to how to resist pressure, he can apply to me. Eh, my love?" He smiled at her and she was passionately grateful to him, both for refusing to admit that the subject was sore, and for thus indirectly reminding her that he had waited for her, avoiding all other betrothals.

More, watching them, thought how mysterious were the ways of God. A loving couple, both seemingly healthy, wedded for more than eight years, dead babies, miscarriages, one living child, female. And the Queen, poor woman, past her first youth, thirty-three at this year's end; beginning to show her age, too.

Katharine was only too well aware of the way in which the gap in age between her and Henry was widening. Her glass was a constant reminder. Disappointment must be accepted and could be borne, but it left a mark. In repose her face now wore a look of settled gravity, of patient resignation. Her smile was still sweet and in moments of animation her eyes brightened into beauty again, and since the sight of Henry always pleased her, this was the face which he saw most often. But repeated pregnancies had thickened her figure and though she wore her stays tightly laced, was careful to preserve an erect posture, kept every fast day and on others ate sparingly, the slenderness of youth was gone forever. Her complexion, thanks to Maria de Moreto, was well preserved.

"My mother," Maria said, "kept her looks into old age." She spoke without fondness or pride, remembering how often she had beaten eggs and oil and honey into a cosmetic paste, when they could be ill spared. Now, with more loving care, she whisked and Katharine wore the sticky mask. "For the hands and neck, to keep them white, there is nothing like lemon juice," Maria said. And though lemons were less easily come by in England than in Spain, they were obtained and the juice faithfully applied. Even more rare and expensive was henna, with which the prophet Mahomet was said to have dyed his beard. It was good for colouring, hiding the fading hairs and brightening the rest, but the silky lustre was not restored. In all this business of fending off the damage of the years, clothes helped. She chose more sombre colours now but the materials were always sumptuous and her fondness for jewels had not lessened. Fully garbed and bejewelled she was a magnificent, if not a youthful, figure. Sometimes she remembered her mother, too busy for vanity, caring only that her clothes should be clean and suitable to the occasion. But the lesson to be learned from that memory was plain—her mother and father had ended as a pair of working partners, and then not always in accord. It was not a relationship which she wanted to establish with Henry; never, not even when they were very old.

Presently Mary was three and there had been no sign of another child to follow next year, next year, next year. There were moments when Katharine felt that she had failed Henry, and England in not providing a prince; but neither King nor country seemed to bear her any grudge. To Henry she was still dear Kate, or my love, and he still took pleasure in her company: with the people she was still popular, the Princess who had somehow caught their unpredictable fancy, the Queen whom they knew to be good.

And there was always Mary, as satisfactory a daughter as any parents ever had. Unlike Katharine in her youth, Mary learned quickly and easily; in that way she was like poor Joanna; but there were no disquieting signs to be seen in that resemblance. Mary was sensible from the first, completely amenable and a stranger to fear. At the age of three, wearing a gown which save for its colour was an exact replica of her mother's, she would face any stranger, however impressive, make a perfect curtsey and say, in English, Latin, French or Spanish, "Welcome to our Court." It was a performance that never failed to charm, and to astonish, since Mary was small for her age. Her parents, who had also appointed themselves as her first teachers, would look on with pride. Katharine would think: God saw fit to deny me a son, but in His mercy gave me Mary. Henry would think: My daughter so gifted, what might my son not be?

9

"As you say, a fine boy," Elizabeth Taillebois said. "And it is a pity that he will have no name." A little malicious sparkle brightened her eyes. She had done what the Queen had failed to do and borne the King a son. This boy was too late to be of her dead husband's begetting.

"He will have a name," Henry said, looking down at the cradle; "the best, after Tudor. Fitzroy. That will be his name; Henry Fitzroy, son of the King." His face darkened a little and he looked stubborn. "If it pleases God to withhold from me a legitimate son, he will have titles too. Duke of Richmond: Duke of Somerset.

More than she had hoped. Duke of Richmond was the title which the child's grandfather had carried when he won the Battle of Bosworth and made the English crown his own. As for Henry begetting a legitimate child, that possibility could be dismissed. It was three years since Princess Mary was born, and not a sign.

"That should go a little way to make up for being born a bastard," Lady Taillebois said. "What a pity that there is not some pretty title that means King's whore; then I could claim the honour."

She had, not wit exactly, but a sharp, almost shrewish way of putting things which Henry found amusing. She had never had and would never have, any emotional hold on him, their relationship was quite unsentimental; she was good to go to bed with, once in a while, and she often made him laugh.

"You wrong yourself," he said, "Or do you? Whore implies

some degree of promiscuity. I suppose," he said, pretending
doubt, "that he is mine."

"Mewed up here as I have been, by Your Grace's order, I
fail to see whose else's he could be. A stable boy's? A gar-
dener's?" She too pretended doubt, squinting at the child. "I
rather think not. To me he does not look like a peasant's get."

"You are a hussy."

"When you say that, you should add, Thank God!"

"Sometimes I do. And I do thank God for the boy . . ." This
was clear proof that he was capable of begetting a son, strong
and healthy. But why, in the name of God, couldn't he have
been Katharine's child, born at Richmond, Prince of Wales?
As soon as Henry's resignation had ceased to be mitigated by
hope, a slightly rebellious element had crept into it. He never
expected to be enlightened; commanding officers did not explain their motives or designs to those under them; on the other
hand even a foot soldier was entitled to mutter and mumble a
bit, under his breath, when faced with a situation that he could
not understand. Henry muttered and mumbled to himself
fairly often. This splendid child, now three months old, past
the most dangerous post-birth period, and with the true Tudor
red hair curling on his head, was a son whom Henry would most
proudly and gladly have presented to the nation. Imagine the
joy! Presumably God knew His own business best—one must
believe that—but what a left-handed way of doing things!
And how difficult God had made it for his true soldier! In order
to give this child his due—and to show the world what Henry
Tudor could produce, it would be necessary to hurt Katharine.
And that he shrank from.

She was no longer the red-gold, pink-and-white princess from
Spain whom he had coveted, envying Arthur, and married,
defying some death bed words. She was a woman, settling down
to middle-age, engrossed in the upbringing and education of
her only living child. Her extreme piety sometimes bored him—
he thought the wearing of a nun's habit was carrying things
to extremes—but she had never done or said anything that
could, in the slightest way, diminish his respect and admiration

for her. She was part of his youth, the first woman he had truly loved, and she fitted him well, in many ways. Her dignity complemented his; she had a sense of occasion that matched his; she had good sense, and magnanimity. He still admired her; he still loved her, but love, like a masquer, had changed its face of late. She no longer stirred *him*, that little, most vital member, once so unruly when in near contact with her that he would assert himself, even during a scolding. He could still take her hand, kiss her, lie beside her but these touches were no longer a preliminary to bliss.

And could a man be blamed for that. *He* was not subject to the will. *He* no longer responded wholeheartedly to Elizabeth Taillebois. *He* had run off and involved himself with a woman as different from Katharine and from Elizabeth as a woman could be.

Her name was Mary Boleyn and she was the elder daughter of Sir Thomas Boleyn, one of the knights who had fought at the Battle of the Spurs. She was lovely to look at, very blonde and she never seemed to be more than half awake. Katharine was intelligent; Elizabeth was shrewd and amusing; both of them demanded some activity above the waistline. Mary Boleyn was, by comparison, a feather bed, a comfortable, almost anonymous receptical.

There were times when Henry thought that perhaps the Turks had the right idea—God forgive him for admiring any infidel custom; but perhaps a man needed three women; one to be good with; one to be bad with; one with whom to be nothing.

Thinking these things he said to the woman who was so fit to be bad with,

"I think when he is six; able to stand up to the ceremony and comport himself properly."

The malice shone in her eyes again. "Naturally it will take longer than if he had been born in the right bed." It was true that had the boy been legitimate he would not have had to wait six years for his title.

"You," Henry said, "will end as a shrew."

"I hope not. I intend to be a sweet-faced lady pensioner; in a lace cap."

That was going one step too far. Katharine had lately taken to wearing a cap made of lace petals—and very becoming it was.

"The Queen," he said swiftly, "will still be short of forty when this boy is six. If by then . . ." He left that sentence unfinished and went on, "Another disrespectful remark about Her Grace and you will get no pension at all." That was a blow in a very vulnerable area; Elizabeth had always been greedy, for gifts, for allowances, property. Still, she had given him a son, she had bolstered his belief in his own virility.

"Mind your tongue," he said, "and you shall have your pension."

He thought of Mary Boleyn, curious girl, going through life like a sleepwalker; asking for nothing, refusing what was offered, even trinkets. Why? he asked. She replied in her soft, sleepy way, that to take anything from him would make her feel like a bought woman. "Besides, people would notice, and talk. And one gaping mouth in a family is enough."

He had tried to conduct his second extra-marital affair more discreetly even than his first. Mary Boleyn had an appointment as one of Katharine's maids-in-waiting, but it was natural enough for her to visit her father, useful, shrewd man who was seldom far from Court, except when Henry sent him on an errand. Mary went to see her father, housed not gloriously, but comfortably, wherever the Court was; the King strolled into those apartments to talk with Sir Thomas whom the old nobility called that lickspittle toady, the gentleman lackey who was not a gentleman at all. So far nobody seemed to have noticed the coincidences of the timing; he hoped nobody would. He had no wish to hurt Katharine again; and he had no wish to seem fickle. All things considered, he had been, where women were concerned, remarkably abstemious; only two mistresses in a reign of ten years; a man should be judged, not only by the temptations to which he had succumbed, but by those he had resisted. And, when he felt guilty, which was often, he remembered that he had never neglected his duty to Katharine;

whenever that small, uncontrollable *he* could be forced to perform, into service he went. For one thing he had not quite
abandoned hope; a woman in her later thirties, even in her
forties, might still bear a child.

He intended to stay away from Jericho; Elizabeth's attraction
for him was outworn and he would have been happy to give
her her pension and discard her. But the child drew him. He
was a doting father; he loved Mary, disappointed as he was about
her sex and the fact that she seemed doomed never to have a
brother; he loved Henry, born of the wrong woman, in the
wrong bed. Both were extensions of himself; their colouring,
shape, mental ability, amusing, graceful ways were like mirrors,
reflecting his superiority. In the company of either—Mary so
apt with the lute and with a phenomenal memory, speaking
good, almost perfect Latin at the age of four; Henry strutting
about on his hobby-horse and flourishing his little wooden
sword—he could momentarily forget that Mary was a mere girl,
and Henry a bastard. Afterwards, when the entrancement ended
and ran full tilt into grim reality, he would think—if only . . .
if only the boy had been born Prince of Wales; if only the girl
had been born on the wrong side of the blanket. If only, if
only . . . The stark fact remained and sooner or later he must
face it. He was King, he could give the little boy a name and
confer titles on him presently. Would the English people accept
him as heir? It seemed improbable.

From such troubling thoughts Henry could turn his mind to
other things; to the making of his Court, by the hospitality
and favour extended to scholars of all nations, the most cosmo-
politan and modern Court in Europe; to his own enjoyment
of hunting and violent sports; to his love of music and books;
and, perhaps above all, to the preservation of his position as
the third, greatly sought after, power in Europe.

It was the day of the young rulers. Joanna's son, Charles V,
had inherited his vast realms and been elected Emperor in 1519,
when he was still only twenty; Francis of France had been
twenty-one when he became King in 1515: Henry, in 1520, was

still only twenty-nine and had ruled for eleven years. Between
the rival powers of France and the Empire, England held the
balance: between Francis and Henry there was a strong element
of personal rivalry that had little to do with politics; it was even
rumoured that Francis was a shade taller than Henry, and
equally expert at all sports which demanded skill and courage.
They were both anxious to meet.

Katharine, not really a politically minded woman, had the
Spaniard's inborn distrust of France and was relieved when,
just before the meeting between Henry and Francis was to take
place, the Emperor proposed to visit England. She had never
seen Joanna's son, but she felt that he must have inherited
something of his mother's charm. Of her vagrant beauty, and
the good looks that had gained his father his title of Philip
the Handsome, she knew from report, that he had nothing. In
her secret heart she reasoned in feminine fashion; physically
Charles was no rival for Henry; therefore Henry would be more
disposed to like him and to listen to him—he was said to be
very reasonable and sensible—than to like Francis.

The meetings between the three young men who held Europe
in their hands, were arranged for the spring and summer of
1520. Charles was to come to England in the spring; Henry
was then to go to France and from there to proceed to Flanders,
part of Charles' realm, for another meeting. Katharine hoped
that thus a true balance would be struck. If they could meet
and talk and get to understand one another, the peace of the
world might be assured; and as she grew older she became even
more pacifist. Her remark after Flodden and the death of the
King of Scots, "It should have been better for him to have been
in peace," expressed a conviction that had not diminished with
the years.

The Emperor's visit to England was delayed by some trouble
in Spain. May, the month in which England was at its most
beautiful, began to expend itself in flowers and birdsong and
Henry said that on the first of June he must set out from Dover
to Calais.

"*I* keep *my* promises," he said. "Emperor he may be; but if he delays beyond the first day of June he will find nobody to receive him."

"Emperor he may be," Katharine said, "to me he is my sister's son, and to miss him by a day or two would grieve me."

But Henry would not wait in London. There was much to see to; this peaceable visit needed almost as much preparation and foresight as the invasion of France seven years earlier had done. No Twelve Apostles but almost as many horses, knights in armour, and tents. And in addition great silk pavilions, a vast display of silver, clothes, jewels and the ladies with all their baggage. For days the shady, sun-speckled roads of Kent were crowded and the dust settled on the pale pink wild roses that wreathed the hedges. The Court took up its quarters under the roof of the Archbishop's Palace at Canterbury; the main train moved on to Dover and everything except the horses went aboard the waiting ships.

On May 26, by which time Katharine was almost desperate with anxiety, a messenger rode in to say that the Emperor's fleet had been sighted. Henry rode to Dover to greet his nephew by marriage and Katharine consulted with her ladies, and with her household officials and the Archbishop's cooks, as to what kind of meal would most please her nephew; and then turned her attention to the question of entertainment. There would be no language barrier; Henry's Latin was perfect, and no doubt, so would Charles' be; she would avoid speaking Spanish, of which Henry had a smattering but no fluency; music . . . Joanna's son would surely have an ear for a tune; and things that held a message to the eye, dancers, jugglers, contortionists.

When he arrived, side by side with Henry, her first thought was: Oh, what a poor little boy! Nothing that any ambassador or visiting Spaniard had said had really prepared her to meet— Joanna's son, Emperor—so stunted, immature-looking, ugly a creature. For the mouth, so prominent a feature in the pale face, she should, she admitted to herself afterwards, have been prepared, for on his first visit to Spain, as heir, some rude peasant shouted, "Your Grace, keep your mouth shut. Spanish flies are very impertinent." The remark had been reported to her and she had given it no importance; she imagined that perhaps at the time Charles had been speaking, and that the peasant was one of those who resented the linking of Spain to the Empire and eased his resentment by rudeness.

But now, face to face with her nephew, she saw the point of the remark. His lower jaw projected in such a way that he could not close his mouth properly. And even as she rustled forward to greet and embrace him she asked herself: Can he chew properly? Was I wise to order beef?

She threw her arms about him and gave the warmest, closest embrace that she had ever given anyone except her mother, her husband, the baby that had lived and the baby that had died, and bade him welcome to England.

He seemed pleased; he called her "aunt," referred to Henry as "my uncle"; was mannerly, unassuming, almost shy, but he never smiled, and he never laughed even when he applauded the musicians and the clowns and the jugglers. Katharine, from time to time, glanced at him, smiling herself, inviting to him to smile. He never did. He praised; he said, "This is very clever." Or, "It is amusing." Or, of the music, "It is beautiful." But above the sagging misformed mouth the eyes, very pale and rather prominent, never changed their expression, an intense stare, almost, but not quite, vacuous.

"A glum fellow," Henry said in the privacy of their bed-chamber.

She was anxious for Henry to like him, so she did not mention something that she had observed; that vacuous-seeming stare missed nothing.

"My sister was beautiful and her husband handsome. You remember them? At Windsor."

Henry remembered; and what had happened just before that visit, and during it; the thrill which the mere touch of her hand could then convey. What happened? Where did love go?

"He had a poor start in life. His father dead, his mother crazed. And perhaps he was tired from his journey and felt at a disadvantage, being so small and plain."

"Such as he is, we must make do with him. Mary will be Empress."

"He will be thirty, and over, by the time she is marriageable. That worries me a little." Otherwise it was a suitable match. It satisfied her strong family feeling; it would bring England into the strong community of the Empire, which would surely make for peace. And if, even now, she should bear a son, it would not be to his disadvantage to have the Emperor as a brother-in-law.

"The gap in their ages will be on the right side," Henry said, unthinking; for although things had changed and *he* no longer leapt, fondness remained, and admiration and respect. Something remained when love had gone as a tree stood after the leaves had fallen. She was still his dear Kate and he had no wish to hurt her.

Charles' visit was necessarily short and Katharine took advantage of that to make it as much like a private, family visit as possible. "We have so little time in which to discuss so many things," she said. Even Wolsey was excluded from the meals and the conversations, and was forced to prowl about in ante-rooms, trying to pry out of pages and serving men some clue as to what the three royal people were discussing. He suspected Katharine of being Imperialist, as she suspected him of being Francophile and he resented the fact that now, on the very eve of the meeting between Henry and Francis, from which he hoped so much, he was being kept in ignorance of what was being said behind the closed doors.

Most of it was being said by Henry. Charles was not given to divulging what went on in his mind. Beyond saying that he was, more than anything else anxious for peace, the Emperor made few positive statements. The pale eyes which seemed to see so little, had seen a good deal—Henry's vast vanity, amongst other things. So he asked questions, invited advice and listened, his mouth hanging open, while Henry answered, elaborated and advised. Then the astute mind set to work upon the evidence gleaned by eyes and ears and Charles realised that his uncle-by-marriage was not to be dismissed as a big, handsome, vain, self-opinionated fellow whose success so far was due to luck and to Wolsey, as people were inclined to think. Henry was shrewd and well-informed.

With the wry humour which nobody ever dreamed that he possessed, Charles thought: One cannot say that there is more in him than meets the eye, because what more could meet the eye? He conceals his real ability behind the show of bluff good-humour, vanity, pleasure-seeking and carnal appetites, just as I conceal mine . . . no, mine was concealed from the day of my birth; at this moment my uncle-by-marriage thinks me a dull fellow; my aunt believes that I am shy . . . Ha! Ha!

He had sensed Katharine's sincere goodwill from the first and so far as his cold, crippled nature allowed, was grateful for it since he, the most richly endowed man in the world, was also without question the loneliest; but he sensed also her complete subjugation to Henry's will, even to his mood. She sat, throughout these meals and conversations rather as though she were watching a tennis match, turning her head to this speaker and to that, smiling sometimes, now and then saying a few words, pleased because her husband and her nephew were getting along together so well. What she said was invariably sensible, but Charles was reasonably sure that once she was in France, as she would be in a few days' time, if Henry fell under Francis' spell, Katharine would turn Francophile too. At Guines, where Henry and Francis were to meet, if ever there was a conversation such as this, she would turn her head from one man to the other, and smile and murmur and be agreeable —as a woman should. His aunt's behaviour was impeccable, Charles admitted, but her influence was negligible. And Charles suspected that unless, at first sight, Henry and Francis took a real dislike to one another, some of their talk would be about war. These physically powerful men were inclined to look upon the battlefield as a tourney ground in which splendid prizes were to be won.

Still, Charles thought, listening and staring, he had one way of linking himself to Henry and to England that was not possible to Francis. Francis was married, he was free. Charles had little

or no intention of marrying a girl almost seventeen years
younger than himself, a bride for whom he must wait at least
ten years; he had his duty to his Empire. But matrimony was,
like everything else, a weapon and every weapon had its use.
He agreed that to make public announcement of the betrothal
would be absurd at this stage; and, in view of the imminent
visit to France, tactless. Let it wait . . . but let it be understood,
between us here, now in this room . . .

He felt a slight shiver of distaste when Katharine embraced
him again and said, "God has seen fit, so far, to withold from
me the blessing of a son, but in future I shall regard myself as
your mother." She could not know that he detested any reference, however indirect, to the mad woman who had borne him.

Charles rode away to join his fleet, now anchored off Sand-
wich, waiting to take him to Flanders where he hoped that
Henry and Katharine would visit him when their visit to France
ended. Henry and Katharine hurried down to Dover to embark
for Calais.

It was seven years since Wolsey had sent to France the best-
equipped, the most carefully provided for army that the world
had seen, but in the interval he had not lost his eye for detail,
or his sure touch. This time Henry was coming to France as a
friend—but as a friend anxious to impress, eager to match hospitality and splendour with Francis, who was on his home
ground.

Wolsey had seen to it all. Since March six thousand workmen
—glad to be employed—had been labouring to build what was
virtually a palace, but a palace out of a fairy tale, in which
Henry and Katharine were to live and entertain, and a town
around it to house the five thousand people, nobles and their
ladies, officials and servants who accompanied them. The main
pavilion and the banqueting hall were based on brick founda-
tions, and although above they were constructed of canvas only,
the canvas was supported on timbers too long for any ship to
carry; they had been lashed together and floated oversea as
rafts and then tugged into place by teams of sweating oxen.
Everything that could be gilded or painted had been painted or

gilded; glazed windows had been set into the canvas walls, and on the inside the canvas was hidden by tapestries and silk hangings and vast plaster wall pieces, mounted on wood, of biblical or allegorical scenes, brilliantly coloured.

On the opposite side of the valley the French had erected a similar palace, a matching town. Between the two, spies disguised as workmen or vendors, went to and fro, telling the French what the English were doing, or telling the French how the English were getting on. Competition and rivalry were strong long before the chief protagonists arrived. The English managed to keep one secret because only experts from London were allowed to enter a specially erected timber enclosure some few yards removed from the front of the main pavilion. When the screen was taken down, about an hour before the English King arrived, it was too late for the French either to match or out-do the marvel. It was a statue of Bacchus, said to have been brought from Italy; its bronze had been freshly gilded and it had been converted into a fountain from which three streams spouted, two of wine, one of clear water, fed from underground sources; nearby was a table furnished with cups, all of silver, so that anyone who came could quench his thirst.

But Wolsey was not only a superb organiser and an imaginative planner, he was a Cardinal, a prince of the Church, and logically, he had reserved the ultimate magnificence for the chapel which opened from the great central hall. Its ceiling and walls were lined and draped with cloth of gold, silver tissue and panels of embroidery, red roses on white silk, which matched the copes of the thirty-five priests chosen to serve there. The organ was of silver, ornamented with gold, and around the walls stood statues of the Twelve Apostles, all of gold and each as large as a well-grown child four years old. When the chapel was in use there would be real children too, three dozen young boys, the pick of all the monks' schools in England, chosen not only for their voices, but for uniformity of size, good complexion, and generally pleasing appearance. There were enough of them so that if a boy grew two inches in a fortnight, as boys sometimes did at that age, or developed spots, or lost the clarity of his voice, he could be withdrawn from the choir.

The chapel, besides being the finest of the many buildings, had another distinction; it was the first known building to have been built far from the place where it was to stand. Its planning and assembling was a task which Wolsey would delegate to no one, so it had been built in England, in sections easily transportable, and then shipped to France, where workmen, like the fountain makers specially skilled, had only to put the numbered sections together and install the furnishings. They had completed the job in one day.

Wolsey had thought of everything; even the four thousand pounds of best wax needed for the making of candles; hundreds of the best sheep, calves and bullocks from English meadows awaited their last hour in French pastures: but, anxious to make this great occasion a flawless success, anxious to impress the French and to please his own beloved master, anxious that the final result of the gathering should be a lasting peace, Wolsey had overlooked one thing. Even he could not make people like one another. In Francis' suite there were knights who, only seven years earlier, had fled from the Battle of the Spurs; in Henry's rode the knights who had pursued them: 1513 was a recent memory; there were older and even harsher ones; it was the enemy who had come a-visiting; it was the enemy who was being visited. And nothing but rivalry, open or concealed, was possible between two magnificent young men, both Kings, both in their twenties, both proud and handsome, fond of show, both set to out-do the other.

The gathering known as the Field of the Cloth of Gold, partly because so much of that material was evident and partly because the French King's temporary town was sited in the Val Doré, was in essence as false and hollow as the grand pavilions where the outer canvas was painted to look like brickwork. Possibly the only genuine outcome—apart from a wary, cautious respect on either side for the power and resources of the other—was the friendship that sprang up immediately between Katharine and Queen Claude. Both were extremely pious women and neither was of a competitive nature; for the honour of their respective countries and to please their respective husbands, both must be magnificently clad, bejewelled, and attended; and generally there was no question of precedence; it was dependent upon in which canvas town they chanced to be. But early on they met in Wolsey's beautiful chapel, before the altar of God, where, in theory, all men were equal in humility. It was the privilege of the most important lady present to kiss a little tablet known as the Pax. Both hesitated and then, moved by a mutual impulse, kissed, not the Pax, but one another.

Their friendship blossomed as they sat and watched their husbands performing feats of arms in the tourney ground—not against one another, but against, with that exception, "all comers." Henry watching Francis, and Francis watching Henry, would each have been glad enough of a confrontation, but Wolsey had said it would be most unwise. "Eventually, Your Grace, you would unhorse him," he said tactfully. "And although he might not resent it, there are those who would."

Katharine and Claude reached that degree of intimacy where, before one of the competitive banquets over which cooks drove themselves crazy, they would pass little feminine questions across the intervening ground: "What colour of gown and what jewels do you wish to wear this evening?" and so arrange that their colours should neither clash, nor, worse, be identical.

In Queen Claude's suite there were two English-born girls whom she had inherited from Mary Tudor when Louis XII died; most of Mary's ladies had gone home with her, but these, for reasons of their own, had not wished to, and both, being now bilingual could stay on and be useful. Each, in due time, was to be Queen of England, but who would have guessed it then? Anne Boleyn, so thin and dark, little altered, save in height, since Katharine had thought of her a changeling child amongst the fair, plump girls of Mary's suite, and Jane Seymour, fair enough but with a receding chin which the passing of the years had not improved. Katharine took pains to seek them out and speak kindly to them: and she was glad that they were in the household of good Queen Claude. Some great ladies—

and some of them professedly pious—had little care either for
the souls or the bodies of their waiting women. In the dormi-
tories of some palaces and magnificent houses there was enormous licence, some of them were little better than brothels.
Queen Claude's ladies lived like nuns. Katharine approved,
little knowing that this fact would eventually work to her own
damage; that if Claude had been less strict, Anne Boleyn might
have been easier game, taken, enjoyed and abandoned.

On the whole Katharine enjoyed this visit to France. There
the usual crop of ugly rumours— With the King and the flower
of his nobility exchanging compliments, gifts and banquets,
the French fleet had secretly set sail to conquer England; ten
thousand Frenchmen, skulking in the hills that ringed the Val
Doré, were waiting to take Henry prisoner and hold him to
ransom; both the water and the wine in the Bacchus fountain
had been poisoned.

With each rumour, as it came in, her heart would jump a
little; her congenital Francophobia taking over from her common sense. Henry was far calmer. Warned about the French
fleet setting out for England he said, "Nonsense! My brother
of France promised Wolsey that no French ship should set sail
on the Channel while we were here. And if they did, and if they
landed, the militia could take care of them!" Told about the
Frenchmen skulking in the hills, he said, "This we *can* put to
the test. I will ride alone, not by the direct road, but the one
that skirts the hills, to pay Francis an unexpected visit." He
did so though Katharine—her distrust of the French coming
uppermost—begged him not to. "I do not believe in the hidden
thousands, but two or three fanatics. . . ." She had dark
memories of Moorish ambushes.

But Henry rode, alone and unarmed, into Francis' camp;
and came home jubilant. Next morning Francis, alone and unarmed, rode over to wish Henry good morning, and declare that
he, and he alone, would hand his shirt and shave him.

On the surface it was all good-humoured and, as Claude said:
"They never completely grow up, these men. I often think
that that is why God entrusted us women with the responsibility for their souls. Their minds are so easily diverted; their

lusts so easily aroused. Children chasing butterflies . . . Holy
Mother of God, what now?"

They were at Wolsey's table. The butcher's son from Ipswich,
having feasted with the King of France and the King of England, had begged leave to entertain them both at his and he
had arranged things—he thought—rather cleverly. There was no
high table, set on a dais; there was a round table, acknowledg-
ing neither head nor foot, set in the centre of a round carpet
which had come from Constantinople, and around it another
vast, circular table with the company seated around its outer
rim. At the inner, circular table, Wolsey sat at one place,
Francis on his right, Henry on his left—that had been prearranged; then two French Cardinals, and the two Queens
whose growing friendship Wolsey had observed with approval.
"A table with no head," he had said to Henry, "like that of
Arthur, at Camelot."

Claude's question, "What now," had been evoked by Henry
pushing back his gilded chair, passing behind Wolsey, seizing
Francis by the collar and shouting, "Come, you shall wrestle
with me!"

For almost a fortnight he had restrained himself; in almost
every move he had made, every word he had spoken he had been
guided by Wolsey's Book of Ordinances. He had watched
Francis, his junior, but more nearly his equal than any other
man he had ever seen, just as wide of shoulder, and that irking
half inch taller, match him, exploit for exploit, against *other*
men. But he was certain that had he not agreed that open confrontation with the King of France was unwise, Francis would
have been humbled. Now, exhilarated by wine, aware that the
meeting was nearing its end, and sure that a simple wrestling
match, however it ended, could rouse no enmity, he was determined to show that though older, he was stronger and more
supple.

Francis was taken by surprise by the sudden assault, and
angered by it; he contented himself for a straining second or
two in merely resisting Henry's attempt to throw him, and
then, suddenly exerting his strength to the full, lifted and
threw . . . Before eyes that were gratified or horrified, the King

of England sailed through the air and fell, full length and with a heavy thud on the carpeted floor.

He was up instantly, face crimson, blue eyes blazing.

"Again," he said, a trifle breathlessly, winded by the fall. But by that time Wolsey was on his feet and between them, saying, "My lords! My lords!" And Claude clutched Francis by the arm, while Katharine took Henry's; "No more, I beg you." "Desist, I pray you. Would you frighten us to death?"

"But he threw me!" Henry said.

"No, no!" Francis said in a loud, carrying voice. "You threw yourself, you resisted so stoutly. I vow I thought you had taken me with you and was surprised to find myself left standing."

Claude's pressure on his arm changed from entreaty to approbation. Katharine said in Henry's ear, "He will not risk a further bout." Wolsey said, "My lords, the next dish is served."

Francis who in the circumstances could afford to be generous, said, "Somebody must cut my meat for me. My brother of England has pulled my arm from its socket."

So, with amiable pretence, the meeting of the Field of the Cloth of Gold, in itself an amiable pretence, came to an end. Henry and Francis were each to reign for another twenty-seven years, and to die in the same year; their relationship was to fluctuate, now friendly, now inimical; Henry always thought of Francis, no matter against what background, as the man who had thrown him and evaded a return bout; and Francis always, in his secret mind, thought of Henry as the typical Englishman who would come up behind you and seize you by the collar.

The Emperor, silent and withdrawn, competing with nobody because there was nobody on earth with whom he must compete, sat waiting at Gravelines for the promised visit of his aunt and his uncle-by-marriage. And they, and the French, had hardly quitted the Val Doré, and men had hardly begun to shift the stuff and the symbols of splendour when one of the violent storms of early July blew up; the wind and the rain could make a sharp distinction between pretence and reality and in a short time the fairy-tale pavilions were tattered, lurching ruins, lacking entirely the sad dignity of buildings once sound and good, fallen on evil days.

10

Little Henry Fitzroy, living proof that, mated to the right
woman, Henry could beget a healthy boy, was two years old
when his father snatched at a chance to act as a Crusader, not
in armed combat against the Infidel, but as a theologian against
heresy. In Germany there was an Augustinian friar named
Martin Luther who for some time had been causing his superiors
concern by questioning the authority of the Pope, the authority
of bishops and some points of Church doctrine. Henry believed,
and Katharine agreed with him, that Luther had read overmuch, and completely misinterpreted, Holy Writ which the
new printing presses were pouring out in vast numbers. His
own extremely revolutionary ideas were also disseminated in
the new print: he held that there were only three sacraments—
the Church observed seven; he did not believe in the celibacy
of the clergy; he said that when the Sacrament of Holy Communion was celebrated, every communicant should take both
bread and wine. Finally he nailed a list of what he called
"protests" to the door of the church in Wittenburg and hundreds of people, already prepared by his pamphlets, began to
call themselves Protestants.

"He is a dangerous fellow," Henry said. "And his protests
should be answered."

"He has been excommunicated," Katharine said.

"For such as he excommunication means nothing. He has
already excommunicated himself. Someone should take all his
arguments and refute them, one by one."

"Someone should," she agreed. "Why not you?"

She was delighted to see that Henry took the suggestion
seriously. The very name of Luther was anathema to her and

it pleased her to think that it should be her husband who would demolish such wicked arguments. It was also important that every possible sphere of common interest between them should be cultivated. She was losing her hold over Henry's body, but they could still share the pleasures of the mind.

In writing his treatise, Henry made use of his education for the Church, his knowledge of Latin, his skill with words: he wrote swiftly and well. Katharine was capable of looking up references for him, and of copying a corrected page, and she was always willing to sit, her hands busy with the needle and listen while he read what he had written. She was free with praise: "A splendid argument!" "That is very clever." As she had hoped, the project brought them together.

Two clerks made the final copies, one for the printers, one for the Pope, who when he had read *Assertium Septum Sacrementorum Contra M. Luther,* bestowed upon its author the title of Defender of the Faith. Henry proudly added it to all his other titles.

But in his heart he felt that he deserved more, a blessing from Heaven as well as from Rome. He still found difficulty in believing that what he wanted was to be denied him. And it was true that in the middle of such disturbance of function as Katharine was undergoing, women did sometimes conceive.

He braced himself to make a sacrifice painful enough to deserve a near miracle. He would give up his comfortable, complaisant mistress, Mary Boleyn.

He knew that in her inarticulate way she was very fond of him and he did not underestimate the worth of what she was about to lose—himself; so he set about making the break with some consideration.

One evening he was able to say to her, "Mary, I have found a husband for you."

She took it calmly. Men preferred a married mistress; and in future the liaison would be conducted behind a husband-and-wife screen, instead of a father-and-daughter one. It would be better; for her father was always nagging her— Ask for this; ask for that; you stupid wench, make hay while the sun shines!

Occasionally, because she would ask for nothing, he struck her.

"Who is it?" she asked with an almost total lack of interest.

"William Carey."

"Oh no!"

"And what's wrong with him? He is of gentle birth, young, good-looking. Granted he has no estate but that can be remedied. He is fond of you, too. Elated at the prospect of marrying you."

"He would be," she said almost sullenly. "He is in love with me. He would be jealous. He would not share me. It would mean the end—for us."

"Dear Mary; it must be the end."

"Why? What have I done?"

"Nothing. But circumstances demand it."

He had never had to do with a hysterical woman. Katharine had taken blow after blow with dignity; Bessie Blount had allowed herself to be paid off with the cheerfulness of a mercenary at the end of a campaign; even his sister Mary, protesting against her marriage to old Louis, had not behaved like this. The sight of Mary Boleyn, so placid, undemanding and easy, tearing at the lace of her bodice, tearing at her hair, banging her head against the wall and screaming, appalled him.

"Stop it," he said, taking her by the shoulders and shaking her into silence. "People will think murder is being done."

As he shook her the tears flew from her face and made dark splashes on his yellow doublet. And her nose was running. He felt for her something of the aversion he felt for the sick and the maimed.

"Will you listen to me . . . I'll knight him . . . You shall be Lady. I'll give him a manor and some good office."

"Keep your gifts. You never bought me. You shall not sell me. I loved you. I love you, God help me. Go away. Get out of my sight."

He had not taken an order from anyone since his father died.

"Very well," he said, his tender care for her well-being and his regret at parting from her all swallowed in rage. He stamped away. If she despised his gifts, let her do without them.

Mary realised that she still had her father to face. She tidied herself and her limited mind moved from the shock of rejection to the problem of how to explain. It was with a good imitation of her usual stolidity that she said to Sir Thomas:

"William Carey has asked me to marry him. And I have accepted."

"Without asking me!"

"He asked the King. He consented."

"Ah!" Sir Thomas said, seeing as he thought, the whole thing. Shrewd, after all, not bothering with little benefits, waiting for the day of settlement. "And what will your marriage portion be?"

"Nothing."

Sir Thomas almost became hysterical himself.

"What, after all this time. All this evil talk. People saying I profited by your shame. I who carried the canopy over the Princess at her christening when you were a green girl. Nothing. You tell me nothing. In God's name, why not?"

"We love one another. We need nothing more."

"You stupid, senseless, improvident wench! You loose-living slut! You trollop!" With each abusive word he slapped her savagely about the head. "You could have had three manors. So marry your pauper and live on love. And starve. From me you will get nothing."

The hoped-for, prayed-for last-minute miracle did not come about.

In May of the year 1522, when the Emperor paid his second visit to England, he noticed a change in his uncle who was far less affable than he had been two years earlier in Canterbury and at Gravelines. His aunt Katharine was, as before, kind and welcoming; the little cousin to whom he was now officially betrothed, was, at six years old, an admirable and accomplished child; but Henry had changed.

Charles, seeming to notice nothing, noticed that Wolsey was in the ascendant and Wolsey, Charles knew, was ardently Francophile. The acute political awareness which was, after his religion, the most lively thing about him, quickened in the young Emperor and made him susceptible even to a change in a tone of voice.

The moment of truth came on an evening when they were discussing Princess Mary's future. Charles had little intention of marrying a child so young, but he needed Henry's goodwill and he needed time. So plans must appear to be made.

"In three years' time," he said, "when she is nine. Then she must come to Spain and be reared as a Spanish princess. And she must bring with her a dowry of eighty thousand English pounds."

"Two years ago I should have agreed," Henry said. "Now I consider the terms ridiculous. She will be Queen of England, she must remain in her own country. And England will be her dower . . ."

As he said that he felt sick. England, his England, part of this dullard's vast Empire. Because I have no son. No lawful son.

"I was obliged to make some concessions over the dowry and the place of residence of the Princess," Charles said. "There were some on my council who deplored the betrothal."

"Why?"

"This is not pleasant for me to say. But some—good lawyers too—professed a doubt as to her legitimacy."

"They did *what?*"

Charles said solemnly, "Ideas, even when repudiated, are not without effect. Within my Empire there are those who question the Pope's authority as a whole. This is heresy which must be put down. But in small ways . . . Nowadays even a good Catholic may ask difficult questions. I assure you, it was a good Catholic who asked whether even Papal authority could make lawful a man's marriage to his brother's widow."

"Of all the outrageous . . ." Henry began and stopped. "You say this in good faith?"

"In good faith. The man who asked the question I silenced. Forever. But the question was asked and the doubt lingers. I think therefore that over the question of the Princess's place of residence and the amount of her dowry, it would be as well not to be intransigent."

Never, not even when thrown by Francis, had Henry known such humiliation. Not to be intransigent. To be told that by this malformed little runt!

With difficulty he mastered his fury.

"It may be that this talk is premature. By the time the child is nubile, other thoughts may prevail. If you are as earnest to root out such heretical notions as I have been and intend to be."

"Yours is a task comparatively easy. You can have no idea what it means to govern an Empire which includes such divergent elements as most Christian Spain, and Germany, which I begin to think, was never even completely converted."

For a moment Henry reverted to his avuncular, advice-giving role.

"Heresy must not be tolerated," he said. "As I see it those who rebel against one form of authority are presently likely to rebel against others. Church and Throne are one." He added, with the sourness which Charles had noted as new, "You may find that it pays you to be—intransigent." He smiled as he bounced back the offensive word, but it was not a pleasant smile. Charles, ignoring the jab, went on to talk of the problem, mentioning the Netherlands as the area most prone to disaffection; so many rich merchants, so many wealthy towns; Spain, poor and agrarian, was far more biddable; though born in Flanders, he always felt more at home in Spain. . . .

He took his leave of his relatives and of England, without realising that into his uncle's mind he had dropped a seed which would bring forth a strange harvest.

11

When Mary was nine she did not go to Spain. Instead she went to Ludlow.

Henry had thought deeply and long about the possibility of persuading the people to accept Henry Fitzroy as his heir. It would not be easy, but his own vast popularity encouraged him to think that what he willed would not be gainsaid. Wolsey's response to the suggestion was not encouraging, the Archbishop of Canterbury's even less so and the Duke of Norfolk said bluntly that it could not be done. But three men did not make up England, they did not even constitute the King's Privy Council. When the boy was six, Henry decided that a preliminary test, at least, might be made.

The boy was six, strong, big for his age, very handsome, when his father brought all his gift of showmanship to the ceremony of knighting and ennobling him. Henry Fitzroy knelt and rose to his feet, Sir Henry Fitzroy. Then he withdrew, to reappear, looking, for all his size, very small between the Dukes of Norfolk and Suffolk, and knelt again while the patent of nobility was read. When he stood up for the second time he was Duke of Richmond and Duke of Somerset, Lord Admiral of England, Keeper of the city and castle of Carlisle. And amongst the titles, spattering down like autumn leaves over the russet head of a very bored but well-mannered little boy, there were some that, for all they meant, might have been mythical. Normandy, Gascony and Aquitaine, once the provinces of English Kings, and still claimed by name, just as Henry claimed to be King of France, though only Calais remained in English possession.

As a spectacle, an occasion for rejoicing, for the rich an

excuse to buy new clothes, for the poor an opportunity to eat and drink at the King's expense, the ceremony was a success, but it failed of its objective. Not one person in all that long day echoed the words that sounded in the proud father's mind— He would make a King. The boy's looks and deportment were praised, but too often there was the unwelcome addition beginning "It is a pity . . ." or "If only . . ."

Katharine, though Henry had never mentioned his plan to her, knew the purpose of all this; particularly significant was the title of Richmond, and of those faraway places ordinarily shared out amongst kings' sons. For her it was a day of deep misery; such a sturdy, composed little boy, so obviously Henry's son. He should have been hers. But she drew comfort from the thought that God, in His infinite wisdom, working out His inscrutable purpose, intended Mary to be Queen, as He had intended Isabella to be Queen of Castile. Mary was, Katharine became every day more certain, something very special, not in looks but in intellect and disposition.

And it was plain that though Henry had not yet fully resigned himself, the people had. They showed it in subtle ways. All day all people of rank had been careful to pay particular deference to the Princess of Wales; and when the crowds, crammed with food and somewhat drunk, roared for the Duke of Richmond to show himself, the demand was no sooner met than there was another roar, incomparably more enthusiastic, "And the Princess of Wales!" "We want Mary!"

England had spoken. The King of England heard.

At the very end the new Duke was tired and dazed; but he wanted to say good night to the Queen. His father had occasionally brought him to Court, unofficially, and the Queen had always been very kind to him and given him sweetmeats. He had sometimes wished, in a blind childish way that she were his mother; and once he said so, "I wish I was your little boy!" Quite the wrong thing to say; she cried and said, "So do I!" And the second sweetmeat had not been forthcoming. She was a lady who set great store by good behaviour, but in a kind way. At home if he said or did anything amiss he was liable to be slapped.

Today he thought that he had behaved very well, and going towards the Queen at the end of it all, he hoped that she would say so. Tonight he did not want a piece of marzipan, he had eaten his fill.

Katharine sat, with Mary on one side and Lady Salisbury on the other. The Duke of Richmond knew Mary, who on his visits had sometimes played with him, putting her books or her lute aside for a little while. He took her by the hand and swung her away and went to Katharine's side and made his little bow and said, as instructed:

"I wish Your Grace good night." Then he added his own words: "I hope you think I have been a good boy today."

Katharine said, "You have been a very good boy." She put out her arm, pulled him close and kissed him in the sight of all. "Sleep well, my lord of Richmond." He smiled up at her.

But later, alone with Henry, she said:

"He will now be about the Court and he must learn to treat Mary with respect. She is Princess of Wales."

The emotions and strains and disappointments of the day had taken their toll; Henry's temper flared; not the hearty, noisy temper that a little shouting and stamping could dissipate; something more deadly.

"Yes," he said, after a little pause. "She is Princess of Wales. And I think it is high time she went to Ludlow and showed herself in her Principality."

The boy had meant no harm; he was only six; Mary was nine; were children supposed to conform with strict Spanish etiquette? Let Mary go to Ludlow, where nobody would take her aside by swinging on her hand.

Confounded, Katharine said, "But she is only nine! We have hardly known a day apart . . . I have supervised every moment of her days; taught her . . ."

"And done very well," he conceded. "But there are things that no mother can teach. Independence is one."

"That is true. But I thought at twelve. Would twelve be not soon enough?"

"Not as things are. The Welsh are always complaining of being a mere appendage. Mary's presence at Ludlow will appease them. And there she will be treated with respect."

She saw where she had made her error and hastened to amend it.

"I did not mean to criticise his behaviour. No other little boy in the world could have done better. I only said that he must learn . . . as all boys must."

He was still clear-minded and fair-minded enough to realise that he was punishing Kate for the disillusions of the day. He said—and it was a lie—for which he would do penance: "What you said had nothing to do with it. I have been minded for two months now to send Mary to Ludlow."

"Have you chosen her governess?"

That was Kate. So reasonable. And of course, had he thought about Mary's removal he would have chosen her governess.

"Yes. The Countess of Salisbury."

"The perfect choice," Katharine said warmly. "There is no one to whom I would so willingly entrust her." Though it would mean the removal of her closest friend amongst the English ladies.

Henry, knowing this, realising so far as a man could what this day had meant to her, remembering how she kissed the young Duke, could but admire her. A woman in a million.

"I would like, with your permission, to tell Mary myself."

"Who else should do it?" he asked. He was off to Hever, Tom Boleyn's Sussex house. He needed something to sweeten his mood after this day's doings. Mary's sister, Anne, was there, her sister but so different that it was unbelievable that they should be related; and he hoped to seduce her.

It was the second time within a brief space when Katharine had been obliged to break what she feared would be unwelcome news to Mary. On the former occasion it had been that the Emperor had broken his betrothal and was to marry another cousin, Isabella of Portugal. She had explained carefully, wondering how much a child of nine would feel rejected. She had spoken of the difference in age, of the long tradition of marriage between Spain and Portugal. She had not mentioned that Isabella of Portugal was to be the most richly endowed bride in the world. She did not herself believe that the dowry had much influenced Charles; age had; like every other monarch he needed an heir and he could not wait until he was thirty before he married.

Mary had taken the news with the utmost calm, simply saying, "But I shall still be Queen of England."

She took the order to go to Ludlow in much the same manner.

"I shall miss you sorely. But you will write to me?"

"Every week. And you must write to me. Not so often perhaps, because you will be busy. The Welsh chieftains are very poor, and very proud . . . I remember. If they kill a sheep it is an occasion and they make a feast of it. I found that they were pleased to be told that there was no such mutton in the world, and that is true. They like their Princess in her best gown and bejewelled. And it is essential to learn their names and say them properly. I found the names difficult. . . ."

She and Arthur had laughed, practising the names over. Madog ap Llewellyn of Meirionydd, to be distinguished from Llewellyn Ben of Senghenydd and all those Ap Rhys's. More than twenty years ago; the young Katharine as much of a ghost as the young Arthur. Laughter, friendly talk, scenery so beautiful that to one straight from Spain the lush greenery had had a fairy-tale quality. And rain almost every day. Looked back upon, the whole brief episode had a wistful, unreal quality.

"Shall I continue my Latin?"

"Yes. Master Federston will instruct you. Write to me in Latin, Mary; that will be good practice for us both."

"I shall write a little every day. How long must I stay there?"

"Not long, darling. Just long enough to please the Welsh and eat mutton with all those who claim descent from Llewellyn Ap Rhys. And Merlin!"

Smile, child, smile.

But Mary, unsmiling drew back a pace, and with a pressing stare that resembled her father's, said:

"Am I being put aside to make way for the Duke of Richmond?"

"Of course not. Who put that nonsense into your head?"

"I heard it said. In a pitying voice. I do not care to be pitied —except by you, when I am ill. And I *am* being sent away."

"Not for that reason, I assure you. Because you are Princess of Wales, and will one day be Queen of England. Nobody can ever put you aside. Nobody."

Mary left, not very cheerfully, but the letters which came with touching regularity sounded happy and soon included a few Welsh words of greeting or farewell, strangely and phonetically spelt. All Lady Salisbury's reports were good. Her Highness invariably comported herself with grace and dignity suitable to a princess twice her age. Her health was excellent; her lessons proceeding well.

Katharine missed Mary and her favourite English lady and then settled down to what she thought life would be henceforth, a peaceful, middle-aged routine. The child-bearing years with their ardours, their hopes, disappointments and griefs were over; she had her religious observances, her public duties, her private charities; she had, if no longer Henry's love-making, his company and all the interests they shared. He seemed to have settled down, too; he made no further attempt to foist Bessie Blount's boy upon the people of England. There was no rumour of his taking any woman as his mistress. Katharine, life's zenith gone, faced the sunset with equanimity.

Presently, she realised, the business of finding a husband for Mary would need to be dealt with. Every girl needed a husband, and a Queen needed an heir. Now and then Katharine hoped that Henry, so hating the idea of England being absorbed through marriage by some other country, would consider and propose the obvious solution—Mary's marriage to Reginald

Pole, the son of the Countess of Salisbury. On his mother's side he was related to the Plantagenets—the only surviving shoot of that stock whose name it was now unwise to mention, in Tudor-ruled England. But it was royal blood; marriage with him would not, for Mary, be a mésalliance: and he was clever, bookish, pious. He was sixteen years older than Mary, but the gap would not matter so much as in the case of the Emperor, for Reginald could never be King. He would be Mary's husband, Consort to the Queen.

But all this could be left for the future; there was plenty of time. Katharine merely hoped that when the time came, Henry, wishing England to be an independent entity, would choose Reginald Pole rather than what seemed to be the only alternative, a French Prince. Philip of Spain, the son of the Emperor Charles and Isabella of Portugal, whom Mary was eventually to marry, was not yet born and Katharine, casting about idly in her mind saw the choice between the French and Reginald Pole and hoped that when the time came Henry would see what was best for Mary and for England.

12

The two English girls who had served Queen Claude had come back to England in 1523 when, for a brief time, war between England and France had seemed imminent. Jane Seymour had gone to her home, Wolf Hall, in Wiltshire, but the Duke of Norfolk had asked, almost begged, Katharine to find a place for his niece, Anne Boleyn.

"She has no real home, Your Grace; my sister died years ago, and Sir Thomas remarried—a farmer's daughter." The Duke's dislike for his brother-in-law was undisguised. "He has never attempted to do anything for either of his daughters; and I . . . I have my own responsibilities. But I feel sorry for the girl and thought that an appeal to you . . . Though I know," he said deprecatingly, "that you have a preference for good-looking women about you."

He had stumbled by chance upon the words which immediately appealed to Katharine; who, if she had momentarily thought that Mary Boleyn's sister was one of the last people she wished to have about her, dismissed the thought immediately.

"I will make room for her," she said.

"This one has sense in her head and has acquired accomplishments. I trust that Your Grace will find her useful."

Having done his duty to a young relative without having to spend a penny, he retired, well satisfied with himself. Queen Katharine was always very generous to her women, and if Anne should marry—the Duke thought this unlikely, she had so few attractions—Her Grace would give her a dowry; and if she failed to find a husband, she would be safe enough; for though Katharine liked her women to be handsome, she never dismissed one simply because she was old.

So Anne Boleyn came to Court and Katharine, at first sight, thought that her looks had not improved much; and that, despite her uncle's words, she did not look like a girl who was ill-provided for. Her dresses were extremely stylish, with an individuality of their own, every colour and fashion carefully chosen to set off her one undeniable attraction, that curious elegant grace. Viewed more closely, the clothes revealed to Katharine—experienced in makeshift—that they had been re-made, turned, mended. And her only ornaments were worth-less; the collar, which invariably encircled her overlong neck, was of base metal, gilded over, the gilt worn away in places, studded with false gems and her one ring was set with a rather meagre piece of amber. Yet they, too, were well chosen.

Katharine was delighted when young Harry Percy, heir to the Earl of Northumberland and a member of Wolsey's household, began to pay Mistress Boleyn marked attention. He was a hand-some young man; he would one day be very rich. Many of the other ladies—not one of whom liked the newcomer—were envious, constantly asking themselves, and one another, what he could possibly see in her.

"She's not even amiable," Maria de Moreto said. "And that great mole on her neck and that extra finger." Nobody had ever made a bid for Maria's hand, and no one now ever would; it was natural that she should feel envious; but others, young, pretty, even betrothed, said things just as sour. Harry Percy could marry whom he chose; why pick on her?

"He sees her with other eyes," Katharine said. But she did snatch an opportunity to speak seriously to young Percy and to say that since Anne had no mother and her father was much occupied with affairs, she felt it her duty to inquire whether his intentions were honourable; because, if not, the way he was behaving was likely to damage Mistress Boleyn's reputation. He said, with integrity shining from his eyes, as well as resounding in his voice, that his one wish in the world was to marry Mis-tress Boleyn. He had asked her to marry him and she had accepted; but Sir Thomas was absent from London just now; the moment he returned his consent would be asked and the betrothal announced.

"We already regard ourselves as plighted, Your Grace. I can think of no reason why Sir Thomas should object to me. We plan to be married before Christmas."

"You brought me news of Flodden," Katharine said. "And in its way this is equally good news. I like my ladies to marry and be cherished. I trust that you will be very happy."

Then something inexplicable happened. The Earl of Northumberland came hurrying down from the north; was closeted with Cardinal Wolsey and emerged to say that his son was already betrothed—had been for years—to Lady Mary Talbot, daughter of the Earl of Shrewsbury; and, a betrothal being as binding as marriage, he must marry her or no one.

Then one of Wolsey's secretaries, a man named Thomas Cromwell, had asked audience of the Queen and told her, in rather roundabout terms, that circumstances being what they were it would be easier for everyone if Mistress Boleyn retired from Court and went to her father's house at Hever.

"It seems harsh to me, Master Cromwell, that she should, in one move, lose the man who loves her *and* her place in my household."

"So it may seem to Your Grace," Cromwell said. He was the son of a blacksmith and to him the world had always been harsh; his first tottering steps had been taken in a place where everything was hard, heavy and dangerous. "My lord of Northumberland would very willingly have taken his son back with him, but he refused to go and being of full age, could not well be forced. His Grace and my lord Cardinal are agreed that to allow the two young people to remain in contact could have disastrous results. They might even find someone who would, in ignorance, marry them. That would cause a scandal; and worse still set the Earls of Northumberland and Shrewsbury by the ears."

There were some people apparently who regarded betrothals

as sacrosanct. In her heart Katharine held to the old ways; she could spare a thought for Lady Mary Talbot and she had no wish to see two Earls at enmity. Old Henry VII had done his best to reduce the power of his noblemen, he had forbidden them to maintain private armies, but the rules were easily avoided; every great landowner in England could still muster a force of retainers. . . .

"Very well," Katharine said. "I understand that Sir Thomas Boleyn is not in London."

"He has gone to see to his estate in Norfolk. Blickling, Your Grace."

"Then Mistress Boleyn shall go there, immediately."

She had known humiliation and disappointment herself and could give the right due to the girl's behaviour in this crisis. No tears; no self-pity. The news had been broken to her by Lady Cuddington to whom Katharine had entrusted the unenviable task, and Anne had come and curtseyed, and asked leave to withdraw. "Your Grace knows upon what cause."

"I do; and believe me, I am sorry for it. God go with you."

And Katharine had taken steps to see that the poor girl did not go unaccompanied; she had persuaded Lady Lucia Bryant to spare one of her serving women, a stern-faced but very reliable woman named Emma Arnett, to conduct Anne to Blickling in Norfolk and to hand her over to her father.

Sir Thomas had another house, Hever in Kent, and when, Katharine thought, as she did sometimes, about the girl who could wear a collar of base metal, studded with coloured glass, and a turned dress, and somehow, for all her lack of beauty, make what was tawdry seem to be real, she hoped that in Norfolk or Kent there had been some hearty, bucolic young man, one of the country squires of a breed only known in England, who would have been attracted to the girl, perhaps a little dazzled by the possibility for having as his wife a woman of little physical charm—except grace, but who had waited upon three Queens, could read and write in French as well as English, could handle the lute expertly, was equally good at the virginal, and could make an old dress look like new.

And then, in 1527, after four years, Anne Boleyn was back in London, back at Court, her sponsor this time not her uncle, but Henry himself.

"Tom Boleyn," he said, "has done me sterling service and I have bestowed upon him the title he coveted and to which he had a definite, though disputed right. He is now Earl of Wiltshire. His Countess is a good little creature, but humbly born and by nature shy; she will not take her place at Court—and wise she is; she cures a good ham and I understand can make butter with the best; but his daughter is not her daughter; she is . . ."

"I remember her well. Four years ago she was removed. Because Henry Percy wished to marry her. Oh yes, I remember her."

"And you would be willing to receive her again?"

"It would be difficult not to; she left in no disgrace. The one thing is . . . she did not get along very well with the others. I could never see why."

"Things will be easier now. As an Earl's daughter she will have her own apartments," Henry said.

He was tired of riding to and fro between London and Hever; he had been doing it for four years. No man had ever wooed a woman so sedulously as he had wooed Anne, or been so little rewarded. Four years earlier, his fancy lightly taken, he had told Wolsey to break up that boy-and-girl nonsense; Tom Boleyn's daughter was no fit match for Northumberland's heir. That had been done and after a little space he had gone down to Hever, set on easy conquest and been rebuffed and eluded in a way that had turned fancy into infatuation. Anne had made it cruelly plain that she would never be his mistress and that, instead of cooling his ardour, had fanned it. He had only lured her back to Court by making grandiose promises, which he intended to keep: and to do that he needed Wolsey's help and full co-operation. He knew that Wolsey would not work his best on the problem if he knew that the ultimate aim was to make Tom Boleyn's daughter Queen; so care was necessary and great discretion; he had not dared to go to Hever one hundredth as often as he wished. With Anne amongst Katharine's ladies again he would at least see her, talk to her, dance with her sometimes without making himself conspicuous.

So Anne was back at Court; no longer a mere knight's daughter, but Lady Anne, daughter of an earl; and the collar she always wore was now of gold, set with real jewels; her clothes were better too; dresses of amber-coloured, or tawny velvet, or of silk, so darkly cream that it made her sallow skin look fairer than it was. She still lacked figure, no bosom at all; and she still lacked the power of endearing herself to other ladies. She was still the changeling.

Wolsey said, "Your Grace, I see Clement's predicament; it is not easy for one Pope to go against a ruling which his predecessor gave under his leaden seal. But the Archbishop of Canterbury and I have gone very thoroughly into the matter and we have decided that there is sufficient doubt to make action feasible. The Holy See has many things to consider; we gave your great matter our undivided attention and our conclusion has been forwarded to Rome."

"Where it will lie on a shelf, gather dust."

"Things move slowly there," Wolsey agreed. He knew why. He should have been Pope—and could, would have been, but for the hidden influence of the Emperor. That influence would also operate against Henry's plea that his marriage was unlawful; the Emperor was Katharine's nephew.

"The questioning of Julius' dispensation," he said, "could be made unnecessary, very simply. I considered it the other night when I lay wakeful. Her Grace is, as we all know, a woman of great piety. If she could be convinced that her marriage was unlawful, she would abjure it and retire into a convent . . . There is a precedent for it. A saintly Queen of France did precisely that, and allowed her husband to remarry. It would be much the speediest way."

"I think she might do it," Henry said, after a little pause.

"She is half a nun already; she wears the habit, under her clothes. She has a room in Greenwich, bare as a cell. She gives time and money to charities . . . My true Thomas, unfailing friend; I think you have hit on it. Will you—as Cardinal—propose it to her?"

In the eighteen years of Henry's reign Wolsey had come to power and more power by making himself indispensable, not only in great things, like the fitting out of an army or the organisation of events like the Field of the Cloth of Gold, but in innumerable, small ways. "I will see to it." "Your Grace may safely leave it to me." But now, though he had no fondness for Katharine, whom he regarded as an obstacle to his French policy, and who had once criticised his way of life, he was glad enough to be able to say, with truth and with feigned regret,

"Your Grace forgets. I am about to leave for France. Francis must be persuaded, or spurred into doing something about this Italian business. If only because while Clement is virtually the prisoner of the Emperor, he is most unlikely to give a decision favourable to you. In case the Queen spurns the suggestion we must make certain that Clement has cause for gratitude to Your Grace and the King of France."

"Rome, falling to Charles' troops, was a stroke of ill luck for me," Henry said.

"And for the world," Wolsey said. "Even for the Emperor, in the long run. Those who sacked Rome were German *landknechts*, little better than heathen, as their behaviour to nuns and monks showed."

Momentarily diverted from his egocentricity, Henry said:

"The Emperor once told me himself that his German subjects were hardly Christian . . . So, must I tell her myself or would the suggestion come better from a woman?"

"What woman has Your Grace in mind?"

"The Countess of Salisbury. The Queen trusts her completely and she is back in London now."

Wolsey looked down at his plump, well-kept hands, the great Cardinal's ring glowing on one finger.

"I should deem that unwise," he said. "If I know women they

would end crying on one another's shoulders and saying that Julius, being Pope, could never be in error. Pious women hold extreme views."

"As usual, you are right," Henry said gloomily. "I must do it myself; but it is a job I have little heart for."

Greenwich was still Katharine's favourite residence, because here Henry had met her in the lime walk and taken her from the room that smelt of the stable to the room that smelt of the past; here she had been married, and here Mary had been born. As she grew older and knew less positive happiness and occasionally felt that she had failed Henry and England, she cherished her memories more fondly.

Katharine was taking advantage of the bright light of a June morning to work upon a shirt for Henry; the linen was so fine and the stitches so small that by candlelight or on a dull day such work was impossible. When Henry came in she thought he had come to pay his courtesy morning call, a thing he never failed to do when they were under the same roof. With the shirt still in her hands she rose and curtseyed, and waited for him to seat himself. He remained on his feet and jerked his head towards her women.

"I have a private matter which I wish to discuss with you."

She imagined that she knew what it was. The new alignment with France was to be enforced by Mary's betrothal to a French prince. Mary had in fact been in London for some time so that the French Ambassador could report upon her appearance, disposition and accomplishments.

Henry seemed to have difficulty in broaching the subject; he told her to sit down; sat down himself; jumped up and went to the window and made a comment about the fine weather.

"Is it about Mary?" she asked, resuming her stitching.

"Only indirectly. It concerns you and me."

She looked up quickly. The light from the window fell upon his bright hair and massive figure. He ate and drank prodigiously, but he took so much hard exercise that it was muscle, not fat that made his bulk. His skin was still clear and ruddy, his eyes bright. Such a handsome man, she thought, and looked upon him with doting admiration. He saw the look, flinched and to escape it turned to the window. Speaking with his back to her he said:

"It concerns our marriage. I have thought long and hard about this, Katharine, and I beg you not to take it amiss . . . I think the dispensation should not have been given. You were my brother's wife. That is why our union has been cursed."

The gist of it jerked out he swung around again and met her look of blank incomprehension. Something in his mind cried: Oh, understand; make it easy for me; you with such a reputation for kindness, be kind to me!

She seemed to have been struck dumb.

"It is plainly set down in Leviticus," he blundered on. "If a man takes his brother's wife, they shall be childless."

Childless? Had he gone mad? Leviticus, a set of laws laid down for Jews. Had he taken a fall and deranged his mind?

"I cannot understand," she said. "Ours is no childless marriage. We have Mary. Henry, are you well? Have you had a fall? There is no sense in what you are saying. No sense at all."

"I am in my senses. I have seen the truth of the matter. So must you. We should never have married. The Pope was mistaken; the dispensation was not valid."

"Your father and mine accepted it. So did you."

"I was in love with you, Kate, and not responsible. My father, on his deathbed, tried to warn me. I gave no heed. I was wrong then and I have been punished. For a King to have no child but a daughter is to be childless."

"There was the boy who might have lived had he not been christened in midwinter."

She seemed calm; only her hands, kneading at the delicate fabric which had been handled so carefully and was now being treated like a dishcloth, betrayed agitation.

"How many children are christened in winter and survive? Hundreds. I see his death as part of the curse. My conscience has wakened. I know now that I have . . . we have . . . lived in sin for eighteen years, and been punished."

"Who put this to you, Henry? It is not true. We have not lived in sin; we have lived in the holy state of matrimony. My marriage to Arthur—as you know very well—was in name only. Pope Julius knew that and gave permission for our marriage. Who troubled your conscience with this nonsense?"

Her apparent calm angered him; he said sharply:

"It is not nonsense. Cast your mind back to Charles' last visit. You were there when he said that some of his advisors had questioned Mary's legitimacy."

"I was *not*," Katharine said. "He would never have dared to say such a thing in my presence. If Mary is illegitimate what am I? A strumpet?"

"No, no. Perhaps you were not there. But he said it. More lately the French have raised the same question and I . . ."

"I think German lawyers, tainted with Lutheranism and the French who have never properly respected the Pope, are responsible for such talk. I think you would be well-advised to ignore it."

"How can I? Two years ago I sent to Clement asking him to confirm or to refute Julius' dispensation. No answer has yet come. More lately the Archbishop of Canterbury and Cardinal Wolsey have gone thoroughly into the matter and say that the legality of our marriage is doubtful."

Two years. All this going on behind her back.

"What then can be done about it? Had Clement found a flaw in the dispensation, he would surely have amended it. It rests with him."

"With *us*. Katharine, the way is clear. We have only to admit that we were in error, that we were never married in the sight of God, and the whole thing would be undone. I would look after you well, you and Mary. You are both dear to me; I would look upon you as my sisters. My *favourite* sisters," he added, remembering the bitter quarrels he had had with both Mary and Margaret. "I would find a kind, suitable husband for Mary and dower her well. You could revert to your title as Dowager Princess of Wales; and you could enjoy all the comfort you now have in any convent that you chose."

"Convent!"

"It would be the best way. An acknowledgement. I thought . . . I mean of late . . ." Embarrassed he turned to the window again. "It would not be so very different from the life you live now. It would show the world that you admitted the invalidity of our marriage. But . . . if the idea of a convent repels you, I daresay it could be managed in another way." He needed Wolsey now. "A public statement, perhaps, admitting that you and I were never legally married. In that case, any manor you choose. Or any palace . . ."

A small part of her confused mind, schooled by eighteen years of having no will but his, of trying to please him, was tempted to yield. Give way, please him, retain some remnant of affection. She stamped the impulse down.

"I can never consent to anything, never say a word or make a move that would make Mary, my daughter and yours, a bastard in the eyes of the world."

"She is that already," he said. She heard the change in his voice; the explanatory, persuasive, almost apologetic note had gone, replaced by something hard and ruthless.

"Not until Clement says so. Until he says otherwise—and if the decision had been so simple he would have declared himself by now—I am your lawful wedded wife, Mary, your lawfully begotten child, and your heir. By that I must stand."

Something in him, not yet lost to grace, tendered its unwilling admiration; it said— A woman of quality and I recognised it from the first; a most admirable woman. But there were, in his mind, other, louder voices reminding him of Anne, that dark enchantress, waiting in the far wing of the palace, her bed for which he craved, forbidden because she would not be his mistress, only his wife, and Queen; reminding him of the slowness with which things moved in Rome; reminding him of his—and England's—need for an heir; reminding him that this summer, part of the sweet summer of life—thirty-six this month—was passing.

He said, "If you obstruct me, I fear you will regret it."

"And if I did not, you might regret it more. Henry, I beg you;

think where this might lead. Julius gave us leave to marry. Clement must recognise the Papal authority of his predecessor, or undermine his own. If you shuffle me aside and marry the Frenchwoman whom Wolsey has chosen for you . . ."

"There is no question of that," he said, "until I am free."

But he was pleased that his real intention was so well concealed.

". . . the matter of authority will always remain," Katharine said. "You might well find yourself with nothing but bastards—if Clement gives you leave to marry again and half the world holds, as I do, that Julius' dispensation was good. I think you have been ill-advised."

That was another thing to which she must hold; he had been ill-advised. It was Wolsey, so pro-French, so anti-Imperialist, thwarted because his ultimate ambition, to be Pope, had failed, who had concocted the whole abominable plot. And suddenly she saw Henry, herself, Mary, Clement, and all the thousands upon thousands of people who believed, as she did, that Popes, though subject to human weaknesses, were in their decisions inspired by Divine grace, all of us, in those plump white hands reduced to nothing but pawns in a game to be played for his advantage.

She began to cry, mopping her eyes with the shirt which she had been making for Henry, part of his birthday present.

On Henry the eighteen years of marriage, ecstatic, and then with the passing years, placid, had left their mark. As her desire to please him had been cultivated, so had his desire to cherish her. Old habits held. He said, "Oh, for the love of God, Kate, do not cry. You know I cannot bear to see you cry." Nor could he bear to be opposed; for eighteen years his will had been law in England. What was to be his curiously ambivalent attitude towards her was born then, when he wished to stem her tears, and wished also to beat her over the head. The whole thing could have been as easy as slipping on a glove; now it would be painful, long drawn out, and public. Anne waiting, nagging, despairing, defiant. God help any man, caught as he was, between two such stubborn women.

Katharine thought: This is a horrible world; one from which, but for Mary, I should be only too glad to retreat: and she sobbed on.

"Well, we shall see," Henry said, unable to bear his conflicting impulses any longer; the beautiful Princess from Spain whom he had loved, who had loved him, lost and gone, even death could not be more irrevocable—*her* he wanted to hold and comfort; but she was entombed, not in stone, but in the body of this middle-aged, stubborn woman.

He went away; and for the first time there was a heaviness, a lack of liveliness in his step.

The whole interview had taken no more than fifteen, at most twenty minutes. He had put forward a proposition which she had rejected. Both were good pious Catholics and they had unleashed, in a small room, forces that were to shape and alter half a world.

Left alone, Katharine cried on, seeing what must be done, but shrinking from it; seeing what had been done and abhorring it. But tears served no purpose except to induce pity in others. She was alone, unobserved. Nobody could weep forever. And she had other resources.

She sent for the Spanish Ambassador, Don Inigo de Mendoza. Dr. Puebla she had never wholeheartedly liked; his successor had lacked tact; Mendoza was, in her opinion, as nearly ideal an ambassador as a man could be, dignified, astute, tactful. He was a member of a noble Spanish family and as a boy had been one of Isabella's pages. He had formed part of the escort which had ridden with Katharine on the first stage of her journey to England and she looked upon him as a friend. When he was appointed, she had imagined that they would have long talks together and she would hear all the intimate, trivial news from Spain. It had never come about. She had observed that, no matter how crowded the room, as soon as she and Charles' ambassador had exchanged a dozen words, Wolsey would make his way towards them and either hover, or make an interruption. She was wise enough to realise that the Cardinal suspected the

possibility of connivance between a Spanish-born Queen and a
Spanish ambassador—though what was there to connive about?
Not to lend substance to the suspicion, however, she had never,
until now, made any effort to see Mendoza in private. But this
was a crisis.

She saw, by his face, his manner, that he was already informed. She had hardly begun when she stopped and said, "You
knew?"

"Your Grace, there have been rumours. In Europe for months.
Lately here, even in taverns."

"And no one saw fit—you did not see fit, Don Mendoza, to
inform me?"

She sounded exactly like her mother, chiding him, years ago,
for biting his nails.

"We all hoped," he said, "that it would blow over, without
the need for Your Grace to suffer a pang. Even the ale-drinkers
would spare you and have hoped, as I have, that the Pope would
give the decisive word, in your favour."

In my favour? As though I were a criminal. What have I
done?

"It was left to His Grace to inform me. To me it was a great
shock. To be asked to admit, after eighteen years of happy marriage that I was never wedded at all, that my child bore the
stigma of bastardy . . ." She would have wept again there, but
the last tear had been wrung out of her; and the lovely June
day had clouded over; she was empty, cold, wretched, greatly
in need of some heartening word.

Mendoza said, "It is all very unfortunate. Your Grace has my
sympathy." And what, at this moment, was that worth?

"I thank you," she said, forcing herself to civility. "But I need
more. As His Grace left me he said, "Well, we shall see." I had
raised every point I could think of, overtaken by surprise as I
was; he was not convinced and those last words have an ominous ring. *His* case was submitted to Rome two years ago. Did
you know that?"

"I have heard of Dr. Knight and his activities," Mendoza
admitted.

"Then some moves must be made on *my* behalf. Someone must speak for me. Whom can we send?"

"It is a matter for lawyers, Your Grace. And I am inclined to think that no English lawyer, despatched without the King's warrant, or the Cardinal's, would get farther than Abbeville, in France." He saw the incredulous look on her face and knew that in a minute she would be thinking, probably saying, that he was imagining a state of affairs that did not exist. He said, hurried and defensive, "The Cardinal has a long arm, Madam; and many friends in France. Last year, making my way here, with every possible letter of credit, every proof of identity about me, I was delayed, for many weeks, in Arques. The Cardinal, for some reason of his own, wished Spain and the Empire not to be represented in London. My papers were examined—by men who could not read, or pretended not to be able; my pro- tests—and my French is fluent—were ignored or misunderstood. Eventually I was allowed to continue my journey; in the Cardi- nal's good time. There were many apologies for the blunder on the part of officials, too officious. But they were acting on in- structions. I do not doubt that the same instructions would apply to any English lawyer who did not carry the Cardinal's blessing."

"Then I must appeal by letter to His Holiness and to the Emperor."

"I fear that the same fate would overtake any courier carrying such communications, Your Grace."

She looked at him bleakly; and he stared at her, apologetic but unhelpful. She knew a swift regret for old Dr. Puebla, that resourceful man.

"Your own diplomatic correspondence?" she asked.

"I have known letters go astray in mysterious fashion. What gets through is read—I know that. Not only read but subject to tests, in case I have used invisible ink."

She realised the weight of the forces ranged against her.

"If I may venture to offer a word of advice," Mendoza said. "The information reached Your Grace only this morning. When one is taken by surprise it is possible to act too hastily. A little time for reflection, perhaps, and some compromise might be reached."

"How can one compromise over such a thing? Either I am married or I am not. One side of the case has already been under scrutiny by Rome for two years. I am not represented there . . . Thank you for coming so promptly, Don Mendoza. You have leave to go."

"I deeply regret not being able to be helpful."

"On the contrary, you have made me aware of dangers that I did not know existed. What a pass for a country to come to! And England where the people regard themselves as the freest people in the world!"

"It happens invariably when too much power falls into the wrong hands, Madam."

As soon as he had gone she sent for Francisco Filipez, her server. He was one of those who had come with her from Spain and had stayed. At Ludlow and for a short time afterwards he had had charge of her horses. One day at Durham House he had come to her and asked if she would allow him to become her server; and that sounded a strange request from a man, no longer young, accustomed to a different life altogether. He had explained that the climate in England did not suit him; being out of doors stiffened his joints. So she had agreed. About a week later the old King, in miserly mood, had decided that she needed no horses of her own. She had sometimes wondered whether Filipez had heard a whisper. He was an excellent server, and although he still spent much time in and around the stables, he had never once brought into her presence the slightest whiff of the odour which always reminded her of her old apartments at Greenwich where hope had so nearly died. After her marriage to Henry, with gifts to give, she had offered Filipez the post as steward at her own manor of Ampthill and he had refused it, saying, "I would sooner stay with Your Grace. Unless, of course, you think my grizzled head incongruous." She had hastily reassured him.

Now she said to him, with brisk practicality:

"Francisco, do you still ride?"

"Every day, Your Grace." A man who, so long ago, had sought an indoors post!

"How long would it take you to get to Spain?" She knew that Charles was in Valladolid.

Filipez reckoned quickly; summer with long days, the roads dry and the rivers fordable.

"With good horses, sixteen, seventeen days."

"And could you carry, in your head, a message that I dare not commit to paper?"

"My memory is good."

"Then it remains to find a reason for your going, and for your haste. Otherwise you might be waylaid."

He knew more about the circumstances than she had done— until ten minutes ago.

"Your Grace, who would waylay a humble man, going home to receive his dying mother's blessing?"

His mother had died so long ago that he had no memory of her and could use the name with no feeling.

The thought shot through her mind that only those who had known a hard upbringing were resourceful. Dr. Puebla, Maria de Moreto, this man; me?

She gave him her messages; one for Charles himself, one for him to forward to Rome. "You will need a passport, Francisco."

"I shall have it, not tomorrow perhaps, but the next day, Your Grace."

"God keep you," she said.

In every way this had been a vile day, even weatherwise; but she was Queen of England, and in the glowering light which made the candles necessary, even on a June evening, she took her place at the supper table, the marrow of her bones quivering like jelly. But after all, nothing had *happened*; only her inner, private world had been overset, her mind rocked, her heart broken. But this was her place and she took it, beside Henry, who was surprisingly amiable. In the course of the long day he had realised that, if Katharine would not give way, sorrow, not wrath would be his best weapon; he must appear to be a man compelled by his conscience to take a course very painful to him. Alongside this reasoning, all through the day, another thought had run, a mounting anger because his sweet Kate, always so amenable and anxious to please, had defied him.

He said, halfway through the meal, with some malice in his voice:

"That server of yours has just applied for a safe conduct to Spain. He claims that his mother is dying. To me he looks somewhat old to have a mother, even dying."

So that resource had failed too. In the bright hall, full of candles and colour, music and merriment, she felt as stranded as though she sat alone on a rock in the sea. But Filipez must be protested.

"There will be others, with similar excuses. My people will see no future here, after what was said this morning."

"Straws show which way the wind blows," he said sententiously. "For your own sake you should think again. Those who take up an indefensible position must expect to stand alone."

"I know," she said, wondering if she could ever be more alone than at this moment.

Henry was so pleased by Filipez's apparent desertion and the opportunity it had given for the delivery of a little homily, that before he slept he had signed papers that would have ensured Filipez's safe conduct anywhere in Christendom.

A fortnight later, beating his own most optimistic estimate by two days, Filipez was in Valladolid, seeking audience of the least accessible monarch in Europe. Unshaven, caked with dust, red-eyed from lack of sleep, he said to one official after another, "I carry an urgent message to His Imperial Highness." "Where is it?" they asked, prepared to take it, peruse it, judge its importance and possibly deliver it. "In my head," he said. Mad? Drunk? Inadmissible.

Filipez had hoped that by some miracle he could gain an audience without disclosing whence he came; it was a secret errand, but in the end, asked for the twentieth time, "Where is it?", he pulled out of his doublet the much-handled paper which had served him so well.

"This is not the message—that is in my head," he said again, "but this is proof of urgency." The black, scrawled, signature, *Henry R.* was recognised and in a short time, Filipez, on his knees before the Emperor, was repeating, word for word, the message that Katharine had entrusted to him.

Charles was not ignorant of the rumours. The King of England plans to put away his wife, remarry and beget a son. There had been no developments; and for a man upon whose shoulders such vast responsibilities weighed, there were a thousand other things to think of. Charles had as little knowledge of, as little patience with sexual traffic as any man alive. He had been betrothed ten times; he had married his cousin, Isabella of Portugal, he had begotten an heir. His uncle-by-marriage, Henry of England, had been less fortunate in that respect and had appealed to Clement to annul his marriage and set him free to marry again. And in two years, Clement had made no move and there had appeared to be no need for Charles to concern himself.

Now here the thing was, cropping up again; in the frantic appeal from his aunt that he should send a good lawyer to represent her at Rome—a request made in this unusual fashion.

He approached the matter cautiously.

"You may stand," he said. Filipez stiffly and with some difficulty stood. "This is a strange approach. I have my Ambassador in London. It seems to me that the Queen, my aunt, could have communicated through the usual diplomatic channels."

"They are blocked," Filipez said bluntly. "Nothing in these days goes in or out of England except what suits the Cardinal. Nothing that Her Grace wrote would have reached Your Imperial Highness."

"Yet you were given safe conduct."

"By accident. Have I leave to speak freely? Unless Her Grace receives help from outside England, her cause is lost because the Cardinal has set himself to ending this marriage and making a new one, between His Grace and a Princess of France."

Behind the vacuous expression, the sharp mind sprang to attention.

"Tavern gossip?"

"My lord, I have lived in England for twenty-six years and I have learned that what the ale drinkers say, though it may be hotly contradicted, is right, nine times out of ten."

Charles was fond of his aunt, who had been kind and maternal to him, and who had not resented the breaking of his betrothal to her daughter; but his nature was too cold, too reasonable to be moved into action by sentiment. Policy was a different matter; he had no wish to see England and France linked by marriage.

"You intend to return to England? When?"

"Tomorrow, Your Imperial Highness."

"Then inform Her Grace that her message was delivered, and noted and that action will be taken. I shall instruct my Ambassador, by letter, to support her in her decision—and offer what comfort is possible."

"May I . . ." Filipez hesitated; it was already late, so much time had been wasted; and it was hardly for him to suggest that the Emperor should sit late into the night writing letters . . . "If you would allow me to carry the letter? I go faster than any courier, and with my safe conduct I get better treatment in France than anyone without it would do."

Charles noted the significance of that remark, not with hurt to his vanity—he had little—but as a circumstance to be considered; in France Henry's signature on a passport meant more than his own!

"The letter will be ready for you in the morning. Her Grace is fortunate in her servant."

"She has many," Filipez said deprecatingly. "All the people of England, save a handful of the Cardinal's men."

Charles noted that remark too.

He wrote to Henry first, a curious letter, more forthright than was his habit, and in tone that of a father rebuking and reproaching a son who contemplated some action not only disastrous but preposterous. Then he wrote to Mendoza, telling him to seek an audience with the Queen immediately and assure her of his support and sympathy. He was sending Cardinal Quinones, a most gifted and experienced lawyer, to Rome on her behalf. The two letters were folded together and addressed to Mendoza who would present Henry's with due formality.

Filipez made the return journey in thirteen days, went straight to Katharine with the verbal message which he made sound warmer and more partisan and energetic than it had been in fact; not because he deliberately falsified it, but because thirteen days of thinking, *The Emperor is on her side,* had coloured his opinion. It was worth the twenty-seven days in the saddle to see her face light up and hear her say "Thank God."

He then delivered the package at Mendoza's house and went to bed for eight hours. Redressed, scoured clean, he was behind Katharine's chair that evening at suppertime.

Henry, with that personal touch, the passing interest in people's affairs which endeared him to so many, noticed and said:

"You! Back already?"

"Your Grace, I got no farther than Valladolid. There I heard that I was already too late. My mother was buried. So I turned about; and the Emperor himself honoured me by entrusting me with a package for Don Inigo de Mendoza. So I rode fast."

"If you were a younger man, I'd say you were wasted at that job." He ran his eye over Filipez; very spare, he'd ride light. Henry nowadays on a hunting day tired out five or six horses; but then who would wish to be like that fellow with no calves to his legs, spindle-shanked in his hose.

In the near-month of Filipez's absence, life had seemed so placid and ordinary that sometimes it seemed as though that terrible interview had never occurred. After the sidelong warning that those who took impossible stands must expect to be alone, Henry had not referred to the subject again, and except for adding to her prayers a request that Filipez might get through safely and that Charles would do what she asked, Katharine had tried to put it out of her mind. She had done what she could; there was no more to do at the moment, she must trust in God and stay calm. Even anxiety showed lack of faith. Act as though all were well and all might yet be well.

But it was strange to sit and stand by Henry's side, smile, make amiable conversation, make one of his summer progresses with him and be everywhere received as Queen, knowing all the time what was in his mind. When the first shattering shock had worn off a little, she could sort out one hurt from another and knew that the lasting wound had been dealt when he said that he had put his case to Rome two years ago. He might be justified in his doubts; she loved him and found it easy to see things from his angle; what Charles had said about Mary's legitimacy was enough to sow a seed. But before a word was said to anyone else, she, the person most nearly concerned, should have been consulted; if necessary they should *together* have asked for a Papal decision. It was impossible not to feel a sense of betrayal. It was almost equally impossible to look upon Henry as a traitor, capable of so base an action. The habit of loving and admiring him was too strong to be overcome so easily. He had remained faithful to her and to his betrothal—not without difficulty; he had remained faithful, save for two excusable lapses, to his marriage vows. Why should he suddenly be so faithless as to go behind her back in an attempt to break up their marriage? It was out of character. So how? So why?

She would reach this point in her thinking and give herself an answer. Always the same. Wolsey. Wolsey was pro-French, against her and the Spanish alliance from the first. And she could well imagine how he had gone about the work of persuading Henry that his marriage was unlawful and his sonlessness a punishment. Those plump white hands with the great Cardinal's ring gleaming, steepled under the double chin, the solemn sonorous voice quoting Leviticus. It was probably Wolsey who had first said that for a King to have only a daughter was to be childless; it was the way he used words, making traps for men's minds. He had done it for years, weaving webs like a spider, leaving it to others to entangle themselves. "Your Grace has no *legitimate* son. But you are still young. With another woman, not cursed . . ."

And why had Henry not said, "On a woman who was not my wife I got a son." Perhaps he had said it and Wolsey had replied with some sophistry about sin between the sheets being less culpable than sin between the ears, sin with Elizabeth Taillebois, completely unhallowed, more easily forgiven than sin with Katharine, Arthur's wife, in defiance of God's law and the more offensive for having the appearance of legality. Elizabeth Taillebois pensioned, her son provided for; Mary Boleyn married off; venial; shallow, uprooted and forgotten; her own case, as Wolsey would present it was altogether different, far closer— If thine eye offend thee, pluck it out. And whether Wolsey was the originator of the scheme or not, he was certainly the source of the secretiveness, secret motives governed him, secret methods were his tools.

It was so easy to exonerate the man she loved by blaming the one she neither liked nor respected, but now and again, clearheaded in a wakeful night she would think in a different fashion. Henry was not entirely incapable of secretiveness; he had learned to keep his own purposes concealed when his father lived; both his extramarital affaires had been conducted with what was called in such circumstances, discretion. Was his desire to end his marriage prompted less by some words in Leviticus than a wish to take some other woman as his wife? Some young Princess, with many child-bearing years ahead of her. French if Wolsey had any say. Princess Renée. Perhaps.

She had, as yet, no knowledge of her real enemy; the one so close, lodged across the courtyard in apartments suited to an earl's daughter, mingling with the other ladies-in-waiting. Henry and Anne had been very careful—not that there was much to be careful about, Henry often thought, angrily: they were hardly ever alone in a room together. Anne was determined that nobody should say that she, like her sister, was a strumpet. Henry was anxious that neither Wolsey close at hand, nor Clement far away in Rome should know the truth. All must be cloaked until Wolsey had persuaded Clement to give the desired answer. And both Henry and Anne had another reason for behaving with great circumspection. He was determined that she should be Queen, therefore her reputation must not be smirched. Anne was afraid that if she yielded an inch the spell would be broken. Only for the seemingly unattainable did men go to impossible lengths.

On Henry with his sensual nature, and now for a long time accustomed to having his own way in most things, the strain was enormous; seeing Anne every day, sometimes many times in a day, always in a crowd, being obliged to curb even his glances; and then, in their brief, painfully contrived times alone together, sometimes permitted a kiss, a caress, but more often being teased, railed at, mocked. For Anne also felt the strain—not of thwarted passion—but of insecurity and impatience. Men would go to great lengths for the seemingly unattainable, but only for a limited time. Suppose that time spent itself while Clement still dithered. Only her maid, Emma Arnett, knew how often Anne's nerves gave way and she would have fits of hysteria, take to her bed, have to be dosed and cossetted. And almost every day, sometimes many times in a day, she was forced to join the ladies around Katharine, the impediment in her path; the woman who could have, should have, retired with grace and made the whole thing easy, and chose not to do so.

To Katharine a form of enlightenment—almost immediately rejected—came on an apparently ordinary evening, when, as the tables were cleared, Henry said, as he so often did, "Now we will dance."

Katharine no longer danced; dancing was for the young and that single, devastating talk with Henry had leeched away the last of her youth. Life went on, day following day, with everyone waiting for the Pope to pontificate, pretending that until the word was given, all was as it had been; but it was not. The strain of waiting that irked Henry's temper and made Anne hysterical had damaged Wolsey, putting fresh lines into his face where the hitherto firm flesh now sagged; and around Thomas More's eyes and mouth there were marks not set there by study and the need to issue fair judgement on legal questions. Three of us, she thought, who love Henry . . . and I am in worst case of all, because without him I have nothing. Then she thought: Nonsense, I have Mary; and her face brightened and lifted as she looked down upon the floor where her daughter was taking her place.

Henry had undertaken to see that Mary rode and danced expertly and could make songs as well as play the lute in the ordinary way and in these arts as well as the more serious subjects she was a credit to her teacher. At the age of eleven she was still shorter than normal, a fact that irked her and for which she tried to make up by holding her head high and by ordering shoes with tall heels; she had inherited her mother's dignity and her father's ability to put dignity away on occasion. This was such an occasion because Henry had given the musicians the signal to play one of the merry tunes which accompanied the dance which the English, with their knack of simplifying French terms, called a "Brawle."

He had his reason for that. In the more stately dances done to tunes almost as solemn as church music, and steps performed in formal pattern, ladies and gentlemen danced in pairs and though the pairs mingled, forming foursomes and eightsomes, the partners always came back to one another and at the end exchanged the kiss with which most dances concluded. A Brawle was different: though it had an almost infinite variety of forms, one movement was repeated at intervals, all the men formed a circle on the outer side and skipped in one direction, all the ladies in the inner circle, skipped in the opposite way for exactly twenty steps and stopped; ladies then faced outwards, gentlemen inwards, the ladies curtseyed, the gentlemen bowed and the pair immediately opposite one another were partners for the next movement, three running steps forward, three backwards, hand in hand; then a swinging motion, in which ladies were often lifted from their feet; then the kiss, and off to the next pattern, the square, the circle, or the running under an archway made by one pair holding their hands high. Then the two circles again. In a lucky evening, with a little jostling, Henry might find himself opposite Anne three or four times, hold her hands, hold her waist and kiss her, all without being in the least conspicuous. There was torment in the joy, but that he did not grudge.

In the soft bright light of hundreds of candles the colours of the clothes of the dancers shone and shifted, blended and contrasted. Henry wore yellow slashed over cloth of gold; Mary was wearing bluish green; apart from their colours they were easily distinguishable, he the largest, she the smallest of the dancers. Other people stood out from the mass, too: Elizabeth Conyers, only eighteen but with hair completely white; it was said to have changed colour in a single night—romantically minded ladies whispered that young Digby's betrothal to another woman had caused the change, Elizabeth herself said that it was due to a bout of fever. Maria de Moreto who occasionally showed an unexpected softness towards girls thought to be love-lorn, had once suggested the use of henna to her and gained no thanks; Mistress Conyers said that she considered her white hair becoming. When her cheeks were coloured pink it was. The Lady Anne was another easily picked out on account of her collar. Other ladies had copied the ornament at one time, held to it for a month or so and then abandoned it. The truth was that it was not becoming, except to Anne whose neck was extraordinarily long; to others the ordinary necklace, lying at the base of the throat, and with pendant jewels, drawing the eye downwards, did better service. Tonight Anne wore tawny and of the jewels in the collar the topazes seemed to predominate.

Henry, in the outer circle, stood level with Anne in the inner one and they paired off; she curtseyed, without looking at him, and rose, taking his hand without the smile which was obligatory, no matter how unwelcome the partner might be. She was a girl who smiled very seldom, Katharine had observed; perhaps the unfortunate business with Harry Percy had quenched some source of merriment within her. Henry spoke to her as they took the steps forward and backward, she inclined her head in her graceful way but seemed not to answer. Then they swung around, Anne's feet leaving the floor; Henry always lifted his partners high. They kissed, made a foursome with Margaret Lee and Sir Harry Norris, the four right hands joined in the centre, and then back into the circles. Henry's partner this time at the end of the twenty skipping steps was Jane Seymour, plain and shy, now back at Court.

From time to time both Wolsey and More seated by Katharine spoke to her, obeying the unwritten law that those who did not dance should converse. They spoke and she answered them, without removing her attention from the floor.

The colours of the dancers' clothes merged, separated, blurred; the skipping rings went round; twenty steps and a halt. Now Henry, who was wide, stood opposite his daughter and Anne Boleyn whom the dance had placed next one another. From where Katharine sat it seemed that Henry was slightly more directly opposite his daughter whose face already wore a look of welcome and delight. Then it happened. Henry did not step sideways—the rules of good behaviour in a dance forbade that, but he leaned so that his bow was made to the Lady Anne who was just about to curtsey to Sir Francis Westleton who stood on Henry's right. It was one of the jostling movements which, because he was King and because he occupied more space than most men, had served him well in the past. This evening it did not because the female partner thus subtly slighted happened to be his own daughter who, with a movement so like his own that in any other circumstance it would have been comic, rose from her curtsey with exactly the slant to her left that was necessary, and rose and took her father's hand. Francis Westleton took Anne's and the dance would have gone on had Henry not raised his hand as a signal to the musicians and said, into the sudden silence, "Enough is enough."

What Mary said was also clearly audible; she had her grandmother's deep, carrying voice. "Oh! I wanted to be swung. Nobody swings as you do."

Henry said, "Swung you shall be," and there in the centre of dancers halted by the cessation of the music, he lifted and swung her, more turns than the dance would have demanded. And with a dark and glowering face.

Anne Boleyn, Lady Anne Rochford. Nonsense, ridiculous. She did not lie at the heart of this miserable plot. If Henry wanted her—and it seemed that he did—she was there for the taking, as her sister had been. The King of England had no need to shuffle off his marriage on *her* account, a woman he could never marry; not even a woman of noble family. Quite incredible. There had been a King of England, the fourth Edward, who had married one of his own subjects and thus offended most of his nobles. Henry would never . . . And yet, and yet . . . That unsmiling face, the inclination of the head, the ready acceptance in an equivocal situation, of another man's hand. Nobody quite like her . . . I knew it from the first when I thought her a changeling. There is something about her, something unusual and strange after which Henry yearns—I saw that in his face, in the outstretched hand and the attempt to push Mary aside. But not to *marry*. A passing fancy; nothing to do with the great matter involving two Popes, two crowned Kings, the Prince who was now King of England, the Princess who was now Queen; their one living child, Mary Princess of Wales. Nothing to do. No. Nothing to do. . . .

She could have asked Henry a point-blank question, and it was pride, not lack of courage which prevented her. Their relationship had altered since the time when she had been able to speak openly about Elizabeth Taillebois—and even then her remonstrance had been futile. Since then there had been the liaison with Mary Boleyn and that she had ignored entirely, largely because in her heart she was not sure, and wished not to be. And that was before the shattering interview in June since when, it seemed to her, she and Henry had been engaged in an elaborate masquerade, each pretending that nothing had changed. But the masks of amiability and ordinariness with which they appeared in public were not dropped when they chanced to be alone together which happened rarely, but did still happen often enough for such meetings to have become as stylised as a puppet show; an exchange of civilities from which every hint of intimacy had been banished. It was as though they were carrying between them some object of such frailty that a misdirected breath could shatter it forever; yet a thing which, if borne carefully enough would survive and finally be put down in a place of safety.

It was therefore impossible for her even to mention the Lady Anne either as his latest light-o'-love, or her potential rival. And this time, if there were gossip—as there must be if even half her suspicion was justified—none of it reached her ears. She did notice that sometimes when she entered a room where her ladies were chattering a curious silence would fall and once she asked why. The answer was prompt— They had been arguing and it was well known that Her Grace disliked disputes among her attendants. Even Maria de Moreto was unforthcoming, though Katharine, feeling ashamed of the sidelong approach, once invited her to gossip, saying, "The Lady Anne tells me that she has discovered a new musician."

"Oh yes, Your Grace. A fellow called Mark Smeaton, taken from the plough-tail, I understand. He is not well-liked."

"By whom?"

"Those with whom she surrounds herself. As Your Grace must know *she* is not much liked among your ladies; but she makes up for it in her leisure hours; her brother, her cousins— one would think they were glued to her; Sir Francis Weston, Sir Henry Norris, William Brereton, Nan Savile . . ."

Once, when there was hope, when there was security, Maria de Moreto had been frank. Now she had no purpose save to comfort. And it was a comfort based on truth; for when the relatives and the friends went to their beds, there remained Emma Arnett, watchful as a dragon . . . Maria knew the whole situation. She also knew that the Pope must move soon and in the meanwhile the less damage done, the better.

So it was left to the ordinary English people, nameless, faceless, to prove the truth of what a dusty courier had once told the Emperor—uninformed ale-drinkers, nine times out of ten, were right.

It was one of those shining autumn days; Katharine and Mary left Greenwich to go by barge to Richmond; and all along the river banks, thronging the steps that joined land to water, they congregated, and they shouted. "God save the Queen." "God bless the Princess of Wales." They also shouted, "We want no Nan Bullen!" "No Nan Bullen for us!"

"You heard the cries, Maria?"
The campaign of comfort brought to nothing; how many times had she said: One word in her hearing and I will tear out your eyes!
"Your Grace, they cry against her as a witch."
A witch; there was no such thing, except in those old tales, told by Joanna in the dying firelight, long ago. Even Torquemada and the Office of the Inquisition, under whose shadow Katharine had been reared, held that there was nothing worse than heresy to be rooted out.
"Maria, you cannot believe that." I do not. The linking of her name with mine and Mary's has another and for me a more sinister implication; more sinister because I do not believe in witches or their craft.
"I do believe it," Maria said. "She bears two marks. The extra finger and the mole on her neck that the collar covers. That is the teat at which the Evil One suckles. The extra finger is the mark of the beast. And then there is the dog. Have you never marked how in company she never names him; she whistles, snaps her fingers and he obeys. But he has a name, one of Satan's. She calls him Urian. And was ever a hair of him singed?"
Katharine had seen the dog's performance several times. A page held a hoop bound about with strips of linen so old, so dry as to be instantly inflammable. The boy held the hoop at arms' length, using tongs and when the flame made a full circle, the Lady Anne would call and snap her fingers or say, "Come to me!" The dog, a mastiff with some other blood, would run, leap through the fiery circle and emerge—as Maria said—unsinged, and put his head on his mistress' knees. It was, in dull moments, a useful entertainment because afterwards several gentlemen—and a few ladies—would endeavour to prove that

their dogs were equally brave and docile. Not one had ever shown itself to be so. But what did that prove, except that the Lady Anne's dog feared the whip more than the fire?

"Maria, how many in the crowd today knew that she was blemished and had a dog obedient beyond the ordinary? They cried against her for another reason, linking her name with mine because they fear she will supplant me . . ."

On me, Maria thought, always the load falls! This time I refuse it! She said firmly, "And how could that be? His Holiness will give an answer favourable to Your Grace and then you will see Mistress Boleyn bundled off back to Hever with no pension and no husband. She is a witch, she has put a spell upon the King—but to one end only; that she should be Queen. Once she sees that is impossible and he sees that he will never have his way with her, it will be over. Like that," Maria said, clicking her thumb and finger with a sound like castanets.

"I pray so," Katharine said. "But even you, Maria, seem uncertain of mind. You say that she is cried against as a witch; and in almost the same breath that she does aim to take my place. Everybody seems better informed than I . . ."

"She *is* a witch. How else . . . Did you ever know *him* to admire a woman with no looks? No bosom. No amiability. Not even young. And of an unyielding disposition. May I say what I think? She had set herself to be Countess of Northumberland and was thwarted. *Then* she took up with the Devil and he, Father of Lies, promised her more. But when did he ever keep a promise? Oh, she may toss her head and walk proudly and guard herself and say the way to her bed lies through St. Paul's. But that will gain her nothing. The Pope will declare for you— and as you heard today, the ordinary people will never accept her."

The conversation had come back to where it started, the cries from the river bank, from the people jostling on the steps and little jetties, all the way from Greenwich to Richmond.

And I kept in the dark; until that moment when Henry passed over his own daughter and looked . . . and looked with the naked, yearning, hungry gaze which once he turned upon me . . . and even then doubting, until today. Maria knowing so much; every blacksmith, baker, butcher, huckster knowing. It was impossible not to feel shamed. Now she understood why the chatter had ceased as she entered a room and why two people, almost whispering together in a passage would look startled at her approach and begin to talk in voices, overloud, about some trivial matter. Everyone knew and tonight she must face them all, for tonight, to mark the move to Richmond, supper would be eaten in public. She thought of the eyes, sharp with curiosity or soft with pity, the tongues, venomous or wondering, and felt that she could not face them. Unless strength were found from somewhere.

"I wish to be alone for half an hour, Maria," she said, and as soon as the door was closed she knelt and prayed for courage, for control, for patience, for the power to remain dignified in a supremely undignified situation and finally for victory. Strength flowed in from somewhere; the Pope, Christ's Vicar on earth would decide rightly and she would be vindicated. In that certainty she could find all the courage and patience and control that she needed.

She sat by Henry's side and looked around the hall and thought: All concerned in this business are here. Mary had her own table at which this evening M. du Bellay, the French Ambassador, was seated, together with Lady Salisbury, Reginald Pole and various other ladies and gentlemen. The Spanish Ambassador, Don de Mendoza, sombre in black velvet, was with Wolsey, splendid in scarlet, and they appeared to be in amicable conversation. The ladies-in-waiting and other Court officials sat at a lower table, from which at intervals sounds of merriment drifted. Anne this evening was clad in crimson and below the never discarded collar she wore a parure of rubies. I know now where she gets her finery! But whence comes her power to fascinate? There are women younger and prettier at the table, but she is the focus of attention, Westleton, Carnaby, Wyatt, Norris, even her own brother have eyes for nobody else. And it is always after something she has said that the laughter breaks out, though she never smiles. I must not stare! I will never, if I can help it, give a sign that she is anything more than one of my ladies-in-waiting.

Henry seemed glum; he did not brighten even at the sight of the sucking pig, brought to table with an almost shocking appearance of life, its eyes made of the whites of hard-boiled eggs with circles of pickled walnut in their centres. Did he envy the merriment at the low table? Had he heard of, and been annoyed by, the calls from the river? He himself had made the journey on horseback, perhaps he had been shouted at, too. She wished that she could think of something sprightly and amusing to say, but she had never been apt with verbal quips and she had already said that Richmond looked its best at this season and that they had had fine weather for their move. She was meditating some remark about Mary when Henry gave up the pretence at eating, shifted a little in his chair and said:

"Well, we have heard from Rome."

Her heart seemed to stop and then moved again, thumping so heavily that the diamond pendant she wore shook and shimmered. The answer was wrong for him, in his present state of infatuation, but right for her, for Mary and for England. She waited, too breathless to speak.

"Clement is sending a special Legate to go into the case thoroughly."

Not what she had hoped for. The facts were there. The Pope could read; he had the best lawyers in the world to consult. What was there to be gone into?

She managed to say, "When?"

"Early next year." Autumn and the Christmas festivities to be lived through; but having faced this evening I can face anything.

"Do you know whom the Legate will be?"

"Cardinal Campeggio."

"I remember him." He had been in England twelve years earlier—on another special errand, urging England, as part of Christendom to join Europe in resisting the encroachments of the Turks. Apart from bringing about a treaty between France

and England it had come to nothing: the age of positive
Crusades was over, but Henry had liked Campeggio who spoke
excellent English, and had presented him with an English
bishopric—that of Salisbury.

For a second or two she thought, feeling hollow and sick,
that the choice was sinister—a man whom Henry had favoured,
being sent to decide upon a matter in which only one decision
would please the King. But she put that thought resolutely
aside; it was unworthy. The Pope would be seeking justice
and it was natural that he should send a man who knew the
language and the country and was, besides, one of the great
jurists of the day.

"He is a good lawyer," she said.

"What we need is less law and more common sense," Henry
said grumpily.

"And that, alas, cannot be hired, my lord."

"No," he said, dragging the word out. The disgruntled look
gave way to one almost wistful. "If only it were you should
have a wagon load, first thing tomorrow morning!" Then to
her surprise he laughed; not quite the hearty booming laugh of
former days; her practised ear caught the sourish undertone
as when a man joins in a laugh against himself. But it was
laughter, loud enough to attract attention. Several heads lifted
or turned. And she smiled, deliberately assuming the look of
a woman who has said something amusing and been pleased
by its reception.

Let them all puzzle over *that*, she thought with a flash of her
mother's combative spirit. Here we sit, a King who wishes to
put his wife away because in his dangerous middle-age he has
met with a woman who rates her virtue too high; and a Queen
who refuses to be put away; but who, coming into this hall,
uninformed, would guess at our predicament? And that is how
it must be, until judgement is given. Early in the new year. Oh
God speed Campeggio's journey across Europe, God guide his
decision, and God grant that in this waiting time I may do
nothing, say no word, cast no look, make no gesture which

would make our life together difficult when the verdict falls
in my favour.

Henry's thoughts were busy, too. He had put some spite into
the remark which hinted that she lacked common sense and
there had been a jeer in his laughter. But it was like trying
to fight a feather pillow. Still, it looked well. Appearing in
public together, talking, even laughing, over their food, bolstered
his claim that nothing but the qualms of conscience had persuaded him that his marriage was not good. And that was a
claim far from being wholly false; nor was it wholly true. Only
very simple minds were capable of making such judgements.
He wanted Anne as he had never yet wanted a woman; he
needed an heir, he doubted the validity of his marriage—and
he was not alone in that. If it had been a sound, lawful marriage
would Clement have hesitated for two whole years and then
sent Campeggio as co-adjutor with Wolsey?

But there were the cries in the streets. Scattered and few,
just sufficient to warn him. Along the river, no doubt, those
whose sympathies were with Katharine and Mary had clustered,
yelling vociferously. But on his own ride a voice had said, "No
Nan Bullen for us," another had said, "God bless the King—
and the Queen," and one had said, "Kill the witch—and her
dog!" And amongst the loyal shouts of "God *bless* the King"
there had been others, "God *save* the King," with an emphasis
which a poet's ear for stress could hardly miss.

And how, Henry wondered, how by Christ's Wounds, had
the secret, so closely kept, leaked out? Who told the common
people that his aim was to marry, not to seduce? Wolsey
would be difficult now; paternal speeches— This I say from concern for Your Grace's good. . . . And the Emperor would undoubtedly take umbrage at the thought of his aunt, a Princess
of Spain being supplanted by one of her own waiting ladies.
Still, Wolsey could be cajoled, and if necessary ordered, and
Charles could be ignored; he had enough on his hands without
taking any practical measures in defence of his aunt. And now
that the secret was out life would be easier; the elaborate
subterfuges could be dropped. Also the very fact that she was

being cried against in the streets would give Anne confidence in the sincerity of his intentions.

Early in the new year. It was now October. January. February. March at the very latest. Five months. In five months' time. . . . And Wolsey's little homilies could be cut short by orders to get to work, use every influence, pull every string to expedite Campeggio's arrival. After that more orders, to see that the right verdict was given.

The year 1527 ran down into the trough of winter. The new year, so eagerly awaited by everyone, began.

13

Cardinal Campeggio was to set out for England at some time loosely defined as the spring of 1528. Wolsey wrote to him, expressing his pleasure that they were to work together, and urging him to make haste. He then brought his talent for organisation to bear upon the arrangements for the journey; he had many contacts, many friends in France and could expedite or delay travel as he chose. Good horses and baggage mules stood at the various posting stages, eating their fill; comfortable places, such as Wolsey himself would choose to spend the night in, were chosen, hired or borrowed and kept in readiness. And Campeggio, as Wolsey knew, travelled light; in fact, when Campeggio had come to England earlier, Wolsey had felt so strongly that his paucity of baggage was unbecoming to a Prince of the Church that he had sent twelve empty coffers, covered with scarlet cloth and with gold furnishings, to augment his poor display for his entry into London. Wolsey knew his countrymen; they admired ostentation.

But that was years ago and Clement had another reason for choosing Campeggio in addition to the facts that he knew his law and spoke English. In the interval Campeggio had become very gouty; there were times when he could not hold his horse's reins, or bear to put his feet into the stirrups; worse days when he could not bear the jolting of a litter; and worst of all days when his eyes were affected and he must lie, immobile, in a darkened room. His journey across France would necessarily be slow, and—Clement hoped—never concluded. The rumours had reached Rome and made it clear that all this bother was less a matter of the King of England's conscience than his lust for Anne Boleyn. Clement knew that men's passions could burn out as quickly as beacon fires; so let enough time be wasted on moves that could offend nobody—Clement knew that he could not afford to offend either the Emperor or the King of England —and all might yet be well.

So Campeggio moved, very slowly towards London, where impatience mounted. Wolsey fretted, this business was making an old man of him; although despite the rumours, he still did not believe that, once free to remarry, the King would actually risk the unpopularity that must come from marrying Tom Boleyn's daughter; Henry fretted at the waste of another sweet summer, another year of his life; Anne was frantic, sometimes actually hysterical under the strain, sometimes rebellious, threatening to retire to Hever. Katharine waited with outward placidity—she had learned to wait—but she too looked forward to the day when the special Papal Legate would arrive and justify her.

But the sweating sickness reached London long before Campeggio did.

The sweating sickness was a disease peculiar to the English. In the Irish Pale where the English settlers lived, in Continental towns where they went as traders, even on a ship the sweating sickness picked out the English with a deadly precision, sparing their neighbours. That Katharine herself had suffered from it, was in her opinion proof that she had become English by marriage. And unlike some plagues, it made no distinction between those who lived in crowded hovels and those who lived in high, airy houses; the well-fed man was as likely to fall victim as a starving beggar, the man who had a fresh clean shirt every day as the fellow who wore one until it dropped to pieces.

Henry was terrified of it; at the first whisper of the sweating sickness abroad in London, he fled; and since the place he made for was one of Wolsey's manors, he thought it wise not to take Anne with him; it would have been too obvious. Wolsey's various manors, The More, Tittenhanger and others were all well appointed, but small, with no accommodation for ladies. . . .

Katharine, sure of the immunity conferred by her earlier experience, remained in Greenwich with a depleted Court, a circumstance she welcomed because it brought a return of close association with Mary, whose household had also dispersed. It was the nearest thing to real family life that she had known since she was young and Isabella had dragged her family hither and thither and they had lodged where they could, sometimes sleeping three to a bed. She sometimes spoke about those days to Mary, who listened intently.

Anne was still resident at Greenwich; still a lady-in-waiting; until the morning when Emma Arnett came in her stead and said:

"My lady is sick—it is the sweating sickness."

Mary was there then and the moment Emma had gone she said, "And I hope she dies of it! That would solve all." The ferocity in her voice was almost frightening.

"I cannot think it right, Mary, to wish death upon a fellow creature. And would her death solve anything? As I see it she is the result rather than the cause of this dispute. The question that is to be settled is not whether the Lady Anne lives or dies, is or is not your father's paramour, but whether Pope Julius' dispensation was good. Whether for nineteen years I have been wife or an unwitting harlot; whether you are heir or not. That is what Cardinal Campeggio is coming to decide and, to my mind, whether *she* lives or dies makes no jot of difference. And she is only twenty—twenty-one—we must not wish her dead."

"I wish her dead and in Hell," Mary said. She jumped up from the stool upon which she had been sitting and began to walk up and down. She was twelve years old, small and spare for her age—as the French Ambassador had said, short, almost squat of stature and of complexion pale—but she walked as Henry did, or as Henry might, hampered by skirts, and her russet head shone and her young voice had undertones of her grandmother's gruffness.

"Oh, I know," she said, "you and my Lady Salisbury and everybody else have tried to hide the truth from me, fearing to hurt me. At the whisper of bastardy, I am supposed to go and cry in a corner. I do not. I am not meek. Our Lord said the meek should inherit the earth; but was He meek when he took a whip and drove the money lenders from the Temple? Was He meek when he stood before Pilate and refused to answer? Was He meek when He hung on the Cross and said to the dying thief who had given Him His *rightful* title, 'Today shalt thou be with me in Paradise.' The word has been much misunderstood. I am meek in so far as I recognise authority. *I do*. Julius gave you and my father leave to marry. He had the power to do so, and to that power I bow. But I will not be put upon. And if Cardinal Campeggio decides against us, I shall not accept his verdict. Will you?"

She swung round and faced Katharine fiercely.

"Dearest, I have already promised to do so. I said when the matter was first mentioned that I would be guided by the Pope's decision."

"But will it be *his* decision? Campeggio already has cause for gratitude to my father—he gave him a Bishopric last time he was here; what bribe will he offer this time? We know what is in Wolsey's mind. Will Campeggio be able to withstand him and his cajoleries? Besides, His Holiness is in no position to make a just and impartial judgement. Since the Imperial troops sacked Rome he has been under the Emperor's thumb."

"That surely is a factor in our favour. Charles is our relative."

Mary made a wordless sound of repudiation.

"Not even the Pope enjoys bondage. Clement looks to my father and to the King of France to liberate him." She narrowed her eyes and her likeness to Henry in one of his worse moods was startling. "If my cousin and the Pope were truly on our side they would have declared themselves at the beginning; not sent a sick old man to waste more time."

She had evidently heard more about the business than Katharine would have wished; Lady Salisbury had tried to protect her; but of course women talked. And much of what she said was very shrewd; uncomfortably so. If, as Henry had said, he had first drawn the Pope's attention to his qualms of conscience two years ago, it would have been simple enough, then, for Clement to have replied unequivocally—the dispensation was good. Why had he not done so?

Such thoughts were useless, and weakening.

"We must have faith, Mary, and hope and patience. It is not an easy situation; but we must not give way to doubt—or to anger."

"Anger is a great heartener. I am very angry—on your behalf as well as my own—when I see *her* flaunting and setting such a high price upon her virtue, which is in fact no virtue at all, simply inordinate ambition. How you can bear to have her about you I cannot understand."

"It was your father's wish."

"Would you jump into the Thames if that were his wish? I know—Lady Salisbury told me—that you consider that you owe him obedience in all matters not touching your conscience. But suppose—just for a moment suppose," she halted her pacing and stood just in front of Katharine with her hands behind her back—another of Henry's gestures—"Campeggio comes and decides against us. What action would your conscience then dictate?"

"Cardinal Campeggio comes as Papal Legate; he will have instructions, perhaps even his orders. I should feel bound to comply. I should do so with great sorrow, but I should comply."

"I wonder," Mary said, "if you realise how the common people feel about all this. We are very popular, you and I. They howl against her in the streets."

"The common people have no say in great matters."

"They are the stuff of which armies are made."

There was such deadly intensity in those words that Katharine's heart jolted. She reached out her hands and took Mary by the shoulder.

"Mary, you must not *think* in such a way. Never, no matter what the circumstances, or what our personal wrongs, must we resort to violence. Sit down and listen to me. I spent my youth in scenes of bloodshed. It was supposed to be a Holy War, a Crusade against the Infidel, and we celebrated our victories and mourned our defeats without much thought to the cost in dead men. The war was necessary and men were expendable. Then, when I was about your age, my sister Isabella lost her husband—he did not die in battle, but of disease—and she came back to Spain. I realised then what the death of a man meant. I had never seen Alfonso of Portugal—but I saw Isabella; and ever after, when I saw a dead man I saw the women who would weep for him. That is something to think upon; not the trumpets and the flags and the brave display. Mary, I speak of what I know. Three years before you were born it fell to me to raise an army against the Scots. Invaders *must* be resisted . . . but always I thought of the dead men and the women whose hearts would break. On no account over this dispute must even one man shed his blood. It would be civil war—the worst of all. And to have men die over what is, after all, a purely domestic matter, the concern of a mere four people, that would be so horrible that it must not be contemplated."

Mary said, with a cool reasonableness more frightening than anger:

"But you say invaders must be resisted. Is *she* not an invader? You speak of *four* people concerned. Mother, it is the concern of *all*. Julius' ruling can be only one of two things—the inspired dictate of the Vicar of Christ on this earth, or the scribbling of a silly old man who wrote what he was asked to write and whose authority can be set aside by another silly old man. Which was it?"

"Mary, you are speaking like a heretic. What have you been reading?"

"Everything that came my way. I am no heretic; but it is better to know your enemy than to blunder about in the dark. I hold Julius' dispensation good. By that I stand. But I also think that this may be the testing time. Just at this minute when Papal authority is questioned, Papal power so much reduced, this which you call the concern of a mere four people could turn the balance. There have been Popes who were renegade, or mad —the Devil is cunning. Clement is weak and hesitant. If Cardinal Campeggio, on the Pope's orders, reverses the dictate of his predecessor . . . what a triumph for those who refuse to admit

that the Pope is anything more than Bishop of Rome. I wake
in the night," Mary said, "and I think upon these things. I
dread Cardinal Campeggio's coming. If he gives verdict against
us, then Julius was wrong and Papal authority is cut down. If
he gives verdict for us, then my father will be angry and there
will be schism. In either case, through us, Holy Church will
be stricken and that is a thought which I find almost unsupport-
able, except when I am angry and think the thoughts which
you say I must not think."

It was pitiable; only twelve years old . . .

"Mary, until you are of age you should not concern yourself
too much with worldly matters. I am your mother; leave decisions to me. Be confident that whatever happens I shall have
a care to our interests, and at the same time do my best for
Holy Church. The interests are not incompatible; as you say,
this may be the testing time. Let us have faith in God."

"I do. And I do recognise my duty to you, my mother. And
then I think . . . I cannot feel dutiful to him who tries to
repudiate me."

He was her father and until this trouble started she had
adored him; handsome, sweet-smelling and merry, tossing her
about in his strong arms, what could any little girl want more
of her father? And later, praise, for the way she handled her
lute, her good memory, the way she rode a horse. His loud voice
and hearty laughter, even his bouts of ill-temper appealed to
something boisterous in her, something which had sometimes
chafed under Katharine's admonitions and instructions and
rules about what a little girl must and must not do.

Her recoil, when she learned what he was planning to do,
was proportionate to her former esteem. The prospect of not
being Queen of England was galling enough; to learn that one's
father had set himself to prove one a bastard was humiliating
in the extreme; but worst of all was the fact that he was hurting
her mother to whom, as she grew older and more sedate, she
had become passionately devoted and whom she looked upon
almost as a saint.

"I think, Mary, that you must try. He still is your father;

he is the same person . . . this is very hard to explain. He has been ill-advised."

"And led by the nose by a light woman." Mary, who was one day to love recklessly and without reserve, spoke with savage scorn.

"Not light," Katharine said. "Had she been light we should not now be speaking of her. And I think we have had enough gloomy talk. We can do nothing except await Cardinal Campeggio's coming and hope and prepare ourselves to accept what comes with resignation and dignity."

"I shall not. Whatever he says I shall never look upon you as other than Queen of England, or upon myself as anything but Princess of Wales. If the Pope himself ordered me to do otherwise, I *could* not. And," she added, "if I play for you; it will not be any of the songs my father made. I never play them now."

"Play what you like, darling."

Henry scurried from place to place, always just one day's journey ahead—or so it seemed—of the sweating sickness. He would leave a place in the morning and by nightfall someone in that place, a resident or somebody of the royal train, left behind to overlook the loading of the last of the baggage, would be smitten.

Anne Boleyn did not die. Henry, when he heard that she was ill, sent his second-best physician to attend her.

Campeggio moved northwestwards, covering on a good day as much as ten miles.

In Spain Dr. Puebla's son, going through his father's papers, came upon a Papal brief, more lengthy and explicit than the original dispensation. In particular it omitted the word *forhans,* the Latin for *perhaps.* The dispensation gave permission for Henry and Katharine to marry even if *perhaps* the marriage between Katharine and Arthur had been consummated. The brief lacked the conditional word and Dr. Puebla's son realised the importance of his find.

In England it rained and rained; a disastrous summer; murrain—a disease amongst cattle, curiously similar to the sweating sickness amongst men—decimated herds and the blighted, mildewed crops lay sideways in the fields.

So the autumn came; and since no journey can last forever, Cardinal Campeggio who had set out in June on a journey which in midwinter would have taken six weeks and had taken him four months, arrived in England on the first of October and went straight to his bed. And I would to God I could do likewise, Wolsey thought, heaving his ailing, failing bulk up to make the necessary visit of welcome and condolence. He had not fled before the threat of the plague; he had laboured away in London, confident in his belief that the sweating sickness, so eclectic, fastened upon the healthy and the well-born. He was no longer healthy and he was a butcher's son who by using his wits and his phenomenal capacity for work, his talent for intrigue and his gift of ostentation had climbed so high that his enemies called him King of Europe.

But he knew that for him this was the supreme test of his life. Henry had made that painfully clear. By hook or by crook the verdict must be made to go in Henry's favour or the blame would fall upon the most faithful, clever, cunning servant any king ever had.

14

When, after some days, Campeggio, accompanied by Wolsey, shuffled into Henry's presence, Henry looked him over sharply and was satisfied that the long-drawn-out journey had not been a trick to waste time. Inside the soft cloth shoes Campeggio's feet were grossly swollen, his puffy, glazed fingers fumbled stiffly with the papers and even his eyelids were swollen and red . . . A sorry sight, the King thought, quickly averting his eyes. Me too? One day?

He looked at Wolsey and because he saw him almost every day, failed to notice how much he had altered lately, the firm red cheeks mottled and sagging into heavy jowls and pouches under the eyes, the nose sharpened. Wolsey was twenty years older than his master and to Henry his servant's physical endurance, his mental energy and clarity spelt hope. Fifty-four this year, and as good as ever.

Wolsey had had several talks with Campeggio already, and to Henry had dropped a hint, no more, that the investigation might be avoided. "He is very secretive, and says nothing outright—one must remember that he is Italian by birth—but there is something which seems to indicate that he has instructions which do not concern the investigation. He said, quite seriously, Your Grace, that he hoped he would not be obliged to winter in England. It is now October; he knows how long a full trial would take to mount . . ."

Henry's hopes ran high, and now, having greeted them and invited them to be seated, he prepared himself to hear that Clement had found a short cut out of this impasse. Perhaps in an hour he would be free; a bachelor again; able to rush to

Anne and say, "Sweetheart, it is over. We can be married tomorrow, tonight . . ."

He said, "Well, my lords?"

He was not perturbed when Campeggio began with a dissertation about the sanctity of marriage. The man was a lawyer and lawyers like preambles. And with everything in this speech Henry agreed. Marriage was a sacrament, making man and wife one in the sight of God.

He listened, impatience well-concealed, but mounting.

"His Holiness has taken into consideration the tenderness of Your Grace's conscience," Campeggio said, and paused; a lawyer's pause. Henry leaned forward, a smile already beginning to form.

"He has, therefore, instructed me to tell Your Grace that he is prepared to amend any flaw in the original dispensation, and to extend it, so that your marriage to Queen Katharine is good and valid, whether or not she was formerly the wife of your brother, and this would allow Your Grace to resume marital relations with a completely clear conscience."

"Christ's wounds!" Henry said. Precisely what he did *not* want. He sagged back in his chair and for a moment or two he looked almost as old, as worn by life as the two men who confronted him. Then he rallied.

"The offer astonishes me. It admits the possibility of a flaw and at the same time ties me down to acceptance of a flawed dispensation. Julius was either right or wrong. I claim that he was wrong. On that my case rests. This is no answer. Mending up a wrong. You sit there and tell me that if Julius was in error, Clement with a stroke of the pen can make it right and I have leave to take to my bed in good conscience a woman past childbearing age who has borne me dead children, or children dead before their navels have healed. Can Clement, lifting his pen, remove the curse of Leviticus?"

"It is a matter of law, Your Grace," Campeggio said. "And if one gives consideration to Leviticus one should give equal attention to Deuteronomy, where a man is ordered to take his dead brother's wife and raise children in his brother's name.

The study of such ancient, Jewish writings leads to confusion—as your case exemplifies. The teaching of the Church, the authority of the Pope are far more reliable guides to any Christian."

"I am a Christian," Henry said vehemently. "Nineteen years ago, acting under the direction of a dispensation which now even Clement admits may have held a flaw, I married, within the forbidden degree. The consequences proved me wrong; I searched my conscience. Can Clement's amendment give me back the lost boys, the lost years?"

"His willingness to amend any flaw should be a salve to any pang of conscience," Campeggio said imperturbably.

Henry looked at Wolsey who had so far said nothing.

"Thomas, what is your view on this? Am I not right?"

"Your Grace repudiates the notion of amendment. It is to be hoped that Cardinal Campeggio did not travel so far, and so painfully, in order to offer a single, so easily rejected suggestion."

Let Campeggio show his full hand; let Campeggio see what it meant to deal with a man like the King of England.

"There was an alternative suggestion," Campeggio said, after a short, tense silence. "His Holiness is fully prepared to absolve the Queen from her earthly marriage, if she retires to a convent and takes vows."

At that Wolsey looked up and his eyes met Henry's. You see! All this running to and fro, all this talk and what result? They now point to the way out which *I* suggested more than a year ago."

"There is nothing new there, either," Henry snapped. "My lord Cardinal proposed it last year; before he left for France. The Queen repudiated it utterly."

"Saying that she would await His Holiness's decision in the matter. Is it not possible that Her Grace might regard the suggestion coming now as it does direct from him, as a decision? She has now had ample time for thinking over her position." And to see how little hope she had. "Have I permission to see the Queen and lay this proposal before her?"

"If that is the best you can do. You might as well save your breath. I've been married to her for hard on twenty years and never yet seen her change her mind over a principle. She looks on herself as my wife and will do so until I get a plain yes or no to my question, put to Rome three years back. Is my marriage legal or not? It warranted a plain answer. And what do I get? This stale stuff."

He glared at them. This would be a fine thing to tell Anne; he could just imagine how she would take it; tears, hysterics, or mockery. God's eyes! People applauded when the old dog went through the hoop. He went through it every night.

"Had the answer been so simple, I should not be here," Campeggio said. All those miles; so much pain.

"Why are you here? This nonsense could have been put on paper. Clement promised me a full investigation."

"Which I am here to conduct. If needs be. But I was ordered to bring about, if possible, a decent, private settlement. We can talk about the trial when I have seen Her Grace."

"That word does not please me. Who is on trial? Kate . . . Her Grace and I are both innocent victims of a Papal error, which Clement could put right with a pen stroke. If he has power to amend the dispensation he has power to annul it." Impotent anger choked him. Then suspicion flared. Campeggio wanted to see Katharine. Alone with her what might he not say? Clement lived under the Emperor's thumb, and the Emperor was her nephew. The long delay, the sending of this slow-moving devious man to make more delay. Part of a plot against him.

"And another thing," he said, speaking to Campeggio but bringing his hard, blue, down-bearing stare upon Wolsey. "You go together. His Holiness yoked you . . . Go when you like. England is a free country. Anyone may talk to whom he wishes. That is all I have to say. I wish you Good day."

As usual, Wolsey thought, the King had summed the situation in a few words. England was a country where all men were free to obey orders.

"I have nothing to say to Her Grace which I should not wish

Cardinal Wolsey to hear. Indeed I hope that he will lend his persuasions to mind to bring about a happy issue, agreeable to all."

Outside the audience chamber Wolsey, matching his step to Campeggio's shuffle, said:

"That was unfortunate. The Queen neither likes nor trusts me. You would have done better alone."

"If we could travel by river it would suit me well. A boat jolts less and we might avoid the crowd."

The crowd had been very vociferous; shouting for the Queen and against Nan Bullen. Campeggio had wondered whether the English had no work to do, no homes or children to tend that at a moment's notice, or no notice at all, they could flock into the streets and shout. He had made only one comment: "His Grace must know how his people feel."

"He has no intention of marrying her," Wolsey said, putting into words his own deep-seated belief. "And while they are shouting against *her*, they are happy." And not shouting against you, or me.

They shouted lustily at Westminster steps where the Cardinals embarked and here and there along the river, and at Greenwich. And today every now and then, after the call, "We want no Nan Bullen," there was a postscript. "Nor no Cardinals neither!"

Campeggio said, with tact, or malice, one never knew:

"I seem to share Mistress Boleyn's unpopularity. They mistake my errand if they think I come to break a marriage."

"It broke years ago," Wolsey said morosely. His disappointment was almost equal to Henry's. Campeggio, after all, had had nothing new to suggest; no easy way out. And the Queen would never yield. A proposition which she would not take from the King, whom she loved, she would not take from Campeggio. Unless that secretive man had, somewhere concealed about him, a definite order from Clement: Get into a convent! Nothing less would move her; and the investigation would go on, taking time. And unless it ends as he wishes, the bell will toll for me. Wolsey thought wearily that God in His wisdom had made women, child-bearing animals or playthings—his own woman, Joan Larke had been both, and he still enjoyed the company and was interested in the well-being of his son and daughter, known as his nephew and niece. But the western world had given the creatures a ridiculous importance; dowries, marriage settlements, rights. The Turks had better sense; a man had only to say, "I divorce you," three times and it was done.

So they came to Greenwich, where the lower steps, washed by every tide, were clean, those above slimy—"I beg you be careful, my lord!" and then a few which except in an exceptionally wet spring the water never touched.

"We want no Nan Boleyn!" The crowd greeted them.

You muttonheaded fools, Wolsey thought, do you think I want her?

You *silly* English people, Campeggio thought, she will be grey-headed and forgotten before His Holiness gives consent; get back to your looms and your counters!

Katharine was at work with her women, stitching away at an altar cloth, a Christmas gift to the chapel of the Observant Friars, when the two Cardinals, with something of a flurry, were announced. She pushed her needle into the cloth, rose, curtseyed to the two Princes of the Church and led them into the little private room on the far side of the apartment. It was her own sanctum, the place where she wrote her letters, sometimes meditated, sometimes prayed. It was, as regards aspect, on the wrong side of the house, lighted only by a narrow, ancient window that never caught the sun. It had no hearth. Walls and floor were bare and it contained the minimum of furniture. Apart from the table, directly under the window and the chair in which she sat when writing, there was nothing except a bench against one wall and against the other a prie-dieu, and that very stark.

Campeggio, taking the whole place in at a glance, thought: This should not be too hard; she is halfway to a nunnery already. For a moment he saw himself, successful in this tricky business, back in Rome before the English winter set in, his task accomplished, taking his ease.

In that same moment Katharine was concerned with a triviality, a matter of precedence. There was the one chair; offer it to either and the other would be offended; and her eye, sharper than Henry's in this respect, saw nothing to choose between them, physically; Cardinal Campeggio was the more obviously disabled, but Cardinal Wolsey did not look well; the high ruddy colour that he usually carried was unequally distributed, separate islands of red and white all over the full-fleshed face; and the lips bluish.

So she seated herself in the chair and asked them to seat themselves on the bench, and said to Campeggio:

"You bring me news of the decision that His Holiness has made in my case?" And she waited as avidly as Henry had done.

Campeggio said, "Your Grace, in this matter a decision is hard to reach. I bring a suggestion . . ."

He did not lecture her on the sanctity of marriage; he made no preamble. He told her, quite quickly and with a bluntness that Wolsey would not have thought him capable of, that the best, the only thing she could do, was to renounce her dubious earthly marriage and become the Bride of Christ. A nun.

Until he said it she had not realised how much she had counted upon his coming; how much she had relied upon the Pope to espouse her cause. All along she had not set her hopes too high, had been careful to say, even to Mary, "If . . ." and "Whatever happens . . ." But her inner certainty that she was right had coloured her thinking; she realised now that in her inmost heart she had been certain that when Campeggio arrived he would bring proof that she was right, that His Holiness, in Rome, had sorted all things out and was prepared to stand by her.

People said, slapping words about like coins on a counter, "my heart sank," "my heart stopped," "my heart broke" and there was, after all, some groping after truth in such expressions. Campeggio's words went into her ears, her mind absorbed them and lower down, in her chest and stomach there was a drop, a stop, an emptying, as though her whole body was suddenly hollowed out. It needed a deliberate, almost desperate effort for her to gather enough force and breath to say:

"But for me to take such a course . . . apart from the fact that I have no vocation for the religious life . . . would be tantamount to admitting that I was not, never had been, his wife . . . And I was, I *am.* I am his wife. The dispensation was granted; we were legally and properly married; all our children were born in wedlock and this talk of Leviticus is nonsense. Mary is alive; her father's daughter and his heir."

"That is," Campeggio said in a very gentle voice, "one view. Your view, and others share it. But . . ." For the first time since his arrival in England he smiled and even Wolsey, watching with a cynical eye, saw how a smile transfigured the undistinguished face. "The nub of the matter, Your Grace, is that the King thinks otherwise, is troubled in his conscience. If you would retire, your honour in no way impugned, your material possessions in no way diminished, there would be no scandal, no investigation, no outcry. There is a precedent; the saintly Queen of France, Jeanne de Valois, retired to a convent in order to allow Louis XII to marry again."

"I am not a saint."

"You are a woman of great piety," Campeggio said coaxingly; "you wear the Franciscan habit under your fine clothes, do much good work amongst the poor. You are a faithful and obedient daughter of the Church. Would it be so great a sacrifice?"

"Does His Holiness order me into a convent?" Behind her clear steady gaze something flashed.

"Your Grace must know that the taking of the veil is a voluntary act."

"And one that I shall never commit. I am sorry for your wasted errand, my lords. I look upon myself as a married woman and shall continue to do so." Wolsey had so far said nothing but sat, twisting his great cardinal's ring upon his finger. Katharine turned to him and said, "This you will understand better than one lately come to this country. I have a dozen reasons, all good, for holding to my position; one is that I have no more desire to see Mistress Boleyn Queen of England than have the crowds out there, or you yourself. You are much mistaken, my lord Cardinal, if you believe, as some do, that once freed of this marriage, the King would not wed her. He would do it within a week. His will is strong and once his heart is set . . ." As once it was on me! She thought of how cunningly and patiently he had waited, avoiding other betrothals and how he had come to her the moment he was master. She remembered the young green of the lime-walk; now the yellow and rusty leaves were falling; soon the trees would be bare. Like life . . .

She felt her throat ache, her eyes sting. In a second she would be crying. What had Mary said about anger being a great heartener? She said, with at least a show of anger, addressing Wolsey still.

"I blame you for this trouble. I once ventured to criticise your voluptuous way of life and remarked that it was strange that Christ, who was so humble, should have a servant who was so proud. From that moment you marked me down. And you hate my nephew the Emperor because he did not support you when you hoped to be Pope. So you are trying to end my marriage. Were I weak enough to be persuaded you would be one of the first to regret it. I say nothing derogatory to Mistress Boleyn herself, but she is surrounded by men tainted with heresy, men who read Lutheran books, smuggled in."

It was all true, Wolsey reflected grimly; on the other hand he must obey the King or fall.

"Your Grace is mistaken if you think I bear you malice." A half-smile twitched his fleshy lips. "If you ever criticised me, I have forgotten it, I have been much criticised. Perhaps rightly. We are all as God made us, and He made me proud and comfort-loving. But that is neither here nor there. What concerns us is that His Grace is determined to obtain a divorce."

"Divorce!" she exclaimed, pouncing on the word. "When he, or you, or anybody else uses that word I am proved right. Where there has been no valid marriage—that is the contention—there can be no divorce."

They were both startled by the swiftness, shrewdness and truth of that statement; it was out of accord with her appearance and demeanour. It had a lawyer's touch.

When Campeggio next spoke the gentleness and coaxing note had left his voice.

"Whatever word is used, Your Grace, the point remains. His Grace is determined. If necessary the case will come to open trial."

"That is what I have always wanted. Not secret talks at York House," she flashed a look at Wolsey, "or secret conferences in Rome. I want an open trial, where men can study all the evidence and decide." And see that I am right.

"Do you?" Campeggio said; and again, into two words he put a vast meaning. "I wonder if Your Grace has *seriously* considered what a trial would involve. The question of whether or not you were virgin on the night of the eleventh of June in the year of Our Lord 1509, will certainly come under close scrutiny. Would that not be offensive to your modesty?"

It would be almost intolerable. She no longer blushed easily and prettily, but she felt the heat in her neck and in her cheeks, just below the eyes. She remembered her first wedding night, Arthur's whispered words, and her own little trick which had seemed so clever at the time. Would somebody find and drag into the open an old woman who had made a bed at Baynard's Castle on the morning of November 15th, in the year of Our Lord 1501? Well, that could be countered, if it came to that, by the evidence of whoever made the bed on the morning of the twelfth of June, eight years later. No need for trickery then.

"It will be painful and embarrassing for me," she said, "but there is too much at stake for me to shrink. I can say to you, my lords, that my marriage to Arthur, Prince of Wales, was never consummated; so I can say it in open court. And mark this; there are many men, nobles, churchmen, lawyers, still alive, who saw my marriage made, accepted Pope Julius' dispensation as valid, did not question it then, do not question it now. Some of them will sit in that court."

Not if I can help it, Wolsey thought; but how could the adherents of one side or another be identified? This was not a tourney, where every man displayed his colours. But his mind, that sharp instrument with which he had carved out a place for himself in a world where the poor and the lowly born seldom enjoyed preferment, looked ahead, beyond the trial—whichever way it went. He saw the rift that could never again be closed, the wound that would never heal. For once he was not thinking of himself but of the far future when he and Katharine and Henry and Campeggio and Anne Boleyn would be lying quiet in their graves.

He got up, took three paces across the narrow room and fell on his knees before Katharine.

"Your Grace, I beg you, think again on this matter. More is concerned than you dream of. The world is already riven in two. Half Germany no longer acknowledges the authority of the Pope. The German landknechts sacked Rome and made monks the target for their arrows, nuns the victims of their lust. To bring Pope Julius' dispensation into question in open court, at this most critical moment, will, whatever the verdict, do the Papacy irreparable damage. I implore you to listen to me, to look ahead. This thing could throw a decisive weight into the scales. Ordinary people have no discrimination, they see things as black or white, right or wrong. If this comes to open trial they will say: If Julius had power to dispense why did Clement not stand by that dispensation; and if Julius had no such power why did Clement think a trial necessary? Your Grace, upon the question of a marriage—to you, I grant, a thing of great importance, but in itself a trivial thing—the whole future of the Church may hinge."

Campeggio thought: Very clever; and what a good actor the man is.

Katharine said, "My lord Cardinal, the embarrassment that confronts me begins here, with you on your knees to me. Rise, I beg you. Stand up and consider. In taking my stand, so far from undermining Papal authority, I am upholding it by every means within my power. I believe that Julius' dispensation was good; and when all has been sorted, it will be *seen* to be good. The marriage that the Pope permitted was a true marriage and will continue—until one of us is dead."

She believed it. She was Isabella's daughter and although she shrank from the thought of physical violence and bloodshed, she was as confident in her cause as Isabella had been in her Crusade against the Moors. Times changed, methods changed; this would be battle fought out on parchment, in argument; but it would be, it must be, a victory of right over wrong.

The sight of a man grown old and heavy with the years who had momentarily cast away his dignity and knelt and been told to rise, his plea not granted, was one upon which she did not care to look. So, as Wolsey scrambled to his feet, she directed her gaze to Campeggio.

"If an open trial is to come about, I shall need legal advice," she said. "You will arrange it for me?"

You, Campeggio thought, need no legal advice; you need a clout, two, forehand, backhand each side of the head. You are right, but right in the wrong way, and everything that Wolsey just said is true; Clement himself realises it. And because you are so obstinate, I must winter in England . . .

"No Nan Bullen for us!" the crowd chanted; and the solitary voice added, "And no Cardinals neither!" This time Campeggio made no comment.

15

"It was so horrible, Maria. You can have no idea." Here, back in the safe familiar room she weakened, put her face in her hands and shed a few tears of sheer self-pity. Unfair! Blatantly unjust! "Not one of *my* legal advisors was there. Nor Cardinal Campeggio. I was completely alone. His Grace once said to me that those who took an impossible stand must stand alone. And it was not merely what I was obliged to do this morning, bad as it was. It is an omen. What happened this morning will happen again . . . My heart, my very mind is shaken."

"Was the King there?" Maria de Moreto no longer called him *His Grace*. He was lost to grace.

"No. Just the Council. Headed by the Cardinal. And they said that if I did not sign, I should be taken straight to the Tower."

"Jesu Mary!" Maria said, her face going greenish. "The Tower? But on what charge?"

"Treason," Katharine said.

"Treason! Your Grace, Your Grace, I beg you listen to me. Let him have his way, before worse happens. You are right, everybody knows that, but he is King and will have his way. Ask yourself how many go in by the Traitor's Gate and ever come out. There is nothing here for us and we could be happy and comfortable, elsewhere. I fear the worst to come."

So do I; I saw this morning how little justice . . . All those hard faces. All the men who give *him* such ill advice.

"Where could I be happy and comfortable, with my daughter made illegitimate and *her* child looked upon as heir."

"The Emperor would find the Princess a husband. We could

all go to Spain and feel the warmth of the sun. He would be glad to see us go. And we should be safe."

Yesterday Katharine would have derided such talk; today it did not seem ridiculous. But the mention of Mary had strengthened her and reminded her of something.

"That is impossible, Maria; but if you crave to go home and sit in the sun, you have my leave to go—and my blessing."

"I shall never leave you. Never."

"It may be forced upon you. Meantime—I promised to dine with the Princess today. I should not wish her to see me distraught. And I have something to do. Maria, go along and make some excuse. Tell her . . . tell her that I am detained. Proffer my apologies. Make light of it."

Really it would be better if Mary were out of London while all this business was going on. Perhaps even Henry would agree to that.

"And tell Griffith to send Francisco to me."

Once again Filipez stood before her, not behind her; a reliable ally, not a server; he was older, stiffer and his hair was greyer, but he looked lively and tough.

"I will tell you quickly," she said. "Concerning the matter between His Grace and me, there exists a very important document—the brief found amongst Dr. Puebla's papers. The Emperor has it in his keeping. I had a copy, signed and witnessed and gave it, with other papers, to those who in the forthcoming investigation will plead my cause. This morning I was called before the King's privy council and told that a copy was not sufficient; the *original* must be sent. They had a letter, all written, lacking only my signature, ready to be sent requesting the immediate despatch of that document to England. Francisco, upon receipt of that letter, which I signed under duress, the Emperor will speed it on its way; I am sure that it will never arrive. My enemies wish it out of existence. If my letter reaches the Emperor *before* the countermanding request, it will be sent and destroyed somewhere and all that I shall have will be the copy, already suspect. Would you ride again, very fast, and this time without safe-conduct, and tell the Emperor on no account, *on no account* to let that brief out of his hands. I know it is much to ask . . . but whom else can I ask?"

"Whom else should Your Grace ask?" Whom but Francisco Filipez, a devoted servant who had a way of getting the most out of a horse.

"I shall be on my way in less than an hour. I think I shall need no safe-conduct this time; they will think of rats leaving a ship about to sink. But, Your Grace, may I say a word . . . as your server? Lately I have been very careful; I have never offered Your Grace a dish, or a cup which has not been tested by myself or by some other person beforehand. I have been aware that . . . some would have found their way smoothed . . . if a dish . . . Your Grace understands me?"

"Poison," she said, shattered for the second time in one day. She had never thought of it. In Italy Medicis and Borgias had used it often against their personal or political enemies, but this was not Italy.

"I will, with Your Grace's permission, choose the man to serve in my place. And may I ask: Have you, amongst your jewels, a turquoise? Perhaps not," he said, as she hesitated. "It is only a half-precious stone, but there is an ancient belief that in the presence of poison it changes from blue to black. If Your Grace would . . . it is unworthy . . ." He began to wrestle with the ring he wore on his fourth, left-hand finger. It stuck below the knotted knuckle.

"Francisco, you will pull off your finger."

"So I would. Every one, if it would serve." He wrestled with it, remembering how once, on the middle finger of his right hand, it had slipped easily up and down.

"I will have it cut off," he said in a fury. "And I beg you, carry it about you, pass it over everything you are offered. Until I am back."

For a day or two after Filipez's departure she lived in trepidation; turned back at Dover? At Calais? Rouen? She followed him, in her mind, on his headlong ride; she prayed for his safety.

Sometimes, waking in the night at the hour when hope was at ebb tide, she imagined him waylaid, or dead.

Then she learned that to fetch home this precious brief, one of her own chaplains had been chosen—a man named Thomas Abell. He was part of her household, but she did not know him well, had never noticed him much. He came and went, performed his duties; a rather close-mouthed, cold-eyed man.

That Wolsey should have chosen one of her own chaplains, and Thomas Abell of all men, to bring back the disputed brief, was dreadfully significant. A letter signed in her own hand, asking for it, a member of her household sent to fetch it. Charles would be completely deceived—unless Filipez arrived first; and without a passport, could he? Could he?

Maria de Moreto, speaking sourly, offered a way out of this predicament.

"That worthless cousin of mine, Juan Montoya, has been engaged to conduct Dr. Abell on his journey," she said. She had not always thought him worthless. She had once been in love with him. That fact lent venom to her voice as she said, "It will be the first honest job he has done for years; but Dr. Abell will benefit. Juan has a knowledge of inns . . ."

An idea that might have come direct from Heaven flashed into Katharine's mind.

"Maria, what kind of man is he—your cousin? One who would carry an urgent message for me?"

"He is an idle fellow, overfond of women, and of wine. He borrows money and does not repay it," Maria said. "But," she added simply, "indubitably a man of honour." Neither she nor Katharine saw anything contradictory in these remarks.

"Could you ask him to come and say goodbye to you; and then smuggle him in to me?"

"I will do that," Maria said; knowing that to see Juan would give her pain, and that he would certainly borrow every penny she had laid by—about ten shillings.

Montoya came and agreed, enthusiastically, to carry a secret message. He had the born scamp's charm and self-confidence and the ability to induce trustfulness.

"Your Grace may rest easy. *Your* message shall be delivered before Dr. Abell's saddlebags are unpacked. And until that moment thumbscrews would not wring a word from me."

So now, if Filipez had failed to get through, Montoya, on an official errand, with everything expedited and made easy, would. And he would keep his promise—indubitably a man of honour.

The two oddly assorted men moved through France less speedily than Dr. Abell had expected or would have wished. He would have pressed on, missing meals, missing sleep. But he was in Montoya's hands. Dr. Abell had never before been out of England and spoke only English and Latin. Montoya knew the road and had an almost uncanny ability to make himself understood everywhere: and he would say, "There is no point in going farther today. The next inn is twenty miles away, and we benefit nobody by sleeping in ditches." Or he would say, "I am not satisfied with the horses. I have ordered better ones, but they will not be here until morning." Such excuses were usually made in places where some response had been made to the lascivious glance which Montoya directed at any woman under thirty and not positively ugly.

Dr. Abell's patience wore thin; and then as they moved south and the food grew worse, his digestion began to trouble him. Even Wolsey's long arm could not make crossing the Pyrénées other than a test of endurance. Montoya seemed to thrive on the smoked raw ham, the barley bread and the sour local wines which—having given it fair trial—Dr. Abell said was no better than horse piss.

One afternoon they halted to eat and change horses at a lonely little tavern kept by a surly old man and his daughter, a buxom girl with what Dr. Abell had come to recognise as *that* way of walking. The ham was even more raw-seeming than usual and the crumb or two of bread which Abell forced down seemed to lodge in his chest and glow like hot coals.

"Come along," he said, after watching Montoya eat and drink his fill. "The horses are the worst I have yet seen. We shall have our work cut out to get to Roncevalles tonight, even if we start at once."

"And who wants to get to Roncevalles?"

"I do," Abell said crisply. "And so should you. You were sent to accompany me, not to delay me. These long overnight stops have already wasted much valuable time."

Montoya, making no move, took another gulp of the unpalatable wine and said, "I am not delaying you. There is only one road to Roncevalles: you will not lose your way. And tomorrow morning, on a horse that has had a bellyful and a day's rest from the plough, I shall overtake you easily."

Had he known only a little Spanish, Dr. Abell would have left immediately. As it was there began to grow in him the dangerous cold anger of his kind.

"You were engaged to conduct me," he said. "Your attitude is no more nor less than blackmail. And do not think that I fail to see through you. I know that the horses we rode today are by regulations bound to remain here, and that the ones provided are poor, very poor . . ." Dr. Abell entertained a certain amount of feeling for horses. "But that is simply an excuse. You wish to spend the night here because you have cast a lecherous eye on that flaunting girl."

"I still have the use of my eyes, thank God," Montoya said, drinking again. He focussed them, a little owlishly on his companion. "And my ears," he said. "Blackmail is an ugly word, not to be used between gentlemen . . . Not that you could be expected to understand that."

Dr. Abell did not even realise that he had been insulted. He came of sound yeoman stock, people who said, faced with any cause for special elation, "I am so happy, I would not thank the King to be my cousin!" With such a background—and a degree gained by hard study—Thomas Abell was immune from any sneer Montoya could throw.

"If the word offends you, cease the practice," he said. "Unless we make better speed than we have done I shall report upon your behaviour in such a way that you will never be employed in any capacity again."

"Oh, I live by my wits," Montoya said, retorting to this reference to his occasional employment as courier, interpreter, go-between. "I drink when I can and whore with any wench who is willing. But I have never yet betrayed a lady whose bread and salt I have eaten!"

His tone and his look made an accusation of the last words; an accusation so unfounded, so completely irrelevant that the innocent Dr. Abell could only say:

"I think you are drunk now."

Montoya had drunk just the amount which, in ordinary circumstances, would have made him cheerful good company, but the little squabble had tipped his mood.

"I am sober enough to see you for what you are," he said. "One of *her* household, sent to do *her* grave damage and unable to do it fast enough. Blackmail is an ugly word, but there is a worse one. Traitor!" Montoya laughed. "And if the word offends you, cease the practice," he said. "God in Heaven, man! Can you not see that you are being *used?* Her Grace, under threat of being sent to the Tower, signed a request for that brief to be sent to England. *You*, one of her chaplains, are sent to fetch it home. A very pretty arrangement. And the moment you hand it over Wolsey will put it in the fire. But," he said, the wine fumes mounting, "you will not do it. That I swear on the Cross." He put a rather fumbling hand on the haft of the knife at his belt. It was, like sword hilts, made in the form of a cross.

Dr. Abell made a gesture, not matching, but reciprocal in its fashion. He reached out and took the jug of wine and emptied it on to the floor. He had asked for water, and water had been brought, in a coarse earthenware jug and he had taken a few sips, to cool the furnace in his chest and no more, because the water here was almost as unpalatable as the wine. But it was cool. Deliberately he lifted the jug and poured it over Montoya's head.

"Now," he said, as Montoya gasped and spluttered, "let us go. It is plain to me we are on the same errand and haste is imperative."

"The same errand . . . you mean the same side?"

"I am for Her Grace. I believed that the brief, in the original form, would help her cause. You have undeceived me and I thank you. But if we dally more the Cardinal will give us up for lost and may send another messenger . . ."

After that they made much better speed and were more at one until the moment when they stood in the anteroom, waiting to be received by the Emperor—"an emissary from England and his interpreter." And at this last moment Juan Montoya suffered a return of doubt and suspicion. Abell, so typically English, could have deceived him. He put his hand to his knife again and said, "Ask for that brief to be sent and you get this, straight to the heart."

"And how could I ask," Abell said, "except through you?"

"In Latin," Montoya said. "One word in Latin and you are a dead man."

"I am for Her Grace," Abell said again. "And if I say a word to wrong or hurt her, cut my throat."

The Emperor had received the request which Katharine had been compelled to sign and was awaiting Dr. Abell's arrival. Now, most confusingly, the doctor said that on no account was the original brief to be handed over. A new, exact, properly attested copy was to be made, if the Emperor so pleased. The man, Dr. Abell, one of Katharine's own chaplains, made this request, in English; his attendant, a Spaniard, translated, but he seemed wary and watchful. Charles thought: All this is in direct contradiction to what she *wrote*; and neither man is completely at ease. Why not? Some conflict of interest? Some English trick?

He said, "At this hour, on a working day, I take my belated dinner, here at this table. I am ready for it now." He lifted the silver bell from the clutter of papers on the table and rang it in the way that alerted, not the pages with the pappy, well-chopped meat, but four stout guards.

"Remove him," the Emperor said, indicating Montoya. "Handle him gently; he has given no offence. I will speak with him later."

Within the gentle but purposeful grip of the guards, Montoya said loudly, "Beware what you say! My knife is ready."

"Speak in Latin," the Emperor said as soon as they were alone. Dr. Abell said, in Latin, precisely what he had said in English; adding, "I did not understand the situation when I set out. My companion enlightened me along the road."

"And is he to be trusted? Could the enlightenment have been planned in order to make you say what you were not sent to say?"

"I think not, Your Imperial Highness," Dr. Abell said after a moment's thought. "No. He was somewhat drunk at the time, and afterwards regretted allowing his errand to be known to me."

"And what was his errand?"

"To forestall me: or by some other means prevent the brief from being sent."

"And it is your honest opinion that it should not be sent?"

"I am sure—now that I have thought it over."

Dr. Abell was led from the presence and Montoya admitted. His story matched; and the details—being sent for by his cousin, the Queen's lady-in-waiting, and commissioned by the Queen herself—were convincing.

"You appear to be of one mind," Charles said. "Why is there distrust between you?"

"I was ready to kill him if he broke into Latin and argued the other way," Montoya said simply. "He is English. But he seems to be honest."

The honest Englishman sat in his lodging, waiting for the brief to be copied, and began to jot down a few arguments that had occurred to him concerning the legality of the marriage. Conviction grew as he pondered and worked; and on the return journey, every night he took out the copy of the brief and studied it. It seemed to him to be flawless; and he could see why the Queen had been anxious for the original not to fall into the hands of her enemies. It was God's Providence which had given him a drunkard and a lecher for guide. And that was a strange thought, leading to some even stranger. Had Juan Montoya been destined from birth to be bibulous and lecherous in order that at one particular moment of time . . . in a dirty little Pyranean tavern . . . ?

All the way home Dr. Abell was very tolerant of Montoya's peccadillos, supplied him with money—Montoya being penniless again—and when they reached the region where the wine was drinkable, sometimes took a glass or two with him in good fellowship. On the whole however, his attention was on the problem of the marriage and he began to plan a book. It took some time to write, and before it was published it had become an offence in England to give Katharine the title of Queen.

Francisco Filipez had said: Until I am back. He was back in a fortnight with a grubby bandage on his head and his right arm splinted to a piece of a broom handle.

"I apologise for appearing before Your Grace in this state," he said, "but I knew you would be anxious. I failed."

"Are you much hurt, Francisco?"

"No. A cracked head and a broken arm. I was set on, at Abbeville."

"By whom?"

"I never saw. They came behind me." There were moments when even the most wary man must turn to a wall for a moment. "When I came to my senses I was on a boat bound for Dover. And I thank God, Your Grace, that I had no papers about me. Nevertheless, my errand was guessed at. I was not robbed. I was sent back to England, admitted at Dover without question. I think it was intended that I should be living proof that no messenger you send will get through." He looked at her miserably.

"I sent another, Francisco, in case you were intercepted. My second messenger travelled with every safeguard the Cardinal could provide. Nothing like so swift as you are," she smiled at him, "but he will arrive. So you need not worry. You must go to bed and I will send Dr. de La Sa to attend you."

"Your Grace, I need no physician. A night in my own bed

will restore me." He had failed; he had two major injuries and a dozen smaller ones, he needed no purgings or bleedings to add to his miseries.

"Your ring served me well, Francisco. It stayed blue all the time."

There was no lady like her; so brave; so kind. Filipez made a choking noise in his throat. "If the other man, for any reason, should fail, I will go again, as soon as my arm is mended. I will go in disguise."

"I hope there will be no need," she said. She did not think it necessary to say to this discouraged man that it would then be too late. By the time he could ride again, the Emperor would have listened to Dr. Abell and to Juan Montoya and decided one way or the other.

But Filipez's return, in such a state, was an indication of the viciousness of her enemies. She felt weak and isolated; aware that somebody—and still she thought Wolsey chiefly—was determined to be rid of her. However, she had spent enough of her youth on the perimeter of battlefields to have learned that minor defeats could be preludes to victories, so long as one did not allow oneself to be demoralised by them. That was the real nub of the matter; not to lose courage, or hope, or faith in God.

On the whole, as the days ran by and the date of the court of investigation, which everybody now called the trial—so wrong, since the word postulated some criminal action—drew nearer, Katharine fared rather better than the others who were concerned. Henry was anxious and pressed hard upon Wolsey who, arranging everything, gathering witnesses, compiling statements, some most contradictory, still felt that Campeggio had some typically Italian trick hidden in his sleeve: Anne, facing the moment that would decide her whole future, was frequently hysterical and always nervous; Mary, her future equally in balance, and her heart concerned, sometimes wept, sometimes raged, throwing books, needlework, her lute away, riding horses to exhaustion.

Spring, in England in the year 1529, came in with its usual

heady promise; daffodils nodding in the grass, bluebells, the cuckoo's call, and the lime trees translucent green. What happened? Where did the magic go? I loved him; he loved me. And now even the consummation has been reduced to words upon paper—some of them, used in any other context, positively obscene.

Those appointed to advise her and to speak for her in court, came and went. They had been carefully chosen so that the watching world might be assured that there had been no flaw in justice and that the Queen had been properly represented. There was Warham, Archbishop of Canterbury, growing old, not in good health and plainly regretting the whole business; he inspired little confidence. John Fisher, Bishop of Rochester, was plainly on her side and was not afraid to show it. She had also Tunstall, Bishop of Durham, a leading member of her own favourite order, the Observant Friars, and her own confessor, born a Spaniard to whom, in happier days Henry had given the Bishopric of Llandaff. Nobody should say afterwards, when the King had won his case, that the trial had not been scrupulously fair. There was even an attempt to give an international touch with the appointment of two Flemish lawyers to help her, but everything, even access to the relevant documents, was made so difficult for them that they cut short their stay in London and went home.

Campeggio came and took from her a statement, under the most solemn oath, that she had gone virgin to Henry's bed. When she had made it, he said, "Naturally *I* believe Your Grace but . . . there is evidence to the contrary." He looked at her and then away again.

"Bedmakers?"

With ill-concealed distaste he moved his hand. "That, of course. But conflicting. Of more importance are the words spoken by the Prince of Wales on the morning following the nuptials."

Two children, playing a game of make-believe, conspiring to

deceive their elders! The little idyll, so soon over, and now dragged out into the pitiless scrutiny of the law.

"His Grace knows the truth, my lord Cardinal. A statement should be asked of him."

"It has been. He merely repeats that you were his brother's wife." There seemed to her to be something of warning in Campeggio's voice and in his eyes, now again bearing upon her.

"And that is true," she said, ignoring the warning. "Nobody denies that the Prince of Wales and I were legally married. I deny that the marriage was consummated; and this His Grace could confirm. But in fact this court should not be concerned with that. All that is in question is the validity of the dispensation which made my second marriage legal." Campeggio said nothing. "Is that not so?"

He thought of all that was involved in that so simple-sounding question, and sighed. If only she had been less clear-headed, more easily frightened or shamed, cajoled, coaxed, persuaded. . . .

Then, in June, with the court already in session, John Fisher came and said, in his blunt, forthright way:

"Your Grace, I have come to say something which you may not welcome, but which my thought and my feeling obliges me to say. It is this: You will not get justice at the Court now sitting at Blackfriars, and you should repudiate its jurisdiction. *At once.*"

He had always been her staunchest supporter; always certain that when everything was brought out into the light of day, the verdict would be for her.

She said, "You must explain to me . . . why . . . and how it can be done. Be seated, please. You do not look well."

"I should be dead," he said. His old rough-hewn face lost for a moment its nobility and solemnity and produced a wry smile, not much different from a boy's grin. "But for my Meg, I should be dead. But that is neither here nor there—except as evidence of what I say."

"Meg is your hound."

"She *was*." He was grave again. "This is of no importance,

Your Grace, though I was fond of her and she of me, and she was sadly spoiled. Last night she sat by me, avid as usual. I took two cuts at my meat. I was in ill-humour. I was wrong, I suppose, but I had little appetite. I threw the meat at her and said: Here, take the whole. She did, and was stiff and dead in less than five minutes; and my two mouthfuls left me considerably indisposed."

"I am truly sorry," Katharine said.

"I am sorry too. Poor Meg. But had she been less importunate . . . Your Grace, somebody wishes me dead because I am the loudest voiced of your supporters. And if someone is prepared to poison my meat to stop my tongue, how have others been dealt with? You must discount this court. You ask how it can be done. On four counts. Your nationality; a place hostile; the possibility of prejudice in the judges; and, most important of all, the illegality of the whole procedure; a case *sub judica* at Rome cannot be tried elsewhere."

"That is law?"

"As it has been understood for the last thousand years."

"And how do I go about it?"

"You are due to appear on the eighteenth of this month. If you agree I will tomorrow make formal application for you to appear and enter a plea, on the fifteenth. And in good faith, Your Grace, I can assure you that your rejection of this court will be welcomed by Cardinal Campeggio."

"Because it will mean more delay?"

Just a trifle too sharp. Even Fisher, completely convinced that her cause was sound and good, prepared to sacrifice his career and if necessary to give his life, felt that momentary repellence, the feeling—quite unreasonable, as he instantly admitted—that no woman should be so clear-thinking, so concise, so ruthless even to herself, even in handling words.

He said, "I do not think that Cardinal Campeggio wishes delay of itself. I have reason to believe that he feels as I do that a more equable judgement might be reached in Rome. Things move slowly there, but there is experience, and impartiality.

The advice I have just given is the best I can offer Your Grace."
"I thank you for it. And I will take it."

When Henry heard of this move he thought, as Katharine
had done—that it was another time-wasting device and thought
—as Fisher had done—that a trial in Rome was less likely to
give the verdict he wanted. He said to Wolsey, "Whether she
acknowledges the court or not it *is* a court, legally constituted;
and it must remain in session. If she refuses to appear before it,
she can be declared contumacious, and be tried in her absence.
I want an answer. And you know what answer I want." The
dangerous, reddish glare took possession of his eyes again. "I
can tell you this, Thomas. If you allow Campeggio to shuffle
this back to Rome, my case is lost. *And so are you!*"

So the court solemnly debated its own legality and satisfied
on that score continued to sit through a spell of unusually warm
weather. The Queen was not expected to occupy the place
reserved for her.

16

"Tighter," Katharine said. "Much tighter."

Concepcion strained at the rigid, iron-stiffened stays. Maria de Moreto watched with disapproval and finally said, "Your Grace, if it is tighter you will not be able to breathe. And it will be hot in that place."

"The new dress is cut to a smaller waist," Katharine said.

It was all so futile and so pitiable, Maria thought. The whole project was absurd and quite out of keeping with the Queen's character; she was not given to hasty decisions, or to sudden changes of mind. One day to go and deny that the court at Blackfriars had any jurisdiction over her; and three days later to be preparing to appear before it. What good could it do? Maria looked at the new dress, royal purple in colour, its low square neckline encrusted with gold thread and pearls; the new headdress of gold tissue with a band of pearls at the front; the new shoes with high heels. All this and the false pink and white of cosmetics, the newly brightened hair; wasted on a roomful of clerics and men known to be on the King's side.

Lady Salisbury who had slipped in to attend this robing, in order to give proof of her sympathy and fidelity, felt the same, but she said, "It is a very beautiful dress, Your Grace. And I think it will fit without further tugging." Concepcion gladly ceased her exertions and tied the cords.

"And what was the King's response to my request?" Katharine asked. Lady Salisbury had not intended to mention that abortive plea at this moment.

"He did not favour the suggestion. He said that if the Princess were old enough to take interest in the proceedings—and to gossip—she was old enough to understand and prepare herself for her change of status." Katharine had asked Lady Salisbury to suggest that it would be better for Mary to go to the country while the trial was at this critical stage.

"Shield her so far as you can."

"I always have," Lady Salisbury said. "But it is not easy. She is mature for her years; and nowadays very suspicious. A conversation abruptly ended, even a euphemism employed and she is alert at once."

"I know," Katharine said. "Let us comfort ourselves that this will soon be over."

Nobody said anything but Katharine was aware of being the only person in the room who retained any optimism at all. But then, she was the only one who knew what she planned to do.

In the great hall at Blackfriars, borrowed for the occasion, Henry sat highest, under a canopy; at a lower level sat the two Cardinals, fully robed and wearing their wide tasselled hats. A little lower still was Katharine's place with the chair draped in gold tissue, and the canopy of royal status. The King's counsellors sat on one side of the floor, the Queen's on the other, at tables covered with tapestry and laden with papers. All around, less comfortably accommodated, sat the nobles of England.

Wolsey felt ill with anxiety and sleeplessness. The road from Ipswich had led steadily uphill and had had its stony as well as its flowery places. To have come so far, and done so much, and now at the age of fifty-four to have his whole career jeopardised, and in such a fashion, made nonsense of it all. The very nature of the case offended his fastidiousness; toothless old crones claiming to remember the condition of beds twenty, twenty-eight years ago; doddering old men boasting that at Prince Arthur's age they had been fully potent, had begotten children. The question of whether a woman could be twice de-flowered and whether the sheet at Baynard's Castle could be evidence directly favourable to the King's cause. It was disgusting.

"If she keeps her threat and does not appear . . ." he said softly to Campeggio, and looked again at the vacant place. Surely now, with the decision within hours of being made, Campeggio would offer some clue of what was in his mind. He did not. He said with maddening calm, "We shall see." Wolsey thought angrily: Yes, you may be placid. Whatever happens you can pack up and go to Rome; I have to stay here, with a maddened bull of a man who is in a witch's thrall. If things go badly, if there is even more delay, I am finished.

There was a stir as Katharine, attended by her gentleman usher, walked in and took her place. At fifteen Henry VII had thought her well-grown and she had been too tall for Arthur; at eighteen a trifle too tall for Henry, but she was not actually tall. She moved however with dignity; her gown and headdress and jewels had been chosen to convey an impression of grandeur, and from a distance, anyway, the cosmetics detracted from her age. The Duke of Norfolk thought: Forty-four this year; that niece of mine will not wear so well; nothing ages a woman like tantrums.

The herald cried, "Henry, King of England, come into the court," and Henry replied in a loud clear voice, "Here, my lords." At the back of his mind there stirred the thought that it was wrong that he, King of England, should have been driven to the point of laying his cause and pleading his case before his inferiors, as though he had wittingly done wrong, instead of having been wronged and then denied justice. But that thought was flooded out by his confident hope that this would be the end. This sweet summer would not go to join the other wasted ones.

The herald cried again, "Katharine, Queen of England, come into the court."

She said nothing, but stood up and, moving slowly, through the silence and the following eyes, went to where Henry sat. She knelt at his feet, drew a steadying breath against the racing of her heart and the merciless grip of the stays and began to speak as though he and she were alone in a room together. Yet every word, spoken in the voice that Henry had once said was like black velvet, carried to the farthest end of the great hall.

"Sire," she began, "I beseech you for all the love that hath been between us, let me have justice and right, take on me some pity and compassion, for I am a poor woman, and a stranger, born out of your dominion. I have here no assured friend. I flee to you, as to the head of justice within this realm . . ."

Henry was completely appalled, both by this unorthodox behaviour, so unexpected, so unsuitable in a court of law; and by her appearance. That mockery of youth! The grease which formed the base of the pink, the white, the blue, had melted a little in the heat of the crowded room on a burning June day and the colours had blurred. And yet, and yet . . . there was just enough of illusion left to rouse the ghost of the pretty Princess whom he had admired enviously at St. Paul's and claimed under the Greenwich limes. And there was also the sharp, shattering realisation of the damage the years did. Me too? One day! Anne also? It was not a situation where a shilling and an order would bring release. But after that one glance he looked away, fixing his hard blue stare on the wall opposite, at a window where, against a heat-whitened sky, some green boughs hung. He tightened his hands on the arms of his chair and assumed the tense attitude of a man bearing physical agony without outcry. She went on and on. She told him how she had striven to love his friends, how she had borne his children. "This twenty years or more I have been your true wife . . ."

Then she looked at him. She knew him well; every mood, every response. She had made this last gamble because she had believed that appealed to as the final arbiter—that would touch his pride, and reminded of a love, once free-flowing, now silted up—that would touch his sentiment, she might even at this last moment, move him.

But she had miscalculated.

She saw that and was, not quite consciously, glad of the iron-braced stays. They supported her while she said the last, most cogent thing, so difficult, so almost impossible to say. But she said it:

"And I take God to be my witness, I was a true maid, without touch of man when you had me first. Whether that is true or not I put to your conscience."

He knew; he knew it was true; he was the only person in the world . . . and he had a conscience, he must admit . . .

He did not. He stared ahead, immobile as a figure in stone. She said, "If you will not, to God I commit my cause." Then she stood up and walked and walked, not to her place but towards the door. There she was glad of Griffith's arm. The herald called her back, but she seemed not to hear. Griffith said, "Madam, you are called again," and she said, in that low but penetrating voice, "This is no court of justice for me. Let us go."

"And now," Campeggio said to Wolsey, "we must listen, I suppose, to His Grace's declaration that if she were adjudged by law to be his lawful wife nothing would be more acceptable to him; and were the marriage deemed good he would choose her above all other women." He was quoting from one of Henry's earlier statements and his voice had a sarcastic edge.

"That display of feminine guile," Wolsey said, "was irrelevant and, as law runs, meaningless. She has proved nothing, except that she is contumacious and must be declared so."

"With that I fully agree," Campeggio said. Now, Wolsey thought, now, surely he must give some indication of the conclusion he has reached, the verdict he favours. Campeggio presently did so. "Our best course, now," he said, "is to conclude this business and advoke the case to the court at Rome."

Wolsey's heart, no longer reliable, began to stammer in its beat. He managed to say, "His Grace will be much displeased."

"There are other considerations," Campeggio reminded him, quite gently. Wolsey knew then that this was what Campeggio had been told to do, should his efforts to bring about a reconciliation fail. But to level that accusation would be useless.

Henry had no such reticence. In a rage which made all his other outbursts look like fits of childish peevishness, he sent for them both and stormed in a way that shook even Campeggio's calm. If Clement, if the Emperor, if Campeggio, if Wolsey thought he was to be put off in this way they were much mistaken. "Seven months to get here," he said, halting in his stamping up and down and placing himself foursquare before Campeggio, "eight months to set up the court! Advoked to Rome where it has been four years already! You hobble home, my lord Cardinal, and tell your master that if he cannot decide, I can. I am not married. I am free, you hear me? Free to marry when and whom I wish."

"Bigamously," Campeggio said.

"Then ask Clement to permit me to commit bigamy! Maybe he can give an answer to that!" He then turned upon Wolsey and accused him of ingratitude, lack of zeal, conspiring against him . . . This tirade Campeggio interrupted, "Your Grace if you would permit me a word . . ."

"More blockhead's talk! Thousands, millions of words, spoken and written and no sense in any one of them."

"It has occurred to me that the Queen will be equally disappointed by our failure to reach a verdict."

"God's name! So she should be. I hope she is."

"She can hardly have failed to see—by Your Grace's demeanour—that she is repudiated. She might at this moment be prepared to concede if Your Grace would make a concession. Throughout I have gathered the impression that she is less concerned for herself than for her daughter. If it were put to her, in good faith, that the Princess Mary's rights would be recognised after those of the child, or children born of any subsequent marriage, she might be prepared to admit that her own marriage was invalid."

And if she would, Campeggio's first mission would be accomplished.

"If that is the best you can think of! Go and try."

Campeggio had underrated Katharine's resilience. The closure of the Blackfriars court, the advoking of the case to Rome had heartened, not discouraged her. She had always trusted that her vindication would come from Rome. Henry's behaviour in the courtroom had hurt her so deeply that a self-defensive process had begun in her mind even before she was back in Greenwich. It had seemed heartless and she could not, would not, must not believe that. She was now well on the way to convincing herself that he had not looked at her because he dared not, and had not answered her because he could not deny the truth of what she had said.

When the Cardinals arrived she was sewing with her women and rose to greet them with a skein of white silk hanging around her neck. Wolsey asked for a talk in privacy and she led them to the stark little room where eight months earlier he, on his knees, had said things which were to haunt her all her life. Campeggio explained the King's offer while Wolsey stood by, his eyes, the shrewdest in Europe, looking like those of a dog begging one merciful word. She had a feeling that Campeggio, though more composed, was begging too.

Her answer was ready. "If my daughter's rights were dubious, my lords, this would be a generous offer. But they are not; her rights are indisputable—and no subject for bargaining. I see how you are placed and, believe me, I am sorry for you. You have your masters to please. I am answerable only to God, and to my conscience."

Wolsey's brain, battered but still lively, produced a cogent argument.

"And to your daughter, Madam. Have you ever asked yourself what her rights would be should you die before the verdict is given. Or if the decision went against you? Correctly worded, signed and sealed this agreement could safeguard her in the event of such contingency."

Very subtle, Campeggio thought with a flash of admiration.

"Such matters I must leave in the hands of God," Katharine said.

On the way out Campeggio said, "Sailors bring home birds which learn a few words and repeat them tiresomely. Her Grace is much the same."

Wolsey said nothing; he was brooding over what the King had said. One sentence stood out: "You fail very seldom, my Lord Chancellor, and you would not have failed this time *had your heart been in it.*"

17

There followed a time that was like a long pause in a chess game.

Remembering the blind, avoiding stare in the Court at Black-friars, Katharine was prepared for Henry wishing never to look upon her again; yet in that late summer and early autumn she accompanied him on his progresses and was with him at Grafton when Campeggio came, accompanied by Wolsey, to take formal leave before escaping to avoid yet another English winter. At Grafton Henry's uncertainty of what next to do was made plain. He seemed to be on the point of taking Wolsey back into favour, put his arm around his shoulders and talked to him for a long time, in a window embrasure, but in the sight of everyone. Then, next day, he refused to speak to him. Anne Boleyn's doing?

To Katharine Henry behaved with a stately civility which deceived some observers to the point where bets were laid and taken. The Blackfriars Court, inconclusive as it was, had shown the King that his case was poor, so he was making it up, and any day now Nan Bullen would get her marching orders. Katharine interpreted Henry's behaviour as being the same as her own—let nothing be done or said which would make life together intolerable once the Pope had pontificated.

Even Mary's removal from Court did not seem to her a puni-tive measure aimed against herself. She had suggested that Mary would be better away from it all, before the Court held its first session. Henry, she thought, was acting belatedly on that suggestion.

Mary was more suspicious. "And why am I to be sent away this time?"

"Because moving about with the Court interrupts your education. Because Hunsdon is your own manor and should be occupied. Because country air is better for you."

"Shall I be back for the Christmas revels?" Mary eyed her mother with a piercing curiosity. "You will keep Christmas with him, as usual?"

"Dear child, I am his wife. Where else should I keep Christmas but beside him?"

"With *her*, just around the corner. I often wonder how you can bear it. Mother, do you never long to scratch her eyes out?"

"Would that benefit us? I am convinced that for you—as for me, Mary—to be uncivil to her would be to give her undue importance."

Mary said impulsively, "I wish I were more like you," knowing the wish vain. She did not realise that it had taken two people to make her and that, within her, two natures would always conflict. She simply knew that she admired her mother and wished to be like her and could, somehow, never manage it.

"Before Christmas," Katharine said, "the answer may come and all will be as it was before."

So they took leave of one another; neither thinking that it might be forever.

Just before Christmas Katharine suggested that Mary should come home. Henry said, "She is better where she is. *But if you wish to go to her, you have my permission.*"

It was the most forthright thing that had been said for months and the implication was ominous. He wanted her away. The Roman courts had reopened in October, but the question of whether she was or was not Queen of England, Henry's wife, had not yet been brought up; and to make one backward step, even so ordinary and human a move as to go to keep Christmas at Hunsdon with Mary, would be to open a breach in the defence.

She hated war and would never voluntarily have anything to do with it, but she still thought in the terms of the war that had been the background for her impressionable childhood years.

Yield an inch over any debatable ground, retreat one step down the ladder of the escalade, and defeat was certain. Hold out a siege long enough and relief came.

She said, "I have no wish to go to Hunsdon—though it seems long since I saw Mary. I shall keep Christmas as usual."

Parrying every stroke, Henry thought with unwilling admiration. And the situation must be painful. For since everyone, even Clement knew of his intention to marry Anne so soon as he was free—and in any case if they dallied much longer—he had taken no pains to conceal his movements. Anne now had a fine handsome house, next door to what had been Wolsey's residence, York House. And York House Henry had "borrowed" so that on these winter evenings he had only a few steps to take in order to be with Anne. To be nagged and scolded; to be charmed. Wolsey no longer needed York House, or Hampton Court or any of his manors. Stripped of secular office, he had gone to York and was attending to his clerical duties, living modestly and piously, the world put away. Strictly speaking York House, becoming transformed into the Palace of White-hall, was the property of the diocese of York, but it was convenient for Henry's purpose, and nobody had protested. The borrowing of it had been his first exercise in the confiscation of church property and if he thought about it now and then, convinced him that the Church owned so much that it could hardly keep check on its possessions.

"Keep it as usual," he said. "I trust it will be happy. It will be your last with me. Kate, you must understand . . . I loved you . . . I defied all advice. I admit it . . . but we had our good years, though the marriage was cursed . . . dozens of learned doctors concur with me now. It will go against you and then I shall be obliged to pity you, as I did at Blackfriars. Kate, we enjoyed an illicit love affair. Call it that, let it go, a song well sung . . . But over. Could not the last note be tunable?"

This was the first time that he had appealed to her in this way. All his former stands had been taken upon the basis of law . . . Papal dispensation, Cardinal's conferring, hard argument. This was more difficult to resist—but it must be resisted.

And she was encouraged by current gossip—now faithfully repeated by Maria—that the Lady Anne, disgusted by the result of Blackfriars, angry with Henry, angry with the whole world, was on the point of giving up and retiring to Hever. It seemed to Katharine that Henry, making an appeal to sentiment, was trying one last desperate measure.

Victory in a siege went to the side that could hold out longest.

Then came the business of the cramp rings.

Night cramp, like toothache, was a common affliction and there were many charms and superstitions concerned with its prevention. There was a belief that cramp could be avoided by wearing a silver ring that had been consecrated by a special ritual in which a Queen of England had played her part. It was akin to the King's touching for the cure of scrofula. Year after year Katharine had watched the silver rings put into a basin and blessed in the names of Abraham, Isaac and Jacob and then signed with the Cross. She had joined in the prayer which asked that the rings might restore contracted nerves. Then she had taken them and rubbed them between her palms, put them back into the basin and seen the Holy Water poured upon them. Such rings were much coveted, worn with pride and regarded as heirlooms.

She was deeply shocked when she learned that this year Anne had sent cramp rings to be distributed to all the men who were in Rome waiting to represent the King when the cause came forward.

"But they will be worthless," she said to Maria. "It is the virtue of the Holy Oil with which the Queen is anointed at her coronation which confers the cure. Besides, what priest could be found to perform the ceremony for *her*?"

"Some renegade."

The truth was that while the common people still howled against Nan Bullen, and her imminent withdrawal was talked of in taverns, those closer to the centre of things saw that Anne's power over the King was increasing. They quarrelled frequently and rancorously, but every quarrel was followed by a reconciliation, marked by some gift or privilege. Weatherwise people followed the King, and at Suffolk House, Anne now kept unofficial Court.

"I wonder at His Grace agreeing to a procedure so irregular," Katharine said.

He had not done it willingly. It was a concession to mend a quarrel in which Anne had accused him, hysterically, of being insincere and half-hearted. If he meant one half of what he said, Katharine would not still be at Court, housed and treated like a Queen. That was one of her recurrent grievances and she refused to see Henry's point of view—that to deny Katharine the outward show of Queenship would seem to be forestalling Clement's decision and thus prejudice his case.

Katharine never mentioned the cramp rings to Henry; except that the recipients would still wake, agonised in the night, the matter had no importance. Anne could wear the Queen's crown and still not be Queen. And to refer to the encroachment would be to bring up the subject which, since his sentimental appeal, had by mutual consent, not been mentioned.

When it next was it was broached by Henry himself. They were seated side by side watching an old morality play in which Virtues and Vices and the figures representing Good and Evil contested so noisily, shouting accusations and counteraccusations and striking blows at one another with staves and clubs and blown-up pigs' bladders, that under cover of the din a private conversation was possible.

"I heard today from Rome. Things are moving at last. We are to be called before the judges of the Holy See."

Thank God. A neutral court. No Wolsey there.

"I cannot attend," he went on before she could say anything. "I foresaw this. My advisors assure me that there is no precedent. No King of England can be called before a foreign court of justice."

She thought: He knows his case is weak; he fears humiliation. She said, "If that is the rule you must abide by it, I suppose. In many ways the English have always been a people apart."

Abstinence hit Gluttony over the head with a dried codfish, hard and solid as wood and Gluttony retaliated by throwing a string of sausages, steaming hot.

A people apart, Katharine thought. And it was due to geography. To their island position. When the Roman Empire broke up they had not been overrun by Huns, Goths, Visigoths —they had enjoyed the sunset period with Arthur and his knights. When they were overrun it had been by Angles, Jutes, Saxons, looking for land to till. They had become English. Then, as conquerors, the Normans had come and been so thoroughly absorbed that except for a few names and some words, all twisted, their very language had been lost. England absorbed all, made its own rules and produced a people who could call a most ferocious civil war by a pretty name—the Wars of the Roses. And could end it with a flowery symbol, the Tudor rose, half white, half red. Certainly, a people apart.

"I must also forbid you to attend," Henry said.

On the floor of the hall Avarice bent over his money bag and Charity gave alms to the poor.

"On what ground?"

"As my subject."

She said slowly, "Am I? If I am your wife, then I am your subject, and glad to be. But if, as you contend, I am not your wife, then I am a Spaniard still; and if called to Rome, must go."

Charity hit Avarice over the head with the bowl and the money bag dropped, spilling pebbles, grass, rubbish.

"That would be a good argument," Henry said, "except that you were Arthur's wife and thus made English enough to take the sweating sickness."

"I was never Arthur's wife—as you well know."

Now on the floor, Lust, immodestly attired, wrestled with Chastity.

"We will not argue upon that point," Henry said. "Nor about attendance at any foreign court. I have, as you know, been at Waltham and there I met a man who seemed to me to have the right sow by the ear. He made a very sensible suggestion—that this matter could best be decided by canvassing a consensus of opinion from all Universities."

"French and German as well?" she asked, as Chastity, all in white, eluded Lust's embrace.

"All Universities. Would you accept their ruling?"

"How could I? A Pope made our marriage legal. Only a Pope can undo it. And I wonder at you! The King of England must not be called before a foreign court, but is willing to accept the decision of foreign Universities."

"Let us not be hasty," Henry said. "This fellow—Thomas Cranmer is his name—is something out of the ordinary." Having said that, he stopped, halted by the fact that for once his well-trained and exercised royal memory for faces had failed him and he had no idea what the man looked like. A negative man, neither young nor old, good-looking nor ugly, bold or retiring. The little that the King had learned about him so far, gave no clue to his real character; born of a respectable family he had married an innkeeper's daughter and for that been suspended from the Cambridge College of which he was a Fellow. She died before the suspension was final, and he had resumed his Fellowship, taken orders and become a tutor in divinity. Again, neither one thing nor the other. And yet this unremarkable man had made a suggestion which no one had offered before, and, brought into Henry's presence to expound, had, though showing some signs of nervousness, spoken concisely and firmly. And he had said one thing which Henry, so orthodox, had first found shocking and then so promising that the mind reeled under the impact. Perhaps that was why he could not remember the face or stature of the man who had said, "It would then be a matter for the ordinary ecclesiastical courts; not for the Pope." What made Thomas Cranmer something out of the ordinary was that he had *vision*. He saw over, or around the problem which others —including Henry himself—looked upon as a blank wall. "If the general consensus of opinion in *all* established Universities agrees that a man cannot marry his brother's wife—and that much, surely, Your Grace, all will agree; then your marriage is null and void."

"But that," Henry said, "is what I have said. All along. From the first."

"But never, so far, in a court composed of ordinary English clergy, not under the Papal thumb." And that was true. Wolsey, Campeggio . . . servants of that dilatory, time-wasting, shilly-shallying fellow in Rome. . . .

To Katharine, as the symbol of Evil, all in black, threw a little ball that burst into flames and stank of sulphur at Good who held up a crucifix, Henry said:

"He is one of the few who can see further than the end of his nose. The best canonists, the best lawyers, the best minds centre about the Universities."

She said with that shrewdness which seemed so out of keeping: "Do they? Are Wolsey, Warham, More *still* at Oxford, centring about the source from which they wish not to be weaned? And is yours not a good mind?"

It was unlikely that Henry would weigh her words against those of this new, visionary advisor, but she felt forced to voice her doubts. French Universities were French—to her, automatically suspect; German Universities were Lutheran; Italian Universities would no doubt wish to return an answer in line with the Pope's opinion, but who knew what that was? If only Clement would decide and waste no more time in shuffling expedients. If only she could understand why a simple question —Was Julius' dispensation good?—could not be answered by a simple yes, or no. Was it because there was some aspect or complication of which she was not aware?

With the final triumph of Virtue over Vice, the entertainment ended and the performers lined up to be applauded. Henry kept his hands gripped on the table's edge, but Katharine clapped—it was not their fault, good souls, that their performance should have happened to coincide with a momentous conversation. Henry looked sideways at her without turning his head and there was something dangerous, something like a goaded desperation in the glance.

"You are," he said, quite softly, "the most damned obstinate woman God ever made. But we cannot go on this way. I cannot accept Clement's latest proposal and you will not accept Cranmer's . . ."

"*Cannot*," she corrected. "Only the Pope's verdict can decide."

"The Universities can give their opinion; and if they decide that we were never legally married, an ordinary English ecclesiastical court can release me. *I shall declare the Pope a heretic and marry whom I like!*"

He spoke with emphasis, but without raising his voice and that set the threat in a class apart; very different from anything he had ever said in a moment of rage. It called up a prospect so appalling that it was like feeling the preliminary tremor of an earthquake. She felt her face go stiff and put up her hands, pressing them against her cheeks, staring at him over her fingertips with eyes gone wide and dark with dismay.

"You see, you cannot win," Henry said, still softly but with venom. Then with an abrupt change to an almost coaxing tone, he added, "But it is not too late. Give in gracefully and you shall never regret it."

Do *not*, he thought, and you will see some changes which you will not relish. Among other things which the featureless man of vision had said, was that it would be wise for the King and the lady who called herself Queen, to cease all appearance of cohabitation. A break between their households should be made. Welcome as such a change would have been to Henry, he was not prepared to make it until some firmer ground was under his feet. He wished to avoid seeming to persecute Katharine.

"Think about it," he said.

She managed to say, "I think of little else these days."

She thought about it endlessly, through the routine-patterned days, and often in the night, too. She no longer slept well. She often woke with the panic feeling that she was about to suffocate, and that feeling mastered, the inside of her head would seem to expand, become a vast, empty space, as large as the hall at Westminster, ringing with ominous phrases. She heard again Wolsey's old voice saying: More is concerned than you dream of. The world is riven. And Mary's young voice saying: Schism. To those, tonight would be added Henry's wild statement about declaring the Pope a heretic. She had only one answer to them all—I have no choice. I honour and am ruled by the decision of one Pope and wait, with what patience I can muster, for another to confirm it. What else can I do? To any faithful daughter of the Church, Papal authority must be absolute—if only because, in the end there must be some unchallengeable authority, otherwise all would be chaos. She faced, increasingly as time went on, the possibility that when Clement pontificated, it might be against her—the lengthening delay sometimes undermined her confidence. In that case she would give in gracefully; accept the verdict, the fact that through some technicality, her marriage was void, her one living child a bastard. But not until . . . not until. Clement could not defer decision forever; canvassing the Universities would take time. God send there would be no need for Henry to keep that terrible threat. God grant that whichever way Clement decides, we may both accept it. . . .

An hour or two of this and she would think: Such fretting shows a lack of faith. God knows the answer. Thousands upon thousands pray: Thy will be done, on earth as it is in Heaven; and His will will be done . . . Upon that thought, she would sleep again.

The Emperor's Ambassador, Don de Mendoza, had found the whole situation more than he could deal with and had asked to be recalled. Charles' choice of a successor for him was significant both to Henry and to Katharine.

To begin with he was not even a Spaniard; he was Savoyard, born in Annecy. He was not of noble birth; he came from an impoverished, middle-class family, the son of an attorney who had died young, leaving a widow and several children. He had made his way by his use of his brains; he was a lawyer, said to be a good one. And he had spent some years in Geneva where new ideas flourished. In the end Don de Mendoza had sided so openly with Katharine that he had been placed under house-arrest; Messire Eustache Chapuys had been chosen, Henry and Katharine felt, because he was unlikely to repeat his predecessor's error.

In Henry's mind this opinion was confirmed at the first interview. Chapuys had a scholar's face, thin, ascetic, with cold grey eyes and a thin-lipped mouth. It was impossible to imagine him being moved by enthusiasm for any cause except, perhaps, the proper application of some legal principle. Logic, not emotion, would be his fulcrum. And if his appearance was reassuring, his manner to the King was even more so; in his rather remote way he seemed to be making an effort to be agreeable, and to skirt skilfully around any subject of a controversial nature. Even when Henry said, "I consider, Messire Chapuys, that your master has dealt shabbily with me," Chapuys said, "Never knowingly, Your Grace. The Emperor respects and admires you more than any other monarch in the world. This is not mere diplomatic talk. I have heard him say so, in various connections, many times."

"Nevertheless he obstructed me. Even over so small a matter as the sending on of that brief."

"But, Your Grace, that was a precaution. He was afraid to allow the original out of his hands. I have seen it, and the copy; they are exact in every detail."

"Water under the bridge now," Henry said, not too easily appeased. "The Legantine Court wrung what they could out of the copy. The fact remains that I was denied what I asked for. However, if your master is truly well-disposed towards me, he can do me a service now."

"I am so certain of his mind that I can answer for him. He will do it willingly."

"Then he can use his influence on the Pope to have the place of trial shifted. I cannot go to Rome. *Ne extra Angliam litigare congantur.*"

"Your Grace wishes for another trial in England?" Chapuys, who had studied the case most thoroughly, put a slight stress on *another*.

"No. But I could attend a court in France. In the interest of peace in Christendom, I have not pressed my claim, but I am King of France. There I should be in my own realm."

Chapuys' eyes remained as clear and as cold as the waters of the lake beside which he had been born, but his mind moved rapidly. That moss-grown old claim had been used for three hundred years as an excuse for English invasions. In theory no Christian king was supposed to attack another, except in defence of his own rights. The English kings who had made use of it had all been touched with megalomania.

"It is a solution that no one else has thought of, Your Grace. And well worth consideration."

He had already considered and rejected it. A French court, a French Cardinal in the chair, the whole climate anti-Papist, anti-Imperialist. Henry would get what was now widely, but wrongly, called his divorce there, and ever after be grateful to King Francis and to France. Quite disastrous!

"I thought Cambrai," Henry said.

"Ah yes. And the Lady Katharine would accept the venue?"

It was the first time she had been mentioned directly and Henry noticed, almost avidly, that Chapuys did not say *Her Grace* or *the Queen*.

"I have not yet mentioned the matter to her. There has been no time."

He had, in fact, only just thought of it himself, prodded on by one of Anne's hysterical outbursts. How long, she had demanded would the canvassing of the Universities take? A year at the very least; any man who claimed to be a scholar could argue six months about nothing; given something to argue about they would argue until they were dead, until Henry was dead, until she was dead! And meantime she occupied this invidious position and Katharine was still housed and treated like a queen. It was an intolerable situation and unless he did something to end it soon, she would. She would go back to

Hever. That was the threat which always cut so sharply and so deeply that there were times when under it he felt a wild impulse to say: Go! And good riddance! That impulse, fleeting as it was, always frightened him it was so akin to that of a suicide who cast life away because life had not given him what he wanted. He always restrained it and soothed her as best he could, with gifts, with promises, with honied words.

Leaving her he had thought again about Cranmer's suggestions. Anne was opposed to the waiting for a consensus of scholarly opinion; Katharine said she could accept no decision but Clement's. And there was something else to be considered. If he followed Cranmer's plan it would inevitably lead to the setting up of the authority of a simple English ecclesiastic court in direct defiance of the Pope. It was all very well, coming straight from Waltham to say to Katharine: I will declare the Pope a heretic, but once one realised the full implication and saw, as he did, that a blow against one form of authority was a blow against all authority . . . that if the Pope could be defied, so might a king be, and bishops, lords of manors, mayors in towns . . . there was no end to it.

So he had thought instead of the swift, decisive court in Cambrai.

To Chapuys he said, "It would come better from you, Messire, than from me. She no longer understands me. She is most noble and honourable, and I swear to you, as I have sworn to others, that were things otherwise, there is no woman in the world whom I would prefer before her. But she is a woman and women have fancies; they can be perverse and very stubborn."

And for that, Chapuys thought, God be thanked. Had my mother not been the most stubborn creature in creation—donkeys not excepted—I should not be here. In his coldly amicable voice he said:

"Your Grace wishes me to suggest a court at Cambrai?"

"Yes. As soon as possible. She is at Greenwich."

Chapuys went to Greenwich a man committed to nothing except his master's service. Charles had instructed him to use his best endeavours to bring about, if possible, even at this late hour, a reconciliation between the King and Queen of England whose matrimonial dispute had assumed absurd proportions. Every time-wasting device had been employed. The King of England's passion for the waiting lady must soon burn itself out— he was forty; his wife forty-five; full time that they settled down. They had a daughter, about fourteen. Charles had a three-year-old son; there was a difference admittedly; but when Philip was fourteen, Mary Queen of England would be only twenty-five, greater disparities in age had, in the interests of political or territorial interests, been compounded in the past.

Chapuys was not surprised to find that Katharine was opposed to the suggestion of a court at Cambrai; and it was not difficult for him—a seasoned diplomat—to make a few remarks which sounded as though he was using persuasion upon her, but were in fact calculated to strengthen her opposition. "It would," he said, "be much the *quickest* way, Your Grace."

"I am in no hurry to be the subject of a wrong decision," she said. He felt that his point had been taken. "I appealed to Rome and the only verdict acceptable to me will come from Rome."

"The delay must be very tedious."

"Perhaps less so to me than to others concerned. I sometimes think, Messire Chapuys—and may God forgive me if the suspicion is unwarranted—that everything is being deliberately delayed in the hope that His Grace's infatuation may die down of its own accord. That is a fatuous hope and underestimates both His Grace and Mistress Boleyn, as much as the hope that long waiting will change my mind underestimates me. You would serve us *all* if you conveyed this fact to the level where decisions are made. If His Holiness pontificates in my favour and says that my marriage is good, it will be a great relief to me and also, I think, perhaps to His Grace, when the anger has died. He has been unfortunate—and only I who love him can see this . . . I know," she said, clasping her hands together and hammering them upon the air, "I know what is said, and believed of him. It so happens that his doubts about our marriage, our having no son, were fomented by evil councellors and coincided with the fancy he had conceived—as many men do—for a younger woman. The timing was bad. And the woman . . . Messire Chapuys, it ill becomes one woman to wish another less virtuous, but had she been less virtuous, less of a bargainer, it would all be over now and we should have been spared much suffering. I do not know, Messire Chapuys, why I say such things to you, except that I hope you will convey to your master, my nephew, the certainty that more time wasted will be wasted indeed and that a firm directive from Rome would be to the benefit of us all."

"And if," the Spanish Ambassador said, "it should go against you, Your Grace?"

"I should grieve for my daughter. For myself, I should accept it, putting as they say, a hard heart against a hard sorrow."

Chapuys knew then. In another place, in another tongue, the only woman he had ever cared for or respected, had used that phrase many times. And once the likeness between her and the Queen of England was recognised . . . Dignity in humiliating circumstances, clear thinking, straight speaking, tolerance just on the wry side, and at the heart of it all a rocklike resistance. Like his mother!

His father had died leaving nothing but a house. To the widow friends and advisors had come, meaning well. Sell the house, they said; buy a modest property; Eustache and the next boy, they said are big enough now to take service, in some merchant's house . . . She had listened, with the very same manner as Katharine had listened to his proposal of the court at Cambrai. She had then gone her own way. The clear, rather chilly air of Annecy was reckoned to be good for people with faulty lungs, and she had turned her house into a place where such could lodge, squeezing her own family into the minimum of space and cooking, cooking, the good simple food that did as much as the air. Her first-born, Eustache, should never be a menial, he must continue at school, proceed to University, become, like his father an attorney. The younger boys, if they showed a gleam of promise, should have similar opportunities; and her daughters should be brought up—no matter at what sacrifice—

to be marriageable within the class they would have occupied
had their father lived. It had been a hard and bitter struggle,
worse than poverty because poverty could always show its sores
and find dogs to lick them. But Eustache, her first-born, taken
into confidence too young—to whom else could she talk
frankly?—had never seen her lose composure, dignity or faith.
The pallid, languid lung-sufferers would die, what was owing
would be disputed; the flour would be weevilly, the onions rot
in the ground, the best milking goat slip its tether: and she
would say, We must put a hard heart against a hard sorrow. And
she would press on, undismayed by the fact that everything in
the world was against her—except Eustache, the dependable
little boy always ready to shoulder any task, even those beyond
his capacity.

Eustache, the man, the Imperial Ambassador, came away
from Greenwich deeply committed.

It was, however, the goodwill of the King that the Ambassador appeared anxious to gain. He made a point of never seeking private interviews with the Queen and in public exchanged
only the few remarks demanded by custom and by courtesy.
But he kept a sharp ear for gossip, however trivial and would
shamelessly eavesdrop on occasion. Now and then, even in a
crowded room, he would slip into the formal conversation a
warning word. One evening he said, speaking in a low voice, but
with no glancing to left or right or leaning forward or any other
sign that he was speaking of anything but the weather or the
quality of the entertainment just ended:

"Your refusal of Cambrai is likely to have unpleasant repercussions."

"I trust God will give me the necessary fortitude."

There had been times when the clean, polished rooms at
Annecy had stood empty; when food was scarce and shoes out-
grown. His mother had never failed in fortitude.

"The Lady is bringing pressure to bear. She wishes you away
from Court."

"I am grateful to you, Messire," she said, with the amiable
look, the gracious inclination of the head with which she might

have received some flattering, ambassadorial words. She was aware of the bystander. Not hovering, as Wolsey had hovered. Henry's new man, Thomas Cromwell, who had been Wolsey's servant and who, the moment his master fell from favour, had ridden posthaste to take his place with the King, lacked the physical dignity, the urbane manner of Wolsey. He did not hover, he approached and stood, his stance a little awkward, his intention of interrupting the conversation plain. Finesse, the art which his old master had perfected, was no longer needed; Katharine's days as Queen, even in appearance, were numbered. Tomorrow, or the day after, she would be informed. . . .

Informed already she was prepared for the deputation which called upon her to demand that she should accept, and appear at, the Court in Cambrai. Cromwell, more brutally direct in spheres where retaliation was unlikely than Wolsey had ever been, had chosen the men who were to form the deputation. The Duke of Norfolk, Anne's uncle; the Earl of Wiltshire, Anne's father; the Duke of Suffolk who, ever since the King had spared his head and taken him back into favour, had been a willing pliant tool.

Knowing what the repercussions were likely to be, she said to them what she had said to Chapuys: For her the only acceptable verdict must come from Rome. And when they had gone she turned back into the apartments—to the rooms where, on a June evening long ago Henry's love had installed her, his forethought kindled fires—and began to make preparations for her removal.

It was a dismal task. This is mine, this is state property; this I brought from Spain; this has been given me since. A severance of bone from bone.

"And the jewels?" Maria de Moreto asked. They had been, for years, her special care and responsibility.

Katharine hesitated for a moment. Then she said:

"They are the jewels of the Queen of England; and until the Pope says I am not, I am Queen of England. They belong with me, wherever I go."

When the order came, very promptly, to remove herself and her personal belongings, out of London and to The More, a manor which had once been Wolsey's, near to Harrow Hill, she took her clothes, the silver and the linen that she had brought from Spain, and the jewels of the Queen of England.

She did not look upon her banishment from Court as final. It was part of the waiting time; and the order for it had been given in part to punish her for not agreeing to go to Cambrai, in part to pacify Anne for the delay which the putting into practice of Cranmer's schemes must involve. The move had something to recommend it; the last period of waiting would be spent in private, away from watchful eyes, pitying or scornful, away from gossip, away from the scarcely veiled insolence of Anne and her friends; but it was also away from Henry and although for a long time now their appearances together had seemed to be a cruel mockery of a former happy relationship, she found herself missing the almost daily meetings. Sitting or standing beside him, on public occasions, she had been aware of constraint, the constant wonder as to his mood, what he would say and in what tone; but there had been many occasions, twice, thrice a week, when anonymous among her ladies, she could sit and watch him and admire, and slip away from this troubled present into memories of the happier past. He still jousted with skill and vigour, and though "Sir Loyal Heart" had been replaced by the cryptic, "Declare I Dare Not," she still liked to see him win. It was the same in the tennis court, where, stripping off his doublet, he revealed one of the fine linen shirts that she had sewn for him. Had Anne ever made him a shirt? She never saw him as a middle-aged man, a little heavier, a little slower, redder in the face, shorter of breath. For her his image was fixed and immutable, and with no danger of a surly, chilling, or merely formal word to spoil the illusion, she could still watch him with love. There would be no more of that.

She accepted the irony of The More as her place of residence. One of Wolsey's properties. *De mortuis nil nisi bonum,* but long before Wolsey, in a dark November had halted, and died at

Leicester Abbey on his way back from York to trial in London, she had forgiven him. Like everybody else, she believed that Wolsey had died of a broken heart, surviving by only a few months the withdrawal of Henry's favour. Wolsey had so stoically concealed his ills, his ominous symptoms, that this belief was current. Sometimes Katharine thought seriously about this —the King turned his face from Wolsey and Wolsey died; he has now turned his face from me and I am not dead, have no intention of dying. Am I less loving than the butcher's son? Put that thought aside. I am not yet forty-six; Wolsey was fifty-five; he had no hope. I have. Clement will issue his verdict and I shall be reinstated.

She held to this conviction so firmly that at Christmas 1531, the first of her banishment, two visitors from Venice, having been entertained first at Court and then, by their own wish moving on to The More, declared that in the latter place the food was better and the diversions merrier.

Only those close to her, and, closest of all, Maria de Moreto, saw that at The More Katharine did not flourish. She grew paler, more susceptible to cold and to little ills. She never lost faith or hope or confidence or even good humour, but there was a difference. Maria de Moreto who had herself survived love's loss, remembered her own lessening of gusto and resilience, her own settling down into resignation. Chapuys, still allowed to visit and more punctilious now, wrote to his master, amongst many other things, "The Queen has aged much in few months."

18

It was life in a void. She was allowed visitors—anyone except Mary. Every time that she considered this restriction it would seem to be an act of spite on Henry's part. But that was so sickening a thought that she could not accept it; such malice was incompatible with the Henry she knew. She would remind herself that years ago she had felt in the same way about Mary's being sent to Ludlow, but Mary's stay there had been good for her, good for the Welsh. One must not cherish destructive suspicions. It was better, surely better, at this point, for Mary, with her passionate nature, to live quietly, to continue her studies and not to be too closely involved in a situation which must—and soon—be resolved.

Other visitors made the twelve-mile journey from the centre of London to The More; but in their manner, in their words, what was said, and what was not said, Katharine detected an unwelcome sympathy, a kind of finality, as though she were stricken with some fatal disease that could only end in death. Nobody had any real news to impart and everybody was just a little too eager to remark upon the amenities of The More, which, like every other place upon which Wolsey had laid a hand, was comfortable, handsome, well-appointed. Doomed to death, but on a good bed, under a soft blanket.

To this general behaviour there were two welcome exceptions. The Countess of Willoughby who had been Maria de Salinas came and did not adopt the death-bedside manner. Far from it. She had no eye for the pleasant view, no praise for the painted ceilings. "You will not be here long," she said cheerfully. "His Holiness must decide soon, if only to forestall this ridiculous scheme of putting so much authority into the hands of the English church."

"That is still spoken of?"

"Constantly, Your Grace. The Archbishop of Canterbury is much opposed to it. But he is old, and ailing. And if things are allowed to drift until Cranmer is appointed. . . ."

"Cranmer?"

"He is said to be earmarked for the honour. May I ask what sounds like an impertinent question?"

"I have known you in many moods, Maria, but never impertinent."

"Have you written to the Pope and to the Emperor, urging a decision soon?"

"Many times. I have written with my own hand: and Messire Chapuys almost always includes some plea for a speedy settlement in his communications."

"I think," the Countess said, "that it would be wise to write again. The King himself blows hot and cold on this matter. He can see where the putting of so grave a decision into an English church court might lead. But when Warham dies and Cranmer succeeds him . . ." She finished the sentence with an eloquent movement of her hands. Then she added, "When promotion results from the putting forward of an idea, that idea will be put forward. And a sheep in wolf's clothing is a notoriously dangerous animal."

"Cranmer?" Katharine said again.

"Cranmer," the Countess said. "He even looks like a sheep. But in return for the mitre he would act like a wolf and carry the King with him."

"I will write yet again," Katharine said. "Maria, you go back to London?"

"On my way home. For one night only."

"Will you take, or send a message to Messire Chapuys for me? Tell him that I should be glad to see him at the earliest possible moment convenient to him."

"Most gladly," the Countess said.

Seeing Katharine, even paler and much preoccupied, writing, writing, Maria de Moreto said, "Is it something that *she* said to worry Your Grace?"

"The other Maria? Oh no. It is something I must do before Messire Chapuys' next visit."

"And that will not be yet. He was here only five days ago."

Chapuys had carefully spaced out his visits, frequent enough not to let the Queen feel that she was neglected, not frequent enough to merit Henry's disapproval. On his visits he never admired the view, the wall hangings or the special scented rushes on the floor—the very same rushes as had been spread, as a tribute to the occasion, on the floor at Baynard's Castle all those years ago. Wolsey had ordered that all his residences should be supplied with them and since nobody had ever cancelled the order and since Suffolk people were slow to change, the rushes were still cut and despatched to all the places which had once belonged to the great Cardinal. The bill was mounting. . . .

Chapuys never mentioned the comfort, indeed the luxury, in which she was housed; he never told her that she looked well. He reported what he thought was relevant and withheld what he thought might disturb, and always managed somehow to convey his belief that her cause was right and that her sojourn at The More would not be long. She had found his visits very heartening.

Chapuys was well aware that Thomas Cromwell who had taken over many of Thomas Wolsey's functions—but not all, and certainly not Wolsey's place in the King's heart—had taken on and even elaborated the Cardinal's spy system, and riding out to The More for the second time within a week, he knew that he should be ready with some excuse that could be offered, not extracted. Katharine handed him that excuse; two letters, folded but not sealed; one to the Emperor, one to the Pope.

"To be despatched in all haste, Messire. That is why I troubled you. My own impatience for a settlement, great as it is, is as nothing beside the need for some positive action before the see of Canterbury changes hands."

He wondered, on the fringe of his mind, who had told her that Warham was ailing, Cranmer almost certain to follow him. He himself had refrained from mentioning such matters. But he was not surprised that she knew. The King might say that if he thought that his cap knew his mind he would throw it on the fire, but there were those about him who, unlike the cap, had eyes, ears, tongues. They might not know his mind, but they could observe his attitudes.

"They shall be sent," Chapuys said, taking the two letters, "and if I can arrange it, make better speed than usual."

"Once," she said, "but before your time, Messire, I sent not a letter, but a message which reached Valladolid, from London in fourteen days."

Impossible. And quite impossible to believe, Chapuys thought. And again he was reminded of his mother. Women, looking back to circumstances happier than their present ones, tended to exaggerate; his mother had often said, "And when your father was alive we had meat every day, sometimes twice."

"I cannot promise such swift delivery, Your Grace," he said. But he looked at the unsealed letters and had a thought, just a little thought. "I will do what I can," he said.

He went straight to Henry and said, "Your Grace I was last week at The More on a routine visit—my master being interested in his aunt's health and well-being. Today I was there again. Summoned to take charge of these letters. I ask Your Grace's permission to send them on."

Henry eyed the two packets, unsealed, addressed in Katharine's unmistakable hand, bold, flourishing, rather unfeminine. He had a faint sickish feeling, remembering how that writing had come to him, with faithful regularity, almost twenty years ago, when he was in France, at war; the news of Flodden. . . .

He said, more petulantly than he had ever yet spoken to Chapuys, "Send them on, Messire, send them on. Do not flap them at me. I am not in the habit of reading letters addressed to other persons."

"I have read them both," Chapuys said. "They are harmless.

Both urge the desirability of a speedy decision. Both refer to Your Grace in terms of respect and affection."

And that, Henry thought, is the very devil of it. The woman I no longer care for, *in that way*, the woman who failed me, regards me with respect and affection; the one I crave for, who might bear my son. . . . No, even to himself he would not admit it. Anne was prudish, cautious, she would not admit that she loved him . . . but he was sure that if only she could be sure, that once their union was sanctioned, once he was made free of her bed, the fires of passion, so long banked, would blaze into an unimaginable glory.

"I agree with the need for haste," he said, "I reciprocate the respect and affection. Despatch the letters, Messire. But do not hope for a speedy answer. Clement's indecisiveness is hereditary. His father could never make up his mind to marry his mother and give the boy a name."

Chapuys was old enough, schooled enough not to wince, but he was shocked by this irreverence. It was true that Clement was illegitimate, but it was not a fact that a faithful son of the Church would mention in *that* tone of voice. More than anything yet—more than the calling of the newly assembled Parliament, the Reform Parliament, more than the intention to appoint Cranmer, such a remark showed what was in the King's mind. Unless the Pope decided soon the English church would be lost to Rome. Perhaps it was already too late. . . .

Chapuys said dispassionately, "Delay is always exasperating. Your Grace, it would speed communication to some degree if my post-bag were not delayed at Dover."

"Has it ever been?" Henry's surprise was genuine. Neither Wolsey who had instituted the spy system, nor Cromwell who had inherited it, had felt it necessary to inform their master of every squalid little trick they practised.

"I can think of no other reason for some tardiness, Sire."

"I shall personally give orders that in future your bag is to be taken straight from the horse to the ship readiest to sail."

"I shall be grateful," Chapuys said, giving no sign of jubilation. In future he would be able to express himself freely, to issue definite warnings instead of conveying hints. He had no doubt that Henry would honour his promise. The King of England—especially where his marriage tangle was concerned—was capable of acting the humbug; though even there he probably deceived himself as well as others: but he was not the man to deal in petty lies or shabby tricks. Indeed, Chapuys reflected, this whole sorry business was the result of a kind of clumsy candour on his part. There were many men in positions of power, known to Chapuys, who would never have breathed a word about the doubt as to the legality of the marriage. An unwanted wife was easily got rid of. One had only to impregnate a pair of gloves with arsenic, exclaim over the resultant rash and offer ointment containing the same poison. Death was then certain, suspicion unlikely. The vanity of women led them to try almost any concoction, however vile, in order to whiten and soften their hands. The dead woman, poor lady, had tried something which produced unhealable sores; and presently the widower married again.

Compared with what he might have done, Henry's actions had been honest and straightforward; and in Chapuys' eyes it was greatly in his favour that in a material sense he had not dealt harshly with Katharine; she was comfortably housed, properly attended, surrounded by her personal belongings, still wearing the sapphires, the rubies, diamonds and pearls of the Queen of England. Many an autocrat, opposed as Henry had been, would have brought some physical pressure to bear on a helpless woman who had so obstructed and defied him.

With his lawyer's habit of looking at every aspect, Chapuys considered the possibility that Henry was anxious not to do, or even to say, anything that would leave unexpungeable bitterness should Clement declare the marriage good, and order Henry back to his wife. This was still possible. Until the break was made, the King of England was a Catholic; it was within the Pope's power to order him to send Mistress Boleyn from Court. But time was running out. "The Lady is all powerful here," Chapuys wrote; Pope and Emperor would know what that meant, Lutheranism, thinly disguised. "The Queen," Chapuys wrote, "is the most virtuous woman I have ever known, and the highest hearted." He urged, with increasing insistence as the year 1532 added week to week, the necessity of a decision before the situation had deteriorated beyond repair.

In May, Sir Thomas More, who had become Chancellor of England after Wolsey's fall, resigned from his office. He pleaded failing health and even Henry, accepting the resignation most unwillingly, could not be blind to the fact that little more than two years in office had taken the flesh from More's bones, lined his face, greyed his hair, made his step heavier. They had not enriched him; he had never taken a bribe, and of the vast sums he had handled not a penny had stuck to his fingers. Henry was concerned for him and knowing that More would never accept an outright gift, moved, secretly and tactfully, so that More was voted by a Convocation of Clergy, a gift of £5000. More said, "Throw it into the Thames," a thing he had said of lesser bribes, and went into private life to live on £100 a year, and that none too certain. "My poor women folk," he said, "must learn to perform the miracle of the five loaves and two fishes. Thousands of other women have."

Everyday some women who had failed to perform such miracles, and men who had no woman to do it for them, gathered about the kitchen door at The More. The good Queen was known to be charitable. The stream of visitors might dwindle, but the beggars came, together with pedlars, hoping to find, in a household of ladies, customers for needles, thread and other feminine gear. And there were entertainers, contortionists, men with dancing dogs and bears, minstrels, strolling players, mixed with the beggars with nothing to offer but their rags and their sores.

Among them were many who, in any age, in any form of society, would have been paupers, but there were others, good workmen now unemployed because the land they had tilled had been turned into sheep-runs. One man could tend the sheep that grazed on land that would have needed twenty to plough and sow and reap. Years earlier More had written, in his fantasy *Utopia*, against the enclosure of ploughland for sheep. "Your sheep that were wont to be so meek and tame, and so small eaters, now as I hear say, be become so great devourers and so wild, that eat up and swallow down the very men themselves." Katharine had read the book, and though More had, about this and other subjects, an exaggerated, poetic way of putting things, there was enough truth in it for her to give orders that so long as there was food in the house nobody was to be sent away unfed.

So in the yard there was always some coming and going. It was beneath Maria de Moreto's dignity to go down and listen and gossip, but Francisco Filipez was usually about, and he would pass on to Maria what he had heard, leaving her to be the best judge of what was, or was not, suitable for the Queen's ears. On a sunburnt August day there was news, highly unsuitable, but necessary to relay.

"The Archbishop of Canterbury died," Maria said.

"God rest him," Katharine said. He had been no friend to her, weak, yielding man, accepting the appointment as one of *her* advisers before Blackfriars, but conniving with Wolsey, wishful to bring about a decision favourable to the King. Dead now and gone to his judgement. God rest him.

"There was more to it," Maria de Moreto said, half-turning away, picking up some lace, just washed and ironed by Concepcion, a girl who needed strict supervision. It was a horrible thing to be obliged to say. But if I do not say it, Maria thought, somebody else surely will and maybe with malice. "It is said that with him dead and Cranmer sure of the office, *she* gave in and took the King to her bed." So tactfully as to seem sly, Maria looked up from the lace, saw Katharine's face and quickly looked away again—as she had looked away when, as a child, she had been taken to see an unrepentant heretic burned in Toledo.

Feeling the searing flame of jealousy, momentarily consumed by it, Katharine wondered at herself: tried to reason. Henry had slept with Elizabeth Taillebois, and with Mary Boleyn. But that had been different; they had received the falling crumbs from a rich table; they had not been wooed, or waited for. Anne had been wooed, Anne had been waited for and when the consummation came. . . . Oh God, God! Deliver me from carnal thoughts . . .

She said, "And who, in our yard, was so well-informed?"

"A button-vendor," Maria said. "He has a cousin, a server at Hampton Court. *They* were there, to watch some entertainment on the river. They left together; the King went to her apartment and did not leave until morning. And that has never happened before." Maria put down the lace, with which no fault could be found and put her hands to her face. She did not cry easily; tears were an appeal for help and she had learned, long ago, that when no help was available tears were useless and merely made your head ache. But now a few scalding drops squeezed their way out and fell over her hands. She shed them partly from sympathy, partly from rage at the injustice of life.

Katharine did not weep at all. Once the fury of jealousy had passed she tried to think coolly over what this news meant and what it implied. Anne had held Henry all this time by saying "No"; to have yielded now must indicate that she was either very sure of herself, or very desperate. Which? And having gained the thing he craved would Henry become more, or less, infatuated? She considered the possibility of their coupling producing a child; a son. Another bastard, she told herself firmly; no different from the Duke of Richmond. I am Henry's wife and Queen of England—until the Pope says otherwise. And Mary is heir.

An answer to her speculation as to the effect of the yielding upon Henry, came quite soon—again through backdoor gossip. The King was going to give Nan Bullen a rank of her own, something no woman had ever had before. She was going to be a Duke or some other thing, very grand. It was going to be a great occasion with free food and wine in the London streets. Maria de Moreto, reporting this, said:

"Did I not say from the first that she was a witch?"

Katharine, with the wry humour which was sometimes her

last standby, said, "If so, she must be very powerful, Maria. To become a Duke she must change her sex; and then where would they be?" But the news—even garbled as it was—was a blow to the small, secret hope that she had cherished; which was that once between the sheets Henry might have found Anne no different, nothing special, just another woman in a bed. That he planned to ennoble her suggested that she had lost no ground by yielding; and it held a darker implication—that he seriously intended to marry her and was providing against the accusation that he had married a commoner. And that would be bigamy; a graver sin than mere adultery.

If those about her knew when this ceremony took place they did not mention it; but she knew; there were several days when the beggars, the dancing dogs and bears and their masters deserted the courtyard at The More and went to the richer pastures of the city streets. Eagerly as Katharine had awaited Chapuys' visits, she had never been more impatient than during that September. He came, disheartened because he had no news for her and because he saw, as clearly as anyone what the recent ceremony might imply, and because here he was, lively, active and committed but chained down to the service of a master with feet of lead. If the Emperor had only moved the Pope would have moved too. The wish to be powerful, in order to help and the realisation of his impotence, took Eustache Chapuys back over the years to when he was eight years old, longing to be a man, to earn, to provide and able only to gather driftwood. He intended not to talk about the ceremony at Windsor, but Katharine herself began to question him about it almost as soon as he was in her presence. Woman enough to ask, "And how did she look?"

"Not beautiful—though there were some who said so, of course. Not beautiful; but impressive."

"I can imagine it. As though she were honouring the occasion, rather than being honoured by it."

"Exactly so, Your Grace."

"And what is her rank now? One hears such foolish things. I was told that she was to be a Duke."

"That I never heard. Marquis, yes; the title has been mentioned since no woman has ever before been created a peer in her own right. But the patent read Marchioness of Pembroke. And there was one interesting omission which has caused some speculation. Ordinarily such a patent of nobility, providing for the title to be passed on to the heir, says *legally begotten*. In this instance the words were omitted. I have thought about that omission . . . and it seems to me just possible that the King is providing, beforehand, for the birth of another illegitimate child."

"I had thought that the ennoblement could be a prelude to marriage. But the omission is certainly significant," Katharine said thoughtfully.

"His Grace must know that any form of marriage he goes through in the present circumstance would be bigamous." He paused for a second and then put into words something he had never actually said before. "Your Grace knows that in this matter I am wholly on your side. Your cause is just and I would stop at nothing to prosper it. Yet there are times when even I feel sorry for the King. Seven years ago he asked a simple question, and still awaits an answer. And at the moment his position is exceptionally difficult."

"How so, Messire?"

"He is about to make a visit to France and he has been informed that even if he takes the Marchioness of Pembroke with him, she will not be received or acknowledged in any way. He was obliged to inform her of this and she felt much insulted. Her reception of the snub is, of course, hearsay, but my sources of information are usually reliable."

"So much unhappiness! And it could all have been avoided had the King only resigned himself and accepted his daughter as his heir."

True, up to a point, Chapuys reflected, but an oversimplification. The Concubine—as he now called Anne in his mind and in his letters—plainly had some extraordinary hold over the King. The cynics who had said that once she abandoned virtue she would be abandoned, had plainly been wrong and in London bets were in favour of a marriage as soon as she proved herself capable of child-bearing. Even Clement, while still hesitating to declare that Henry was lawfully married to Katharine, had openly said that should he marry Anne Boleyn he would be excommunicated. What a muddle!

Before the end of September the Dukes of Norfolk and Suffolk came to The More with a request which showed Katharine how far Henry was prepared to go in the effort to soothe Anne's injured feelings. They had come, they said, by the King's order, to take away the Queen's Jewels.

Considering what she had already lost, Henry's love and companionship, her place at Court, the society of her daughter, the removal of a few coloured stones, however valuable and pretty, might seem a trivial thing; but she had always taken a pleasure —almost sensuous—in jewels, and these ornaments held symbolism. They had always belonged to and been worn by the woman who was Queen of England and by nobody else. And Henry himself had poured them into her lap in those first days of love. She did not intend to part with them without a struggle and taking advantage of the fact that the Dukes carried no written order, she sent them emptyhanded away.

Next day Henry's own Groom of the Stole, Sir Henry Norris, brought a written order signed by the King. He was one of the young men who cherished a romantic passion for Anne and managed to blurt out that the Marchioness of Pembroke had not asked for the jewels; she had never asked anything of the King, except marriage. But there were, Katharine knew, other ways of demanding than reaching out a hand and saying, "Give me." She could imagine Anne saying bitterly, "So, if I go with you to France, I go as a camp follower," and Henry saying, "No. You go wearing the Queen's jewels."

So the lovely sparkling trinkets were taken away and she was left with the gold collar she had brought from Spain and her wedding ring. Looking down on *that*, she thought with a certain tartness: This is the only Queen's jewel of any real value and it is mine until. . . . Oh, God, move Clement to decide soon. . . .

Chapuys wrote to his master that if things were allowed to drift further, only war could prevent schism. And the drift went on.

19

News that Mary was ill, simply ill of no recognisable sickness, brought dismay and concern, but no surprise. She had always tried to think of Mary, at Hatfield, at Beaulieu, as removed from the main, turbulent stream, sheltered by Lady Salisbury, busy with her books. But Mary's outburst at Greenwich could not be forgotten. Mary was not one to be easily sheltered or to take refuge in self-deception.

The one thing above all others which girls facing the onset of womanhood needed was a centre of security; and that Mary lacked entirely. Her father had failed her; her mother was separated from her; her status was in the balance; she was either Princess of Wales and heir to England or an illegitimate child, ineligible for marriage, lucky to be provided with the necessities of life. Katharine, considering these things, could look back and see how fortunate she and her sisters had been, at one stage in their youth. They had known what the future held and they had not foreseen upheaval or disaster; disaster had come, but at least not until they were full grown.

When she wrote to Mary she wrote cheerfully, urging patience and trust in God; and Mary's replies had been loving, cheerful, and completely unrevealing. She had never mentioned the situation in which she and her mother found themselves, or her health, except to say that it was good. Now she was ill.

Chapuys, bringing the news, hastened on to say, "But the King sent his own physician—Dr. Bartelot. And he is a brave man. He said that the Princess ailed nothing that he had a cure for. She was in low spirits and suffering from the separation from Your Grace, her mother. For this information the King gave him twenty pounds. And volunteered an excuse for the separation. He said that to allow you to be together would increase the hardness of heart towards him."

"There he is mistaken. The one thing I have always urged upon Mary is obedience. I have myself set an example. Save in the one matter, which is one of conscience, I have never been other than subservient to his will . . ." She thought for a moment and, as always, the better aspect of Henry came uppermost. "He sent his own doctor . . ."

Chapuys, whose own attitude had hardened lately, said:

"Is that to be wondered at? The Princess Mary at this moment is the only legal heir he has. Talk in London is rife, and wild. The Concubine is now with child—that I can say with certainty. With less certainty I can say that there is talk of a marriage, last month, in January. This I cannot, with all my resources, verify. Who performed it and where, I know no more than you. But I do know that the new Archbishop of Canterbury is proposing to gather some kind of court together and to declare the marriage legal—even retrospectively."

"Is that possible?"

"Anything, in these days, is possible. Your Grace, may I speak with a frankness that may, to you, sound brutal?"

"You have always been frank with me, Messire Chapuys. Brutal never. But I am listening."

"To what I am about to say, I have given most serious consideration. The present situation, as we have just seen, has had an ill effect on the Princess' health, and it would be idle to pretend that the separation and your mode of life here have done anything to improve your own. And things are likely to worsen." He looked around the handsome, well-furnished apartment, and then back at Katharine's carefully controlled face. "I know that the King is utterly determined to have this child born in wedlock, or at least in such semblance of it as will be acceptable to the English. To this end the new Archbishop of Canterbury proposes to set up a court in some out-of-the-way place—Dunstable has been mentioned; and there, with all speed, your marriage will be declared null and void. This will have a very unfavourable effect upon your position. I fear that you will suffer much humiliation, possibly even some discomfort." He paused deliberately.

She said equably, "I have been humiliated already. And I spent my early years in circumstances where comfort was the last consideration. I must accept what comes, having no alternative."

"But, Madam, you have." He leaned a little forward and his cool eyes glittered. "I have gone through the formality of resigning my post. I have begun to pack. I have bespoken passage for myself *and my household* on a German ship, sailing from Tilbury on Maundy Thursday. No questions will be asked as to the identity of those who embark with me. The Princess will be at Hatfield, you will be here. A long, hasty ride for you both, but not, I think, beyond your powers."

"You are proposing that my daughter and I should run away?"

"Escape," Chapuys corrected. "While there is time. Once on the Continent, you can appeal in person, to the Emperor, to the Pope. The fact that you have been driven, by intolerable circumstances, to seek refuge will shock them both into a proper realisation of the seriousness of what is going on here. Your Grace has written, I have written; I can only conclude that in the press of multitudinous concerns neither of them has properly estimated the danger. I am certain that your appearance and that of the Princess, as refugees at the Imperial Court will lead to immediate action to reinstate you. It is a desperate resort, but the only one left to us now."

She said, "Allow me to think for a moment." She closed her eyes and placed one hand over them. God, God, help me to think clearly, to decide rightly. . . . This man is my friend, he is well-informed, experienced, cool-headed, should I be guided by what he says?

It was a long moment. Then she opened her eyes and folded her hands in her usual posture.

"You mean well, Messire, and for your care for me I thank you from my heart. But to such extreme action I see no end but war. I could only be reinstated by armed force. The last thing I desire. This is not a matter to be decided by who can put the most men into some battlefield. It is a legal business, to be settled by lawyers."

"It *was*," Chapuys said harshly. "It is beyond that now. Your case is about to be decided by a procedure absolutely outside the law as we understand the word; outside the Church that we recognise—a court of English ecclesiastics owing no allegiance to Rome will take its directions from Cranmer whose only law is the King's wish. And this court you will be called upon to attend. It will be argued that for your own convenience you should move to Ampthill, a place within easy reach of Dunstable."

Ampthill was her own manor; she had once offered the stewardship to Francisco Filipez. The man appointed, when Francisco refused, had said the house was too ruinous for occupation, and that was years ago.

She said, "If I am ordered to Ampthill, I shall go. I shall not attend Archbishop Cranmer's court. A case still *sub judicia* at Rome cannot be tried at Dunstable, or anywhere else in the world."

Admirable; immensely courageous, but utterly foolhardy. He said as earnestly as he had ever spoken in his life, "Madam, I do *beg* you to consider. For five years you have obstructed the King—he has been—I will not say magnanimous, but cautious. He has sustained himself with the hope that Clement's final decision might free him. He knows now that by this secret marriage and the setting up of a court to justify it, he has put himself into a position where no favourable verdict for him can ever be given. And the Concubine, never at any time gentle, and now about to bear, perhaps, a prince, will take vengeance on you. It would surprise me very little if the word *contumacious*, applied to you at Blackfriars, very shortly became *traitorous*."

To that she said nothing and he went on. "Even I shall not be allowed to visit you freely. Ambassadors do not wait upon private ladies. Your Grace, unless you set sail on Maundy Thursday, I foresee nothing for you but hardship and misery."

"For a time," she said. "Until the Pope decides. And you, Messire Chapuys, I shall always regard as my especial friend; and although I cannot avail myself of what you offer, I shall always be grateful for it."

"You reject the plan entirely?"

"I must."

Inconsequently he felt as Campeggio had felt, a strong desire to hit her. A good plan, cunningly made, backed by reason, expediency, good sense, brought to nothing.

"I do hope," Katharine said, "that in your next post, Messire, you find no such difficult problems."

He said bleakly, "My resignation was a blind. I shall stay in England now until I am recalled. And that will not be soon. My master may not heed my letters, but he knows my worth. I shall see this thing out. And since you cannot find it in your heart to avail yourself of the escape I offered, there is one more thing that I should mention. Had you been prepared to come away, I should not have bothered you with it. As it is: Has anyone ever, at any time, suggested that you should have contact with a nun of St. Sepulchre's, in Canterbury?"

The abrupt change of subject confused her for a moment.

"Elizabeth Barton. The holy nun of Kent?"

"That is the woman. Did Your Grace ever receive her, write to her?"

"No. She once—this was when I was still in London—sent a message, offering to use her prophetic vision on my behalf. . . . There was something, just something Messire Chapuys that made me feel that for all her talk of conversing with angels and being able to locate lost property, she was fraudulent; or at least, if not fraudulent, more inspired by devils than by angels. I refused to see her, or to communicate with her."

"Thank God for that," Chapuys said. "Sir Thomas More and Fisher of Rochester were not so careful. Her visions, her prophecies and ecstasies attracted them—among others. And she, poor silly woman, will be used, when the time comes. Cromwell seldom misses a trick. Unless I am very wrong in my reckoning she will be arraigned as a witch; and those who have consorted with her will be, with her, condemned. Her latest pronouncement was that if the King marries in your lifetime, he will die, within seven months. That—and the consorting with a woman who said such a thing—could easily be regarded as treason, of another sort. I am glad that you avoided that trap."

"Sir Thomas More," she said, "could talk himself out of a foxhole and have all the bystanders laughing as he did it. Bishop Fisher's integrity is graved on his face. As for the King . . . No. That I will not believe. She cannot know. God alone decides the hour of our death. . . ."

Chapuys had been right about Dunstable, right about Ampthill. In May 1533, May always in England thought to be the merry month, the beginning of summer, but this year cold and wet, more dismal than any, even old men, remembered, she was ordered to remove to Ampthill.

It was a part of England that she had never seen before; rather as though England were showing another face, flat, sparsely populated, infinitely dreary under the grey skies and the rain; only the oaks, standing solid and putting forth as oaks always did in spring, the reddish-ochre hues of autumn, redeemed the bleak landscape and the decaying house from complete desolation. Dunstable was about twelve miles away in distance; the court about five days distant in time.

But hard on her heels, so close behind her that they arrived before she had arranged herself, her household and her belongings, came the Dukes of Norfolk and Suffolk, bringing as Norfolk said gruffly, her last chance to behave reasonably. "His Grace calls upon you, Madam, as his *subject*, to obey him and renounce the title of Queen. If you will be amenable, he will deal with you and your daughter more generously than you could expect."

It was a last-minute attempt to avoid the coming together of the Dunstable court and it showed that in his heart Henry was not sure of the legality of what he was about to do. He might brag and bluster and threaten, but he had no real desire to make the breach with Rome.

"His Grace already knows my answer, my lords."

Inwardly Norfolk groaned; he had known it was useless; a man might as well talk to a stone. But he was a pious, orthodox Catholic and viewed with dismay the changes about to take place. It was useless for the King to argue that no fundamental change would be made, that the English Church, with himself as its head would hold the same beliefs, follow the same ritual. When one said, "I believe in the Holy Catholic Church," it meant the one, indivisible Church of Rome; not some half-baked, mongrel affair devised by Cranmer.

Norfolk, having a little trouble with his own conscience, looked at Katharine with distaste and thought: All because I persuaded her to take that flibberty-gibbet niece of mine into her household. All because two stubborn, stupid women want to be called Queen. Devil take them both.

Suffolk said, "Disobedience to such a direct order can be regarded as treason. It could take you to the block."

Her eyes narrowed a little and the corners of her mouth lifted. "From you, my lord, such a warning must come from the heart." He had been near the block himself, actually in the Tower, for marrying Henry's sister.

"Times have changed since then," Suffolk said, answering the half smile and the thought, not the words.

And that was all too true. There had been a time when Henry's rage died of its own violence, the stamping and the shouting acted as a purge.

"If you are still set," Norfolk said; "you must take the consequences. You will henceforth be known as the Princess Dowager. Your income will be cut by three-quarters; your household reduced. And you will be held in custody. Lord Mountjoy, who has served as your Chamberlain, will in future be your custodian and govern everything."

This was what Chapuys had foreseen when he urged escape while there was still time.

She said, with an infuriating placidity, "Fortunately my needs nowadays are small. But I would assure you, and my husband, the King, that if I am reduced to begging in the streets, I shall do so as *Queen of England*—until the Pope says otherwise."

Suffolk seemed about to say something, but Norfolk pulled his sleeve and said, "Let be. Enough time has been wasted."

Katharine said, "This is desolate country; food for men and bait for horses is hard to come by. Allow me to offer you hospitality while I am still in a position to do so. We will not speak of things likely to ruin digestion."

Norfolk thought: That niece of mine, Tom Boleyn's daughter will never attain queenliness if she wears the crown for fifty years. Suffolk, who had married a Royal princess, thought sourly: It is something they are born with!

To Lord Mountjoy, uncomfortable in his new role, Katharine said, "I trust, my lord, that to me you will be as good a custodian as you have been Chamberlain. I am afraid that upon you will fall the task of making ends meet. Despite some practice at the art, I was never good at it." Her acceptance of the new situation made him more uncomfortable than ever. He had no intention of acting as gaoler to a lady already deeply wronged. Making ends meet was another matter; sometimes in the past he had wondered whether she could even count. He would stay long enough to get her affairs in order and then resign.

With the minimum of fuss and publicity, Cranmer opened his court in Dunstable, the little market town where another Henry—first of the name—had founded an Augustian Priory and built a palace. The Priory still stood, the palace had fallen to ruin, and all about Dunstable the wind, blowing from the Chiltern slopes, tugged at the growing corn and lengthened and strengthened the straw, making it desirable for thatchers. In that quiet place the verdict was given. The King of England had never been, could not have been, married to the wife of his deceased brother. Therefore his marriage in the previous January—he being a bachelor and Anne Boleyn a spinster, was sound and legal. The offspring of this marriage would be legitimate.

"So here we are," Maria de Moreto said grimly. She looked around the dilapidated place which, even in its best days, had been intended more for defence than for comfort. Beyond the windows the countryside lay flat under the rain; indoors in addition to the pervading damp there were places where the moisture leaked in. "With Your Grace's rheumatism growing worse every day and everybody sneezing and coughing." It seemed to her that life had made a full circle, she was back where she started, living in penury and discomfort; but it was worse in this detestable, sunless climate.

"We are no worse off than before," Katharine said, meaning that the court's decision had altered nothing. "And Lord Mountjoy has promised me that he will urge a move to some healthier place."

Maria did not doubt his goodwill but she felt that if a move were made it would be to some worse place.

Certainly Ampthill was not healthy. When Katharine stepped out of bed on to a pin which had lodged between the floorboards, the trivial little puncture did not heal; a circle of swollen, purplish flesh surrounded a green-lipped, festering hole; and she was in bed, in considerable pain when Lord Mountjoy, obeying instructions direct from London, came to tell her that she must recognise the Dunstable court's verdict. For the first time he addressed her as Your Royal Highness, and Katharine raised her hand. Since his change of function he had been very tactful, therefore she now spoke to him gently:

"My lord, I am Queen of England, and this is my bedchamber. Those who enter it and wish to have speech with me, must address me correctly."

He said plaintively, "It makes things very difficult, for everyone. An order direct from the King is not lightly to be disobeyed."

She would not look at him or give any sign of hearing what he said. She stared at the wall. Her foot throbbed.

"My position is untenable. . . ." he said. "His Grace has ordered me . . ." Finally in a desperate bid for her attention, by way of curiosity, he said, "And there is news from London. . . ."

She thought, as she always did: Mary! The Pope? But she had said that she would not listen to anyone who denied her her title, and she continued to ignore him. Mountjoy, who shared the affection felt for her by most people who came into close contact with her, who admired and pitied her, felt a flicker of exasperation. It was all so futile. She had put up a splendid fight, and been beaten, being one against many and with no ally of any worth. Continued resistance now would only injure her further, whereas a grain of amenability . . . Well, perhaps, when she heard the news, she would realise. With this in mind, he said, "Your Grace. . . ."

"I hear you," Katharine said.

"Queen Anne was crowned on June the first . . ." Not—the purely feminine thought would intrude—all in virginal white, with pearls, wearing the Orient crown.

"To deny her title is now treason."

"I do so deny it, my lord. In Christendom a man cannot have two wives, or a country two queens. His Holiness has not yet refuted my claim to be wife and Queen."

"Your Grace," having said it once, he could say it again, "if I may say so, this is an unreasonable stand, and can only do you damage. May I tell you something—it is not something I was ordered to say, but it is a little straw showing how the wind blows. Gossip, but it should not be underrated. The lady whom I am compelled to call Queen Anne, for her progress from the Tower of London to her Coronation, chose to use your barge. She had your arms and insignia burned off and her own painted on . . ."

"Natural enough. Compared with a husband, a crown, a barge is negligible."

"But His Grace was *enraged*. He said she had no right. He said that the arms were yours, as a Princess of Spain, and though a properly constituted English court could, and did, deny that you were Queen of England, that you were Princess of Spain nobody could deny . . . There was a quarrel of some ferocity. Your Grace, does this not indicate to you that His Grace retains respect, affection . . . things which in the future could be put to good purpose? I am a simple man, neither cleric, lawyer or politician, but it is clear to me that with the modicum of acceptance, you could vastly better your situation."

"But I have known that all along." The slightly self-mocking smile which made those who saw it think how pretty she must have been when she was young, lightened her face. "His Grace told me years ago that if I would say I was not his wife, he would treat me as his sister. But I am his wife. And you, my lord, are temporarily in Satan's guise, offering comfort in return for sacrifice of conscience. And to you I say: Get thee behind me, Satan."

"I was endeavouring," Lord Mountjoy said, "to make it plain that His Grace is not ill-disposed towards you. What I fear is that if you continue intransigent, you may winter here."

"And that is a matter of no importance."

Exasperated again, he said, "But there is another way of looking at it. It is now an offence, a capital offence, to apply to any court outside England."

She shifted the burning, throbbing foot into the temporary solace of another, cooler area of the bed and said, "That can hardly apply to me, unless every act—like a bigamous marriage —is to be made retrospective. My appeal to Rome was made years ago."

Yes, Mountjoy thought; and it was never answered, it never will be. And from here onwards things will worsen for her. And I will have no part in it. I will do her, if I can, one last service, to get her moved from here. . . .

He went about it cunningly, or so he thought. No appeal, no mention of the house falling to ruin or the rain seeping in. Reporting in person to Henry his failure to persuade Katharine to meekness, he said, "Your Grace, Ampthill is the Princess Dowager's own property; and there is an old country saying that every cock crows loudest on his own dunghill. A move might be advisable."

Any move, Mountjoy thought, could only be beneficial; and when he learned that Katharine was to be moved to Buckden, to a palace belonging to the Bishop of Lincoln, he felt that he had done her at least one good service.

20

The move, like everything else that was done in miserable summer, was made in pouring rain. Northeastwards the diminished company plodded through the mire. It was July and the hay, which should have been safely gathered a month since, stood in the meadows still, mouldering and rotting side by side with the fields of barley, wheat, oats and rye, beaten flat and unripening, with harvest only four weeks away.

So they came to the place to which she had been ordered; Buckden, in Huntingdonshire, one of the properties which since ancient times had belonged to the Bishops of Lincoln. It was half fortress, half dwelling place; and passing through the outer gateway, across the moat, under the archway of the inner gatehouse and across the courtyard to the Tower, Katharine, and all those with her, thought that this was a vast improvement upon Ampthill. Solid red brick walls, giving out even on this desolate afternoon a warm glow. Completely deceptive. The rooms assigned to her—called the King's Lodgings—and which King of England, she wondered, had ever lodged there—were as damp as those at Ampthill. The Tower stood with its feet in the moat and the bricks had absorbed the moisture, so that even in the hall, six feet or more above water level, the plaster peeled from the sweating walls and the hangings, some of them old and beautiful, were so rotted that they were unsubstantial as a spider's web. In the room above, her bedchamber, within a week there was mould on her shoes and everything taken out from the heavy clothes chests, leather covered, cedar lined, had a clammy feeling and a mouldy smell. The pains in her fingers and wrists and knees grew worse and the stairs tried her sorely; they came up, very steep and sharp, in a spiral inside one of the round turrets at one corner of the building, and there was no handrail, merely a groove in the sweating wall. Francisco Filipez, helped by the local blacksmith, drove iron stanchions into the wall and slung a rope by which she could haul herself up or steady herself down. On such a stairway no human arm or shoulder could avail, the stairs were too narrow and too cramped. Everybody who mounted or descended them must go alone. Often, on evenings, summer evenings that should have been so warm and kind, as she went down to the chapel, or to the hall, and then came up again to bed, she saw a kind of symbolism in those stairs; the loneliness— and the mute support of the slung rope which faithful hands had rigged.

Outside Buckden, all over England, people facing a ruinous harvest and a winter when bread would be scarce and dear, said that nothing had prospered since the good old Queen was put away. And in London, wherever Anne went, the crowds were silent, sullen and hostile. Henry could not make them cheer; nor could he bear to see Anne fret over the coldness of her reception by the common people and the withdrawal of all the old nobility from Court, on this or that feeble excuse. One day he said to her, "Sweetheart, I shall order the Princess of Wales to come and join your attendants. That will bring the rest flocking back."

Anne said ungratefully, "And who *is* the Princess of Wales?"

"That," he said, "was a slip of the tongue . . . My daughter, the Lady Mary."

Katharine, at Buckden, heard that Mary had been recalled to Court and received the news with mixed feelings. She retained sufficient faith in Henry's paternal fondness to feel that it would be good for Mary to be where he could see her and talk to her rather than be shut away and forgotten. Mary had done nothing to offend him so far, and would, Katharine hoped, be discreet. But, at the same time, being at Court, obliged at every turn to yield precedence to the usurper, would be an ordeal for

Mary, so young and so proud. In many ways Mary's position was worse than her own, she had lived more than half a lifetime and known great happiness; she could afford to await Clement's verdict. Mary was seventeen, an age when girls' thoughts turned to marriage and motherhood—and what suitable match could be made for a young woman in her invidious position? Sometimes, when Katharine's thoughts took this trend, she thought of Reginald Pole, with his good looks, his great gifts and his Plantagenet blood. He had been one of those despatched by Henry to canvass the opinions of the Universities of Europe and was still abroad, in Bologna. He had not married; nor had he taken priest's orders. Katharine knew that Mary was very fond of him, and he would be a suitable husband for her whichever way fortune went. However, from Buckden's semi-imprisonment, she could do nothing except write Mary heartening letters which always included the injunction to obey her father in all things except those respecting conscience.

She also wrote to Chapuys, requesting him to ask for her removal to some other house, less damp and cold; to winter in Buckden, she told him, would impair her health and that of her faithful servants. But although Chapuys went about the business of getting her moved before winter, and used all his diplomatic skill, she was still there in December of 1533 when the Duke of Suffolk came on another special errand, this time ominously accompanied by a posse of armed men.

In September Anne had borne her child—a girl. Henry refused to be daunted; the baby was alive and well, she would have a brother next year. The child was named Elizabeth, after his mother, and given as stately a christening as though she were the prince Henry had hoped for. She was to have, from the first, her own household at Hatfield, and Mary was to be one of her attendants. Mary, stripped down, seeing the honours that had once been hers showered on the harlot's child, was torn in her mind. The baby was innocent of all wrong, and very attractive, especially to a girl who should have been having a child of her own; but to call her *Princess* was to deny her own legitimacy and to make nonsense of Katharine's long, lonely fight; so she said, "I will call her sister and no more."

Henry was touchy; marriage to Anne had not conferred the joy he had expected. No hidden fires had burned. That slender, lithe body, for whose possession he waited so long and given so much, was, once between the sheets, no different from any other.

However, she had cost him so dear that even in his darkest moments he could not bring himself to admit that he had made a bad bargain. He had defied the Pope; he had made himself Head of the Church of England, all in order to put Kate away and marry Anne, who must, must surely, next year, give him the son he needed. He had set his course and must go on. His complaisant Parliament had passed the Act of Succession and everyone of any importance, down to the most petty official, must swear to observe it, to recognise Anne as Queen and Elizabeth as Princess.

Katharine and all her servants must swear. And it was the Duke of Suffolk who was commissioned to force the oath upon them; he set out saying that he would sooner break a leg than go on such an errand.

Arrived at Buckden, he installed himself in the Great Chamber which lay between the Tower and the Chapel, sat himself down with his back to the fire and decided to begin on the servants, feeling that it might give him some advantage if, when he came face to face with her, he could tell her that if she resisted she would be alone.

Her confessor, Llandaff, set the pattern. He could rightly claim to be a Spaniard by birth and therefore unconcerned with oaths of allegiance to anyone other than the Emperor.

"Stand aside," Suffolk said.

The next chaplain was Thomas Abell, who refused point blank.

"I thought that my views were made clear in my book. I hold that England has only one Queen, and that Queen Katharine."

"Stand aside. No; on the other side."

Her doctor was a Spaniard though he spoke perfect English. He had come, he said, to serve, first the Princess of Wales and then the Queen of England and he could not regard anyone else as Queen.

Maria de Moreto, her English perfected years ago, pretended not to understand a word; with Spanish gestures and a fluent flow of Spanish she defeated him entirely. Even when he said, "Stand aside," waving her to where the other Spaniards stood, it needed the doctor to take her by the arm and pull her into position.

So it went on. Stupid people. A kitchen maid, "Sorry, my lord, but if I swore to this, Her Grace'd never forgive me. And when my hand was scalded . . ."

A fluttering little woman, a sempstress, or a laundress. "No, my lord, I don't think I could. I've worked for Her Grace for twenty years. To me she is Queen. I'm sorry to be so disobliging."

He ended with two groups, the Spaniards for whom there was some excuse on one side, the English for whom there was none, on the other. Only three people and they all officials appointed by the Bishop of Lincoln to have a care for his property during the occupation, took the oath. And it was long past dinner time. The short December day was beginning to darken.

"Take the lot to the gateway and lodge them in the alms room." He could no longer bother to distinguish sheep from goats. Let them all cool their heels. "Go across there," he said, indicating the place where Katharine lodged, "and bring the Princess Dowager here to me."

While he waited he went nearer the fire, warming his back and determining to take a high hand with Katharine from the first moment. Women lived too long, that was the trouble; they should die with the bloom of youth still on them and before they learned to be headstrong. He scowled as he remembered his last encounter with a woman over forty and set in her ways. Arrogant, unyielding old bitch. But the Dowager Countess of Willoughby had to be deferred to, the Princess Dowager was in no position to dictate.

Henry's sister, Mary, who had married him for love and whom he had neglected and left alone in a remote manor in Suffolk, had died in June, setting him free to marry for the fourth time. His choice had fallen upon the Countess' daughter, just fifteen, pretty, well-dowered. Her abominable old mother, after raising a number of objections, one absurd—that at forty-nine he was too old—had at last mentioned a most astonishing condition as the price of her consent. Worsted by her and still smarting, Suffolk was prepared to deal harshly with another female who had lived too long.

His messenger came back alone. "My lord, the Queen . . . I ask pardon . . . The Princess Dowager says that she is prepared to receive you."

The distance between the main hall and the Tower was not great, but across the flat plain of Huntingdonshire the wind blew keenly. Under its bite, and the feeling that he had been summoned like a lackey, Suffolk's mood hardened still more.

In the hall of the Tower it was not much warmer and Katharine, huddled into some woollen wrapping, her face pinched and bleached, looked smaller than he remembered and far from formidable.

"I am here," he began without ceremony and speaking in a loud, hectoring way, "to administer to you the oath that all must take or be reckoned traitors. Raise your right hand and say . . ."

She could still, when necessary, speak with authority.

"Stop, my lord. Someone should have informed you. I hold no conversation with those who do not approach and address me correctly."

"I am not here for conversation. I have already arrested your household and if you refuse the oath I shall arrest you, and take you to London with no more regard for your comfort than that of any other traitor. You have been dealt with very leniently but this state of things cannot continue. Now you have been warned. . . ."

She stood still and gave him one hard defiant look, a mute

answer. And then she turned her back and looked out of the window. From it she could see the end of the chapel and beyond it the flat countryside. Sleet was falling now—and if Suffolk kept his threat to drag her to London as a common traitor, she might very well die.

"Take your time to think it over," Suffolk shouted. "You have had five years—but take your time!"

When he saw that she was deliberately ignoring him, red rage exploded, colouring even the whites of his eyes. He began to shout abuse at her, using coarse terms that made her understand how sheltered her life had actually been. And she was sure that Suffolk was exceeding his mandate: Henry had never visualised, and would never countenance this. She almost wished that she had not, by her own resolution, cut herself off from talk with this upstart. She could have turned and with a few words silenced and reduced him. As it was she thought: I must avoid being taken; give him time to come to his senses and remember that though the King does not regard me as his Queen any longer, he still remembers that I am a daughter of Spain and Princess of Wales. The man is railing at me as though I were a fish wife who had given bad measure. And she thought: He is ungrateful too; I pleaded for him when he was in danger of death for marrying Mary . . . But that is neither here nor there. I must get away before, having shouted himself out, he lays his hands, or calls for some minion to lay hands on me. Such an affront I do not think I could survive.

". . . and the King would thank me," Suffolk said, "for ridding him of an obstinate, contumacious bitch."

To her left, only a few paces away, was the door that opened upon the spiral stairs. A strong, heavy door which she had never yet opened for herself—now that she came to think about it she realised that she had never opened any door. . . . But I think I could . . . She took the few swift necessary steps, hauled at the door, felt its weight, thought—I am done—pulled again; slipped through and safe on the far side shot the bolts home. Suffolk heard them screech and beat on the door, yelling and cursing, but the four inch slab of solid oak, heavily nailed, had been designed to resist sterner assaults. It would take a battering ram. Or fire.

"I'll smoke you out, you vixen."

Katharine stood at the foot of the spiralling stairs, trembling and breathless and aware of pain; not the familiar, accepted pain in her knees and fingers and neck, a new one, and worse, in the left side of her chest. She attributed it to the strain of opening and slamming the door. She drew some careful, steadying breaths and then climbed the stairs to her bedroom where silence lay heavy.

For the first time in all her life she was entirely alone. Always before someone had been within call. Now Suffolk had arrested her whole household. She would never see them again. That was a thought to bring tears. She cried a little and then sought her usual refuge—faith in God. She knelt down and prayed for her servants, that they might be spared hurt, or, if they must suffer, be given strength to sustain them in their ordeals. For herself she asked courage to face whatever might happen next and that her faith might not fail, that, whatever the evidence to the contrary, she should continue to believe that God had not deserted her. And as usual, she prayed that the Pope might be guided to pontificate in her favour. Despite everything, she was still convinced that once this happened, Henry would see his error, do penance for his sins and resume life with her to whom he was lawfully wedded.

In the hall below the sergeant who had charge of Suffolk's small force, hurried in, "My lord, come and look!" Some urgency in his manner prevented Suffolk from asking what was to be seen. They hurried to the outer gateway and climbed some stairs. Suffolk went to an aperture in the wall and looked down into the village street.

A crowd of men, work people by their clothes, stood staring at the gateway. They stood silent and still and the only sign that they had come to do anything more than gaze, was the fact that every man carried a weapon of some kind; an axe, a sickle, a hammer; three or four had bows and arrows. The threat was plain; and they already outnumbered the force which Suffolk had judged sufficient to intimidate and if need be, arrest, a few recalcitrant servants.

Suffolk leaned from the opening and shouted:

"Good people. I am the Duke of Suffolk; here on the King's errand."

Not a hat was doffed; not an expression changed. They stared. Suffolk was a man of courage and knew that more dangerous crowds than this had been dispersed by words and a show of confidence.

"I call on you to disperse. In the King's name."

Nobody moved: but one man cleared his throat and said:

"Sir, that b'ain't for you to say. You b'ain't our magistrate."

"Who is?"

They moved then, shuffling, heads together in muttered consultation, murmurous as bees. The spokesman said:

"*Could* be Mr. Alington. Some think different. Who'd you reckon, Bill?"

The names of several local gentry came out in a confused spate; Gostwick, Tanfield, Hynde, Malory, Mordaunt. And there were comments, "Been dead a year, you fool!" "He winter in Huntingdon."

Suffolk recognised with fury the age-old peasant trick.

"Anyway," their leader said in a consoling way, "we don't need none. We b'ain't doing nothing. Just looking."

Two men, better dressed, strolled up; one carried a fowling piece, the other a musket.

Then, from around the bend in the road, came the rattle of hoofs. Relief on its way. There were three riders, a gentleman and two servants. They reined in abruptly. Suffolk shouted. The gentleman took no notice, but bending over the man with the fowling piece, exchanged a few words; turned his horse and rode quickly away followed by his men.

"Who was that? You there, with the fowling piece. The name of that gentleman?"

The man removed his cap.

"My lord, how should I know? He asked was this the London road. I directed him." There was a little subdued laughter.

It was one of those who had authority and had refrained from using it. And Suffolk knew why. The country's sympathy lay with *her* and unrest was rife. People were glad enough not to have to pay dues to Rome any longer but all the other changes were resented and further changes were feared. In such an atmosphere a few blows struck in a remote village might precipitate a crisis. Blows must not be struck here.

"What are you waiting for?" he roared at them. "Nothing is happening here. I have come to ask some questions and carry back the answers. Go to your homes."

"We're just watching," the spokesman said.

Suffolk climbed down and went to the alms room in which the prisoners were huddled.

"Send out the physician and the waiting woman, Maria whatever her name is."

He spoke sternly to Dr. de La Sa. "Your mistress has done a foolish thing. She has locked herself in the turret of the Tower and will not listen to me. You are to go in and make her see reason. If she does not open up she will starve. Persuade her to come out and your own offence shall be overlooked."

"For her own good I must persuade her," de La Sa said, not seeing exactly how it could be done.

Maria broke into a flow of Spanish.

The doctor said, "Women are always concerned with the unimportant. She is concerned that the kitchen fire, left untended, will be out."

"She may look to it. Tell her to be quick."

Maria was quick. The three crossed the courtyard and went towards the Tower. De La Sa gave evidence of his wish to be helpful.

"It would be better, my lord, to call from here so that the Queen may look out and see for herself. Also, this way she has more chance of hearing." So, in full view of her window, they stopped and called that they had permission to visit her and Katharine called back that if the Duke retired to the far side of the courtyard, she would come down and admit them. Even so she was cautious, asking again from behind the barred door if they were alone and then opening it so little that they had difficulty in squeezing through.

"He released you?" she asked breathlessly.

"We were sent to persuade you to submit, Your Grace. And I speak now as your physician. The Duke spoke of allowing you to starve and, as you know, I have always held even a fast detrimental to your health. Would it not be possible for you to take the oath, with spiritual reservations, as is permissible under duress."

"My daughter would not know that it was with spiritual reservations that I had sworn away her birthright."

"I thought you would say so," Maria said and began pulling from inside her clothing the bread, the wedge of cheese that she had snatched up. Dr. de La Sa looked at her with displeasure. It would merely prolong the misery; and the Queen needed no encouragement to be headstrong.

"At best enough for four meagre meals. What will you do for water, for candles?"

"He will leave when he sees that I am not to be shaken."

"I fear not, Madam. And I fear discomfort and privation for you."

"Go down, Dr. de La Sa and tell my lord of Suffolk that I shall remain here until he withdraws, unless taken by force."

He looked indecisive and unhappy. But there was nothing he could do here.

"I shall stay with you," Maria said.

"If I thought it likely to be a long siege, I should order you to go. But you may stay."

Suffolk had gone again to the place of temporary imprisonment and ordered out cooks and servers. The larders and buttery were pitiably ill-stocked; his men were hungry. Tomorrow he would have to send out a raiding party, who would, he knew, find very little. Peasants were skilled in the hiding of provender if there was a soldier within ten miles. The wives of those oafs —who were still watching—would by this time be driving livestock into the woods, pushing food up chimneys or under strawstacks.

When Dr. de La Sa brought him Katharine's message, he groaned inwardly. He could take a battering ram to the door or light a fire against it; but he knew that any unusual noise, flames, smoke, a female scream would change those who watched into something dangerous. And when the door was down, what then? Who could, with impunity, lay hands on her, even to drag her to safety? Searching for an answer to such a question one must take the King into account and there had been so far no sign that he would take any rough handling as other than an assault upon royal dignity. He had once or twice reminded people that though Katharine was not Queen of England she was the daughter of Spain. And when a fawning courtier, thinking to please, had spoken of her in a derogatory way, the King had snarled, "You should wish yourself so chaste a wife!"

Dr. de La Sa said, "Her Grace has provisions for ten days and a spirit of the utmost hardihood."

Outside, though the people behind the faces had changed perhaps, the faces had not; bovine, impassive, and growing in number more rather than less, the peasants, curse them! watched. His own men wanted to be home for Christmas, and so did he—the laxity which the season permitted was delightful for a man who, if past his first youth, was still handsome. And if this solemn Spanish doctor said that in her tower Katharine had provisions for ten days, it meant that she could hold out for twenty; in times of famine, in besieged cities, or boats cast adrift, women survived.

In the morning he said, "Sack the place. To every man what he can carry. We leave in an hour."

Most of Katharine's personal possessions were in the great chests which she had brought from Spain and which could not be carried up the spiral stairs. Suffolk's men took most of her clothes, all her household linen, the silver and plate which, banished from Greenwich she had felt right to take with her.

They ripped the old, beautiful tapestries from the walls, and got little good by that, for they were so rotted by damp that they split, ragged and useless, except as wrappings for other things, the kitchen utensils, pots and pans, spithooks. Suffolk loosed, into the ruined house, all Katharine's Spaniards. Dr. de La Sa and a comparatively humble fellow, Francisco Filipez, in saying that this had nothing to do with them, that only the Emperor had claim to their allegiance, had struck a note that Suffolk, angry as he was, recognised. But Abell, another chaplain named Baker, and half a dozen other people, born English, were bundled onto the spare horses.

The watchers watched. Did they never, Suffolk wondered, need to sleep or eat or even blink?

"I shall know her," the man with the fowling piece said, "I was that day in Buckingham and saw her plain."

So they watched. She was not taken or Master Falconer would have given the prearranged sign. But her gear was taken. Poor lady, left without so much as a change of linen, or a spithook.

They waited, in case it should be a trick; but the train took the London road and pursued it.

Katharine waited too and then came down to the ruined house. She had withstood the brief siege and the enemy had retreated; in the stripped hall she stood, victorious in principle but on the practical level upon which life must be maintained, defeated. Nothing to eat; nothing in which food could be cooked. And the only bed that offered any comfort, her own.

Disheartenment and despair were not far away. Even Maria de Moreto looked grim and Dr. de La Sa said reproachfully, "How long can Your Grace live in such conditions?" The others, with one exception, looked at her helplessly. Only Filipez said, "We must go out and beg or borrow."

There was no need. All that day those who had watched and then scattered came drifting back, bringing offerings, half a sack of flour, a flitch of bacon, a peck of dried peas, a couple of fowls tied together by the feet. There were also some touching attempts to replace the goods that had been filched; a silver spoon and a glass of Venetian make that had come home in some soldier's pack after Agincourt and been kept as too precious for ordinary use; a spit which a young blacksmith had made in his second apprentice year and which his proud mother had hung on the wall, her old one being still serviceable. There was an iron pot, too large for a couple whose children had all left home, and a wide pewter dish that had been cherished in memory of the grandmother who had bequeathed it.

When she realised what was afoot, Katharine insisted upon going out, receiving each gift and thanking each donor. She did so in considerable style, wearing the second best dress of those that remained to her because they had been in her bedroom, and her gold collar. It might seem absurd to stand thus arrayed in order to accept two goose eggs from an old woman clad in homespun, but her instinct was sure; these offerings were being made to the Queen of England and as Queen she should receive them.

Nobody could replace the wall hangings which, frail as they were, had excluded the worst of the draughts; and when, just before Christmas there was a heavy snowfall, snow drifted in through some of the cracks and lay for a time unmelted on the floor. But, as Katharine said, "The Christ Child was worse housed."

21

In the ill-equipped household with its diminished staff, something of formality had had to be sacrificed, but Francisco Filipez had never yet come into any room where Katharine was wearing no doublet and with his shirt sleeves rolled up as he did on a bright May morning of 1534. He rushed in, halted and stood still, staring at her, his jaw jerking. He was under the stress of some emotion which rendered him speechless.

She imagined that what she had been expecting, ever since December, had come about; for it had been a shocking year for those who opposed the King. More and Fisher were in the Tower with many others; the Nun of Kent had been barbarously executed; religious houses whose heads refused to acknowledge Anne as Queen and Henry as Head of the Church, were being closed. It seemed to Katharine that she was unlikely to escape, and that what Filipez could not bring himself to say was that men had arrived to take her to the Tower.

"Try to tell me, Francisco," she said gently. "I can bear it, whatever it is."

He fought the rigor of his jaw and said, in a voice so breathless as to be almost inaudible,

"The Pope . . . he has declared . . . in your favour." He began to cry.

She reached about like a blind woman and found a chair, one of those that Suffolk's men had smashed and Francisco had mended.

She had known all along that this would be the answer, yet now that it had come she was dumbfounded and dizzied. She had so often imagined this triumphant moment, what she would say and do: and now she could only sit and stare and think: Thank God. Five years. Pray God it is not too late.

Presently she asked, "Who told you?"

"The fishmonger. The news was in Huntingdon. The Bishops are on their way. He rose early and travelled fast." Bishops rode as befitted their age and dignity; the fishmonger's load was perishable.

"What Bishops? Francisco, use your sleeve . . ."

He did so, but the tears came faster than he could wipe them. When had he last wept? So long ago that he could not remember.

"I beg Your Grace to forgive me. So long a time, and then the fishmonger . . . and I to be the one . . ." Something like a laugh coincided with a sob.

I feel like that myself, Katharine thought. I could laugh and cry and pray and sing and dance all at once. She sat calmly and repeated her question.

"Of York and Durham. And the flags are out in Huntingdon."

"It was right that you should be the one to tell me. You carried my first appeal. Come, kneel with me and let us thank God."

God forgive me the moments when I almost despaired, the fears I harboured, the tears I shed, the anxiety of the sleepless nights. Unto Thee, oh God be all glory, honour and praise . . .

When she rose from her knees she was herself again; and busy. An Archbishop and a Bishop bringing news of such moment must be properly received. And she must make ready to return to London; thank God again that it was fair weather, daylight long and the roads good. She would be back in London; she would see Henry . . .

That thought stopped her breath. She had long ago put away the memory of his repudiation of her in the hall at Blackfriars; the petty persecutions of the succeeding years she had excused and forgiven almost as soon as she suffered them. That was not Henry. He had been ill-advised first by Wolsey, then by Cromwell, he had been infatuated by Anne and angered, as a child would be, at not getting his own way. She would not have admitted that she herself suffered an infatuation deeper and more lasting than any Henry could ever know; she simply loved him, with the love that could forgive seventy times seven; and she had managed to convince herself that the only thing that stood between her and her husband was his conscience. Now set at rest; so that life could be resumed; the more easily because bigamy had not brought forth a prince.

She would wear the dress that she had worn at Blackfriars and never since, the garment of her humiliation; now the garb of triumph and vindication, the royal colour. The jewels she had worn on that occasion had been snatched from her and given to Anne; but she had the collar which was her mother's parting gift; and she had her wedding ring. Nobody had ever thought of demanding that—perhaps because they knew that to gain possession they would have to hack her finger off.

Buckden for an hour and a half was in a happy tumult; all those who had stayed faithful kissed her hand and some wept; and they said that of course they had known it all along, right must prevail. Good faithful friends, how they should be rewarded! And within a week she would see, not only Henry, but Mary, who had been staunchest of all.

Lee, Archbishop of York, and Tunstall, Bishop of Durham, coming into the hall where the best that Buckden could offer was spread, found their task made easier by being confronted not with the ailing, broken-down old woman of popular report, but by one who looked younger and more vigorous than she had done just on four years earlier at Blackfriars. The Spanish Ambassador was always saying that the flat, damp country was ruining her health, and even Suffolk, to soften the report of his failure, had said that she looked ill and would not last long. In fact, as she welcomed them, there was colour in her face, and a light in her eyes and she moved lissomely.

Of the two, Tunstall felt the worse about the business because he had been one of those assigned to her defence in 1529 and had seen the validity of her case. But he was no hero, he did not wish to be a martyr and in such upset times, with everything moving so swiftly and so inexorably what could a man do when forced to choose between his bishopric and the Tower?

Katharine was not surprised that as she greeted them, both men looked sheepish; many people would in the next few days. It was not easy to admit that one had been in the wrong. She would be very gracious to all—even to Anne . . . She greeted the two men very graciously indeed:

"My lords, I bid you welcome. I understand that you have news for me."

Get it over and done with, Lee thought.

"Madam, the Bishop of Rome has declared in your favour, but his word no longer carries any weight in England. Therefore we, Edward of York, now call upon you, the Princess Dowager, to take the oath of allegiance to our lord the King as Head of the Church of England, and to acknowledge the validity of his marriage to Queen Anne and the legitimacy of the Princess Elizabeth."

Everything, the grave clerical faces, the bare wall, the window from which the light streamed in to fall upon the set table, receded, darkening and reeling. Mary, Mother of God! She fell into the dark, spiralling down. Dying, unconfessed . . . God, to you I commit my spirit, have pity, have pity . . .

The everlasting hands of the Almighty caught and held her and there she was, not dead; she was lying on one of the leather covered chests which were too big to be carried upstairs. The nails which made a decorative pattern around its rim and formed the letters *KR*, her mark, Katharine Regina, felt like stones beneath her, and under her nose Maria was waving stinking smouldering feathers.

What a plight to find oneself in.

She pushed the feathers away and struggled into a sitting position, "That will do, Maria. Help me to my chair."

"A momentary weakness, my lords," she said of a spell of unconsciousness that had lasted ten minutes. "You have more to say?"

They had both, in those ten minutes, entertained thoughts

of fantasy, riding at all speed to London with the news that she was dead.

"A warning, Madam, that the penalty for refusing is death and that you are not immune."

"If you have a commission to execute such a penalty upon me, I am ready. I claim only the ancient right, to die in the sight of the people."

Traitors, or those accused of treachery, had this one right; their bodies might be mangled, their property confiscated, but they must die in public, their last words heard by all who could get within hearing distance.

"We have no such commission. We were told to inform you, and to warn you," Lee said.

Tunstall broke in, speaking hurriedly. "Madam, before Blackfriars, I was assigned to advise you. I do most gravely advise you now. The decision of the Bishop of Rome has hardened His Grace's determination. Where formerly there were words and arguments, there will be bloodshed . . ."

Afterwards, looking back, she realised that this had been the real parting of the ways, the moment of truth. Give in now and there would be the long, easy downward slither into heresy. She remembered again Wolsey on his knees—saying more was concerned than she dreamed of; the world already riven. But to give in now would be fatal; a halfway stand was worse than no stand at all because it implied recantation.

"Then my blood must be shed," she said. "His Holiness the Pope—that newfangled term, Bishop of Rome sits awkwardly on your tongues and upon your hearts, I doubt—His Holiness has proclaimed my case good, my marriage legal, my daughter legitimate. And by that I will abide."

The Archbishop and the Bishop went back to Huntingdon where now almost every house was decorated with a flag, a streamer of new woven linen or a green bough.

London, too, had shown signs of rejoicing, Henry noted grimly; but people were mistaken if they thought that Clem-

ent's decision would influence things. He was angered by it
and felt that he had been unfairly dealt with. That he was also
thoroughly misunderstood was proved by something that the
Spanish Ambassador had said, or rather by the way he spoke
and looked. The conversation purported to be about Katharine's place of residence, but there were undertones.

"If there is any impairment in health, premature demise or
other misfortune," Chapuys said, "the deepest suspicions would
be aroused." He felt that he would now be justified in referring
to Katharine as Queen, but he avoided doing so; there was no
purpose in annoying the King who was very easily provoked
nowadays.

"Great God in Glory! What do you think I am? A poisoner
of helpless women? I resent that, Messire. I resent it very
hotly."

"Your Grace, how could you place such an interpretation
upon words that held no such intention? I was urging a removal
from Buckden, which for some people seems not to be a healthy
place. Nothing more I assure you."

"She shall be moved as soon as I find a suitable residence."

"My master will be relieved," Chapuys said detachedly. "May
I—since Your Grace has made mention of the matter—say one
more word, well meant?"

"We have always spoken openly so far as I know."

"Sire, Henry II did not desire the death of St. Thomas à
Becket. As the story goes he said, 'Will nobody rid me of this
turbulent priest?' Your Grace might well make a similar remark, substituting *troublesome woman*. And there would be
those ready to do what they believed, wrongly, to be your will."

"That," Henry said, "is not a thought to keep you awake at
night, Messire. Have you ever heard me say a word against her?
Has anyone? She is the most damned stubborn, obstinate woman
God ever made. But that is her only fault . . ."

And was that a fault, he asked himself, indulging in a momentary feeling of self-distrust. Clement had pronounced the
marriage good and in the eyes of half the world at least Kate
had been not obstinate or stubborn, but *right*.

Chapuys thought: This should never have happened to him. He is one of those who flourish best in sunshine; healthy, gifted, handsome, he was not prepared for anything to go wrong for him. Given a son all would have been well with him, with Queen Katharine, with England. It was all a great pity, one of God's mysteries.

But Eustache Chapuys had done his best which was all a man could do. He went home to write to Katharine, advising her, despite what Henry said, to be very careful of what she ate and drank; for now, he suspected, the Lutherans would be busy; they looked to Anne, they would want her, before the next child was born, to be Queen beyond any question. Clement's verdict might well have been Katharine's death sentence. But not, of that Chapuys was reasonably sure, by any connivance of the King.

Henry went straight to Cromwell's office.

"The Princess Dowager must be moved. The Spanish Ambassador has been at me again. Buckden is not healthy. If she dies of ague or malaria it would look ill. Get your map."

Turning towards the open shelves where the maps lay, neatly rolled into cylinders, Cromwell said:

"A move is advisable for other reasons, Your Grace. Buckden is too accessible—as my lord of Suffolk discovered."

He found the map, unrolled it and weighted it flat with a book at each corner.

"Not more than half a day's journey away," Henry said. "Long processions tend to invite demonstrations."

Cromwell had been about to make that very statement. He moved a thick finger in a circle, the radius half a day's ride from Buckden.

"There is Kimbolton, Your Grace." The map was a new one, marked with little secret signs; prominence given to any place capable of being held in the event of trouble. On it Kimbolton was marked as more important than many a sprawling, open town.

"Before the late wars," Cromwell said, "it was a manor. It

was fortified during the troubles. It is remote. It is now a castle, with . . ." he peered at the signs, "a moat and drawbridge."

"How near is the moat to the dwelling? I am tired of complaints about dampness."

"It stands on a mound, Your Grace. To the south I should say," he made a rapid calculation, "between thirty and forty feet. Away from the moat, that is, and well above it. To the east the same. North and west at least double that distance."

"It sounds . . . suitable."

It was also final; The More, Ampthill, Buckden, all temporary, places where—he hoped—she would come to her senses, and the moment she did he would have installed her at Greenwich the place she loved and which he no longer could endure. Now, supported by that weakling, that vacillating, dilatory Clement who did everything too late and then wrong, she would never give in. In consigning her to Kimbolton he felt that he was putting her into her tomb. The thought was enough to hurt a little, still; and in response to the hurt anger flared, directed, paradoxically, at Katharine who had made difficult what should have been so easy.

"She is to have no communication with anyone," he said sternly. "And those in charge are not to be likely to sympathise, or even listen to complaints. You understand?"

Cromwell pondered for a moment. "May I suggest Sir Edmund Bedingfield as Steward, and Sir Edward Chamberlayne, perhaps as Chamberlain?"

"Well chosen," Henry said. Both were known King's men; they were unlikely, even within the fastnesses of a lonely castle to call her anything but Princess Dowager. They were also decent men, equally unlikely to treat her harshly.

So that was dealt with. Henry and Cromwell went on to talk about the dissolution of the religious houses which still regarded the Pope as the ultimate authority. For Cromwell this was a profitable business; he was frequently approached by Abbots who felt their establishments to be in danger, and offered a bribe in return for leniency, or delay. He would accumulate a fortune. He was less spendthrift than Wolsey, architects, builders and painters did not find a patron in *him*. He had seen what happened to his old master. When Thomas Cromwell grew old, or fell from favour, he would have something to fall back upon, money soundly invested in the City of London, or with merchants in Germany and the Netherlands.

The move to Kimbolton was made in late May, in cold driving rain, for after opening with promise this summer showed signs of being as inclement as the previous one. And everyone knew why. Before the Pope had decided, there had been an element of doubt in the business, the faintest shadow of excuse for the King's behaviour; now there was none at all. Katharine was Queen and the majority of the people genuinely believed that there would be no good times, no good harvests until she was restored.

Despite the weather a menacing crowd gathered again by the gate at Buckden. Suspicion was allayed, even some hope engendered, when they learned that she was on her way to Kimbolton. That was a grand place, a fit residence, even for a Queen. Few of them had actually seen it, but they knew about it; it dominated the countryside and, to a degree, their thoughts.

It was not, like Buckden, in the heart of a village. It stood, as Cromwell had said, on a mound, completely isolated from the few humble houses that seemed to crouch in its shadow.

The moat, much wider than that at Buckden, had the dull gleam of pewter. The drawbridge was lowered with a crank and a creak, and as they rode in the hoofbeats sounded hollow and doomful. She had a sharp feeling of prescience: For me that bridge will be lowered only once more, when I go to my burying. I have not been sent here for the sake of my health, but to be out of sight and out of mind.

She was still unwilling, or unable to think ill of Henry. This was the doing of Anne, and her friends. She remembered wryly how on that dazzling morning of promise, when she expected the Bishops to bring her recall to London and the throne, she had determined to be gracious to Anne—to propose that she should have The More—a place which she herself wished never to see again—and an adequate pension; and how, presently, she would treat the young Elizabeth exactly as she had treated the Duke of Richmond.

I was born to suffer disappointment.

No, I was born to bear what God sees fit to ask of me. And bear it I will, with God's help.

She was strong again as they arrived in the large inner court-yard and the bustle of moving in began. She had less baggage now. Once she had needed twelve great chests to carry her clothes and her personal belongings; now two sufficed.

The rooms assigned her were to the north and west, and the accommodation was better than any she had had since she left The More. There was a sizeable room with a wide hearth and opening from it at one end a small one, which she intended to make her own private retreat, at the other two, medium-sized ones. The Chapel, surprisingly beautiful, was close by, backing on to the small room; and the stairs, part of the old manor house around which the fortifications had been built like a shell, were of wood, with shallow steps and a stout handrail.

It was as well that at first sight she should be contented with the rooms assigned her; for within a few minutes of arrival she had confined herself to them for so long as she was in Kimbolton.

Sir Edmund and Sir Edward came to welcome her officially, to express hopes that she was satisfied with her accommodation and to inform her that supper would be served shortly in the great hall across the courtyard. Civil and courteous; but they addressed her as Your Royal Highness and she said:

"Sirs, I am Queen of England. If you cannot bring yourselves to address me correctly, I can neither talk nor eat with you."

"Madam, we are sworn . . ."

"And so am I. In this part of the house I am Queen, and those who enter it acknowledge me. No other arrangement is possible."

It was as though the moat had been diverted and now lay, impassable between the two households.

Both the knights had been prepared to deal justly with her. In the great hall across the courtyard the table was set, her place at the head of it—she was Dowager Princess of Wales, the widow of that pale, fair-haired boy long dead. And, as Henry had thought, in Cromwell's meticulously neat little office, these men were likely to be just. But the snub rankled.

Sir Edmund said, "Madam, this will be awkward. There is no kitchen on this side."

"Then, unless I and those who acknowledge me are to starve, food must be sent to us."

It will be sent over, Sir Edmund thought furiously, but it will not be to your taste! He thought sourly of the preparations made, the orders given, the pains he had taken for the proper treatment of the Princess of Wales. What came across the courtyard for the woman who insisted that she was Queen of England, would be the worst of every dish; those who refused the first cut must be satisfied with the scrag end, and lukewarm at that.

She could have reigned in a minor way, wearing her purple dress and her jewelled collar; she was the daughter of Isabella of Castile and Ferdinand of Aragon; she was the widow of a Prince of Wales. From a wide area, people adjudged by Sir Edmund and Sir Edward to be "safe" would have been very glad to come and visit and stare and grovel. She was allowed no visitors, but no such embargo applied to the two knights. As it was she lived in a gaol of her own making, in an isolation of her own choosing; and as the year tipped downhill into autumn, in increasing discomfort, for fuel as well as food came from the other side of the courtyard, and the logs brought over were mainly green, giving more smoke than heat.

The single link between the two households, apart from a few careless pages, was Francisco Filipez who was drawn to the stableyard and stood about there, at first quietly and then throwing out a few laconic words which showed that he was knowledgeable about horses, and then lending a hand, giving advice, until he was part of the scene. If he had cause to refer to his mistress he invariably gave her her title, and this caused no offence. He was a Spaniard, he was old. He was also half-crippled with rheumatism but astonishingly spry, therefore admirable, and he was friendly, the only one "from across the way" who was. Nobody in the larger establishment envied anyone in Katharine's or, given the option, would have joined it, but simply because it was so rigidly exclusive it exerted a certain charm and Filipez, coming out of it with a civil word and a grin, seemed to be conferring a favour. He had tales to tell, too, of campaigns in Granada when he was young and although some of them must be taken with a grain of salt, his listeners thought, they helped to while away a wet afternoon. In yet another rain-drenched summer in England it was not unpleasant to sit in the shelter of stable or smithy and hear an old Spaniard speak of droughts in Spain when trees as tall as those on Kimbolton Hill died for lack of water, and rivers wider and deeper than the Ouse ran dry. In return he was made free of any story current in the yard, mainly kitchen door stuff, what a page had overheard between Sir Edmund and Sir Edward last night at table; what was being said at the little ale house on the London road. It was none of it momentous, but to Katharine who would not speak to anyone who would not give her her proper title, nor set foot in any place where she was not acknowledged, Filipez's little gatherings provided human interest, a breath from the outer world.

22

In the outer world a great deal was going on and Chapuys was in the thick of it. He had many visitors, some coming boldly in open daylight, some secretly by night. They all said the same thing. He could with truth and confidence write to his master, the Emperor, that England was on the verge of revolt; that the Pope's declaration in Katharine's favour had brought many waverers to her side; that though in and around London the new ways were being reluctantly accepted, the North and East were for Katharine and the Pope. Now, if ever, Chapuys urged, was the time for action; if the Concubine bore a son, fickle public opinion would veer. All that was needed was firm and positive leadership. The old nobility, some of whom had taken the oath from expediency, were willing to rise, so were the peasants; of the merchant class Chapuys was doubtful, but if the Emperor would only forbid all trade between Flanders and England, *because* of the way the Queen had been treated, even the London countinghouses would take notice.

Occasionally, usually when he was undressing before going to bed, Chapuys would mentally step back and take a look at himself. *Eustache Chapuys what are you about? What has happened to you?* Men entrusted with ambassadorial duties were supposed to act with impartiality and, unless given orders to the contrary, to promote goodwill between countries. He was unable to plead either youth or inexperience in his own defence, yet here he was behaving like a novice Knight instead of a seasoned diplomat.

Such moments of self-examination never lasted long; he had only to think of Katharine, wronged for so many years and now since Clement's verdict, wronged more than ever, and the crusading spirit was lively again. Increasingly, throughout that summer he spent time and energy and cunning and money which he could ill spare, in testing public opinion and making contacts. He could not lessen his allowances to his family, he was the only one of his mother's children to have made any sort of headway in the world, so he entered a period of self-denial and it was often not from policy alone that he dined or supped wherever Henry was keeping Court.

He saw clearly that the pivot of all his plotting was the Queen herself. In the days when he was allowed access to her he had suggested flight, and later resistance. She had replied that she would never do anything that would lead to war. She had also said, with that smile which so changed her appearance, "Imagine my position if I resorted to force and then had the decision given against me." Being vindicated might well have changed her point of view; Henry's ignoring of the Papal verdict might have disillusioned her at last. But Chapuys had no means of knowing. He had requested permission to go to Kimbolton and been refused, civilly but firmly, not once or twice but several times.

In September he asked and was given private audience with Henry, and after greeting him said:

"Your Grace, I am in need of advice in a very difficult position."

"Tell me your trouble," Henry said. He liked giving advice.

"I fear that my master will be displeased with me. Your Grace, if a relative of your own were incarcerated in some foreign fortress and your Ambassador there *appeared* to do nothing, would you not incline to the opinion that he was idle, or puerile?"

Henry saw the point. "Would you like a certificate to witness that you have made a number of applications for leave to visit the Princess Dowager?"

"That would be better than nothing. An actual visit would be better still. As Your Grace knows I have been careful to maintain neutrality in this matter, but I think the Emperor is justified in wishing to hear, through me, that she is well-housed, in good health, and perhaps—even—resigned."

"She is well-housed; she is in good health. Resigned she will never be. We know that, Messire. And I cannot allow a visit. I said that she should have no visitors and I cannot make exceptions, even for you."

It was the answer Chapuys had expected, and he had come prepared.

"Then I wonder . . . It is much to ask, I know . . . but if Your Grace would connive with me a little. Permit me to make a gesture. Allow me to set out from London, openly, even with some ostentation. Then when I am near Kimbolton, halt me with an order to proceed no further, giving as your reason that such a visit might disturb the lady's peace of mind, or that my noisy suite had caused a breach of the peace in your realm."

"An extraordinary suggestion. Is it, Messire, that by appearing negligent you risk recall?"

"That, amongst other things."

And Chapuys might well be replaced by someone far less personally agreeable, more meddlesome, critical and biassed.

"Very well; to strengthen your position we will indulge in this piece of mummery. But—you will not get nearer than five miles to Kimbolton."

"Five miles from the place Your Grace's messenger will overtake and halt me. My gratitude is unbounded."

So he went about London, saying that he was going to Kimbolton to visit—and if he never said "The Queen" he also never said "The Princess Dowager." He invited a number of people to go with him. There were Spanish merchants in London who could well afford to fit out their servants with fine new liveries, to buy good horses and great silk flags embroidered with the arms of Spain. With his own money he hired trumpeters and drummers.

Cromwell said, "Your Grace, this is open defiance. The man must be mad."

"Rest easy and see what is to be seen," Henry said.

"I see it now, Sire," Cromwell said. He thought he did. He believed that Henry was tired of Anne, so unpopular as Queen, so unsatisfactory as a wife—a daughter and a miscarriage—a difficult and demanding disposition. The King was going to allow a reconciliation with Katharine to appear to be *forced* upon him. Very clever indeed! Devious himself, Cromwell admired deviousness in others; and what could be more devious than this?

September was unseasonably warm, just as June, July and August had been unseasonably wet. A cool, windy month would have served the harvest better; as it was the sunshine caused the flattened ears of corn to start sprouting; there would be little to gather in but straw. An unlikely season, part of, symbolic of, the troubled times. But there was hope; the Spanish Ambassador was on his way to Kimbolton to bring the good old Queen back to London; so people thought, as they gathered on every village green, at every crossroads, to see the gay cavalcade go by, the flags hanging limp in the hot air, the music calling, calling . . . A pity it had been left to the Spaniards to do, a pity it had been left so late, but better this than nothing; better late than never.

Chapuys, who amongst other motives had planned this as a test of opinion, was delighted by the response. Spaniards were not well-liked, even in country places where no Spaniard had ever been seen, but it was astonishing how many geese, fattening for Michaelmas, were killed untimely, mute offerings, and how many voices, once they were out of London, shouted for Katharine and how many men oddly armed, came up and said, "If you need any help . . ." and how many owners of manors and yeoman found themselves able, even in such bad times, to offer shelter and food for man and horse.

Chapuys had his own cynicism; many of these people felt the threat to the monasteries as a threat to themselves; monks were, on the whole, lenient landlords; as for the gentry, every possible closure would affect them, too. Younger brothers, second sons, sisters and daughters for whom for various reasons marriage had not been possible, had taken to the religious life, permanently provided for. At least half of the enthusiasm and goodwill could be attributed to self-interest in one way or the other, but even self-interest could be used; and the other half was formidable, men and women, even children, on their knees, weeping "God bless the Pope!" "God bless the Queen!"

In his assessment of popular feeling he had been right. And after St. Neot's, drawing near to his five-mile-limit, the flood of gifts became almost embarrassing, ranging from bunches of flowers from cottage gardens to a silk dress: "So that Her Grace may make a good appearance . . ."

Out of St. Neot's and nearing Kimbolton, Chapuys began to cherish hope and fear, so evenly balanced as to be almost insupportable. He had tricked Henry; had Henry tricked him? Was he, after all, to be allowed his visit? Or were he and those with him moving towards a trap? Of the conversation with the King there was no record, save in their minds; he was openly defying the order, no visitors to Kimbolton; he had acted as no Ambassador should, and if tonight he found himself lodged in a dungeon under the castle, taken prisoner by a force pre-warned, whom could he blame but himself, and what defence could he make? Worst thought of all, what, as a discredited Ambassador, could he do for that poor lady?

The scheme which he had concocted with such care seemed suddenly worthless. Locked up for open defiance of the King, he would be worthless, too. He sweated more heavily than even the heat of the day warranted.

But the King had kept his word. Precisely five miles from Kimbolton, when Chapuys was considering calling a halt, the messenger arrived. Messire Chapuys was not to go one step further along the road to Kimbolton.

"Then I must stay here," Chapuys said imperturbably. "But news travels faster than men, and the poor lady there may already have heard of our coming. I will send a man on to inform her."

"There is no need. I shall carry the word myself," the man said and spurred on.

That was a setback. Chapuys' somewhat shaky little scheme

had depended upon getting one of his men, armed with this valid excuse, if not into Katharine's presence, at least into the castle, where, under the pretext of speaking nothing but Spanish, he was bound to be brought face to face with one of the Queen's household.

Now he must plan anew.

"We will rest here for a while," he said. There were trees by the roadside, limes still green, chestnuts beginning to turn colour. Into the shade the cavalcade moved and dismounted.

Sir Edmund, at Kimbolton asked, "How many?"

"Sixty at least."

"Armed?"

"Not openly; but the Spanish are tricky."

"And they did not turn back?"

"No. The Spanish Ambassador said that he would stay there. I looked back once. They were dismounting."

Sir Edmund gnawed the inside of his cheek. Sixty men could not take Kimbolton, but they could raise the countryside. It needed only a spark now.

He went across to the other side, where an indifferent dinner had just been eaten and cleared away and said to Filipez, "Where is your mistress?" Filipez indicated the little room.

When the door opened and revealed Sir Edmund, who said, "Your Highness," and bowed, Katharine, holding to her rule, ignored him; but the pain in her chest leaped. It must be something of grave importance to bring him here. Mary?

"I must ask you to listen, Madam. The Spanish Ambassador with a considerable force is now within five miles of this place. A message from His Grace halted them there, but they did not turn back. A message from you might deter them."

It was all very confusing. Messire Chapuys knew that he was forbidden to visit her. Why had he come? Why had he not been halted sooner? And what was a considerable force? She looked at Sir Edmund and saw that he was suffering some agitation. She broke her own rule.

"Do you think, Sir Edmund, that a message from the Princess Dowager would be effective where one from His Grace was not?"

"They look on you as otherwise." And there were times, in the dark of the night, wakened by cramp, when he had some curious thoughts himself. Two Popes had been concerned, one in the making, one in the confirmation of her marriage; and even in her present miserable circumstances she behaved as Queen. Such thoughts, highly unsuitable to one the King trusted, did nothing to endear Katharine to her gaoler during the daylight hours.

"Send and say that there is no purpose in their delay," he said. Get them out of the district. If trouble threatened, let it not be near Kimbolton. "Send that fellow of yours who is so good a horseman."

"Fetch him to me," she said. "And I should wish you to overhear the message I entrust to him."

It was of the utmost correctitude. "Please tell the Spanish Ambassador that I am sorry he has come so far for nothing; but that in obeying the King's order to withdraw he will be pleasing me. I think it might be permissible for you to inquire after the health of the Princess Mary."

Chapuys was entirely unprepared to see one of Katharine's own people. He had been so busy planning his next move. At the sight of Filipez, so obviously at home on a horse, he leaped to the next objective. He hardly listened to the message which was meaningless, anyway.

"Tell me," he said urgently, "is there any person that you know of, in this district, allowed access to the Castle, and friendly to Her Grace?" One of his purposes in this seemingly fruitless journey was to establish some secret contact. It might have taken days, it might have failed altogether. As it was it was settled in a minute.

"Only one," Filipez said. "And she has no access to the Castle. She is faithful; I know because whenever I go there . . ."

"*You* go? Where? How often?"

"I get out when there is a horse to be tried out. The place is a little tavern; about a mile that way." He nodded in the direction from which Chapuys had come "*The Goat and Compasses.*"

"I will try . . ." Chapuys said. "Tell Her Grace that I will try to arrange that she has news, regularly. You must get out as often . . ."

"I shall not get out again if I delay now," Filipez said.

"Tell Her Grace to be of good heart . . ."

Filipez nodded and disappeared in a cloud of dust.

Chapuys after a second said to himself: You blundering fool! You could have given *him* the letter. The truth was that this entirely unexpected, God-sent chance of possible operations in the future, had driven this day's doings out of his mind.

So back to plan two.

He had been concocting it ever since his offer to send a man with a civil message had been forestalled.

He said to his fool, "You understand me. Fail in this and you are no longer my jester."

To the eight picked men, all young, he said:

"You understand me. Your object is to entertain and draw attention from the fool. You must look as harmless as you are. Ride without hats and in your shirts. If ordered to retire, do so, a little way, but continue to make a show."

The Spanish Ambassador, the banners, trumpets and bugles had been turned back; but it was just permissible that eight high-spirited young men should go on a sunny afternoon, out of curiosity, to see the place where the woman who was a Princess of Spain was held, and to offer, by a show of Spanish horsemanship, an hour of entertainment in what must be a life of superlative dullness.

"You did not even ask, Francisco. The one thing I most longed to know."

"Your Grace, there was no time. *They* know how long it takes to ride five miles and back. I was neither trying a sick horse nor schooling a young one. And Messire Chapuys talked of other things. Of sending news through Jennie Turnbull."

"The kind, very kind woman who sends the food?"

"That woman, Your Grace."

The little tavern was nothing to look at but it had resources. To the rear a duckpond and a dovecote, a row of beehives, pigs in a sty, two cows, a productive garden and an orchard. Filipez always rode in that direction and he never came back without some token of goodwill from the landlady for the poor lady shut up in Kimbolton for no fault of her own. Jennie Turnbull, like most married women, was wholeheartedly in sympathy with Katharine.

Whether her sympathy was deep enough to lead her to engage in surreptitious handling of messages, Filipez was not sure; it was a service of rather different order from the sending of what Jennie called something a bit tasty for the poor lady's table.

The eight young Spaniards—one with a clown perched behind him—arrived. The drawbridge was up, and they looked harmless enough, but Sir Edmund went out and shouted to them to go away. One called back that they had only come to show off their horsemanship, while their elders rested, could they not have permission to do so? Life, even for the gaolers, was dull in Kimbolton and soon Sir Edmund was watching as eagerly as the rest of its inmates, as the Spanish trained horses showed their tricks. Then one of the young men took the lute that was slung on his back and sang, a Spanish song. A voice from the battlements congratulated him, in Spanish. He said to the clown, "There is your mark." Then he sang again, Spanish words to an English tune, one of Henry's own. It was an eerie experience to hear, "Pastance with good company I love and shall until I die," rendered, the tune faultless, as "The Princess waits upon the babe and keeps her dignity; When at a doorway she yields place, each time she says: It is my father's will that I obey."

Katharine said, "Men's voices carry better. Dr. de La Sa, ask is she well? Are her spirits cheerful?"

Across the moat question and answer. Somebody called, in Spanish, "Watch the clown!"

Nobody not particularly instructed to do so would bother to watch the clown, who, in truth was not very good except at turning somersaults, which he did so near to the moat's edge that he seemed likely to fall in—and serve him right. When the horses, having rested, drew away a little and resumed their display, most eyes watched them; and the clown fell into the moat and struggled, throwing off his motley coat, letting go his stick with the bells, one shoe, then another. Then, with a deadly accuracy, for he had no wish to end his days competing with dancing bears in Cheapside, he aimed the little casket. Maria de Moreto caught it and pushed it, wet and dripping green slime as it was, into her bodice.

In English and in Spanish he shouted for help, he was drowning. He was happy to realise that nobody was paying him any attention at all.

"Poor man, he is drowning," Katharine said.

"He swims like a carp," Maria said. It was true. He struggled out and with an oriental gesture, put his hands to his brow and bowed.

Chapuys and the main party rode back to the little tavern, and with a brusque, "Wait here for me," he dismounted and entered alone. He asked for ale which Jennie Turnbull served, her temper already ruffled. Why had only one of the fine gentlemen come in? Why did that one ask for ale? She had hoped, watching the party rein in that all would enter and demand wine, of which she had a small store, though it was seldom called for.

"Would the other gentlemen not like something to drink?"

"Probably," Chapuys said haughtily, "but it would be unfitting for them to drink with *me*. You could not know that, my good woman. I am the Spanish Ambassador."

There were a few people—all local gentry—entitled to address her thus, from a foreigner the term was offensive; and the idea that nobody was good enough to drink with him angered her. Chapuys knew the English well; they were as riddled with class-consciousness as any people on earth, but they did not like it to be mentioned. He completed his task of enraging her by drinking her ale without a word of praise and with an expression of faint distaste.

"If it's not to your taste there's wine to be had."

"This sad drink is more suited to my mood," he said. "I am disappointed in my errand. I had hoped to see the prisoner at Kimbolton, but was turned away."

The woman's neck reddened, a sure sign.

"She got a name, you know. And if you're scared to call her by it there's no need to say *prisoner* . . . as though she'd done something bad. The bad's been done *to* her." She had not been angry in quite this way since she found her husband in the hay with the serving wench. She turned and began to flounce away. There were times, Chapuys noted, when a starched petticoat or apron or whatever it was could rustle and crackle like the stiffest silk.

"That is a matter of opinion," Chapuys said.

"Oh, is it?" Jennie said, turning again. "No wonder you couldn't get in. She won't speak or look at anybody that can't give her her name. And I don't blame her. When I married Tom Turnbull I took his name and anybody that couldn't call me Jennie Turnbull after that I wouldn't talk to neither." Often enough, when she thought of Katharine, Jennie equated her case with her own. If, when that young slut had her claws on him, Tom could have got rid of his rightful wife just by saying so, he was fool enough to have done it. Pity the poor Queen couldn't have snatched up a pitchfork and clouted Nan Bullen with the handle and broke her nose so no man'd ever want to look at her again. That was what Jennie had done to her rival; and given Tom one for good measure.

"You misjudge me," Chapuys said. "It is because I am prepared to give her her rightful title that I am not permitted to see her."

That needed thinking over; Jennie did not move in circles where attitudes changed from one minute to the next; in and around *The Goat and Compasses* you knew what a man would say minutes before he said it.

"You mean you're on her side?"

"I am. And so, I think, are you."

That could be a trick. Foreigners were full of tricks. And this one, coming in here and first making her angry so she let her tongue loose, and now changing his tune. And all those men outside, waiting. Arrest? More unlikely things were said to have happened. The red faded from her neck, and even from her face.

"And how do you make that out? All I said was she got a name and like to be called by it, like any woman would. And I said that under my own roof. And nobody heard but you. It'll be your word against mine."

"I rather think," Chapuys said, "that in you I have found what I was looking for. I am not allowed to see Her Grace or to communicate with her. I understand that one of her friends comes here from time to time." He waited; the woman said nothing. "If I found a way of sending a verbal message, or even a letter here, would you be willing to pass it on?" He looked outside the window. "Perhaps inside a duck or a dove. Fresh food is hard come by in winter; and nine women out of ten in England would wish to send the Queen a tasty morsel, if it were within their power to do so."

He then made his first mistake; he opened his pouch.

"I'm not taking your money," she said. "And I'm making no promises."

He would not have been surer of her had she sworn on the Cross.

"Any messenger I send," he said, "will carry one of these buttons about him. And now, let my company come in. They are mainly Spaniards and will choose wine, thereby depriving themselves of the best ale in England."

In Kimbolton Katharine and Maria forced open the casket which was locked, but had no key and Katharine read the letter which had taken Chapuys a long time to write since every word must be set down with double intent—to enlighten and confuse. He praised the English virtue of sympathising with the oppressed; he said that it was embarrassing for him to have no real news of her because wherever he went the first question everybody asked was how was her health; of mind and body; and had there been any change of late? The Princess Mary was in good health and good heart so far as he knew. Then there followed a passage of peevishness; in all his life Chapuys had never known people so boastful as the English; one could understand the Lords Darcy and Dacre, far to the North, with the border in their keeping, saying boastful things about their power, but surely it was a national mania for grandeur that made a tannery owner count his retainers! He said that he hoped to have some real news of her before he sent his next letter to the Emperor who was greatly concerned about her. And so, on and on . . . It was a letter which, falling into the wrong hands, would have done Chapuys little harm, and Katharine none at all.

Out of the deliberate obfuscation the message rung clearly, and was answered, in her mind, even as she read it; there was no need for her to think about it even. She would never encourage war. But what of Mary? Were seductive whispers about Darcy and Dacre and armed tanyard workers reaching her? Were there people, meaning well, who would perhaps suggest to Mary now that it was her duty to head any kind of rising that would set her mother free? She must, somehow, communicate with Mary. But how?

Then she noticed in Chapuys' letter the strange assumption that it would be answered. Yet he knew her circumstances.

She sent for Filipez.

"Can you get out tomorrow, or next day? One of my letters is very important."

"I can always lame a horse," Filipez said.

In the morning it was Sir Edmund's favourite mount which limped and was restive. It was at best an ill-tempered animal and pain had not improved it. Filipez's offer to try it out was gladly accepted.

Once he was well out of sight of the Castle, Filipez dismounted and pried out the bean that was the cause of the trouble and the horse ran smoothly and swiftly to *The Goat and*

Compasses, where, watching his moment, he took two letters from inside his doublet and offered them to Jennie who said:

"Letters are useless to me; I can't read."

"May I leave them with you, Madam?" What she had liked about him from the first was his mannerliness. Francisco would have been surprised to know how often, lying on the fat feather-bed, beside her snoring Tom, she thought, even dreamed of him; not as he was now, old and growing decrepit, but as he had been once, when she also had been very different.

"What people leave here is their business," she said. "A man once left a goat. I fed it for a fortnight before it was called for."

"You have a heart of gold, as I have said before."

"I've got sense enough to know that if these are left to lay about they'll get dirty. I'll put them in my lockfast place." That repository of sweet things gone sour; the first fairing Tom had ever brought her, a curl from a dead child's head, a corn-dolly made by another child who had lived longer but not long enough; her grandmother's charm against toothache, a chicken's wishbone, broken and put together in the form of a crooked cross. It had not worked, despite the connection between chickens and teeth—a chicken having none—and the old woman's muttered incantations. Every time Jennie Turnbull opened her lockfast place to add a coin, sometimes two, to the hoard which Tom knew nothing about, she wondered why she kept such a lot of old, sad things.

Francisco had hardly gone when a pedlar came in. He was a poor one; the kind who if he earned two pence in a day, spent three. She knew his kind. And today he was plainly short of money; she could have anything that he carried in return for a mug of ale. He carried nothing that she needed or fancied and she told him so, bluntly.

"I have some learning, mistress. I could write a letter, or read one." He stood humbly, cap in hand, as so many had stood; too many of them thought that taverns could give ale away. But in his ragged greasy hat, a silver button shone.

That was quick work, she thought, not realising that in An-necy, if you were the eldest and wished to help your overburdened mother . . . if you were a student at Turin, with your own work to do and the work of other, luckier, lazier young men to help with, in order to eat, you learned to be quick. And the habit stayed.

She went, for the second time in less than an hour, to the haunted lockfast place; she took the two letters, and a mug of ale and placed them before the pedlar, saying no word.

He was a quick worker too. She turned the pig meat that was to be ham in its bath of brine and honey and came out. The man and the letters had gone. The mug was drained and beside it lay a knot of red ribbon and a length of lace, wound about a spool. Twenty years earlier, eager to attract Tom Turnbull's attention, she would, God forgive her!—have given her soul for such trimmings. As it was she picked them up quickly and added them to her collection of sorry little things, best forgotten.

But Chapuys had made contact with Katharine. He proceeded to find a way of communicating secretly with Mary.

23

When Chapuys received Katharine's letter he was agonised. He had imagined that the months in Kimbolton would have induced a different state of mind. She must realise how things were trending and that her passive attitude could not be maintained forever. He wrote to his master: "She is so scrupulous and has such great respect for the King that she would consider herself damned without remission if she took any way tending to war." But even as he wrote he considered the scruples excessive and the respect misplaced; and he could think such things without any diminution of respect.

The letter to the Princess had been addressed to her, but sent to him so that he might find means of delivering it and as he stared at it, he faced one of the major temptations of his life. He could guess its tone. Expediency, commonsense, worldly wisdom, even his loyalty to Katharine herself, urged that the letter should be destroyed and Mary left to make her own decisions. Mary, torn between her understanding for the need of immediate action and her mother's urge towards inaction, could only take refuge in delay, and delay would be fatal to the cause.

Twice he carried the letter to Mary towards the fire, and each time he held his hand. The Queen had trusted him and if he— even in her own interest—betrayed that trust, he would rank with the others who, in large matters or small, had betrayed her in the past. So he sent on the letter by Lady Jane Rochford, the wife of George Boleyn who was one of the Concubine's ladies, her sister-in-law and deadliest enemy.

Chapuys' experience had taught him that apart from a few exceptional cases, hatred, malice and grudge-bearing were fully as powerful and slightly more reliable than love and devotion. The pedlar who had so soon appeared at the *Goat and Compasses* was actually a respectable young wool-buyer who had hoped to marry one of Katharine's English maids, taken from Buckden by Suffolk. So long as his resentment lasted—that is until he fell in love anew—he could be trusted to use his legs and his wits in order to do the King an injury and therefore the Queen a service. My enemy's enemy is my friend, was a sound and workable principle upon which Chapuys relied.

Jane Rochford's motive for hating Anne Chapuys had never fathomed; but she did hate her so much that when, shortly after the birth of Elizabeth scandal about Anne had been circulating, her accusation was most disgusting of all; she said that her marriage was ruined because of her husband's unnatural passion for his sister. It had not been said openly and what Chapuys called "the filth campaign" had been withdrawn; but a woman who would say that about Anne would be the friend of the Queen and of the Princess.

Jane Rochford was useful because she had access to Mary. Anne went to visit her daughter and her ladies went with her.

Mary, reading her mother's letter, was dismayed. "Dear daughter, I urge and command you, stay still and do nothing, remain in obedience to your father in all things save those of conscience. To those who advise otherwise, be deaf. Of violence no good ever came, or will; patience and time sort all things. It is by tribulation in this world that we reach happiness in the next . . ."

It was the letter of an aging woman, resigned, to a young one, unresigned. It was the letter of a woman, never very politically astute, and now shut away behind walls, to a girl who, faced by insecurity too early, tended to confuse, and always would, politics with personalities, and who for some time now had lived, if not at the very centre of events, on the immediate periphery. Mary's world, except for one small space, was occupied by people good or bad, by notions right or wrong. Black, white, friend, enemy. The exception was the child Elizabeth, too young and too enchanting to be dismissed from or included within any narrow category.

Mary spent a good deal of time in the ordinary, eventless days, in trying to make Elizabeth walk. She was a sharp, knowing little thing, with an astonishing vocabulary and a will of her own, but so many people were anxious for the honour of carrying her—and thus taking precedence of all, when the cry came, "Make way for the Princess Elizabeth"—that she was extremely lazy. And what would happen to her, Mary wondered, when the time came when nobody craved the honour of carrying her?

That time could come by two roads. A rising in England which would restore Katharine to the throne and Mary to the position this child now occupied: or Father, tiring of the Concubine— there was a good deal of talk about this—might put her away, and in that case as Mary put it to herself—we shall both be in the same case. Either way it was advisable that Elizabeth should learn to walk well and strongly, against the day when there would be no eager arms.

So she would set Elizabeth against some solid object, take some steps backwards and squat on her heels, "Liz, come to me. Come to Mary. Come!"

"Mary carry!"

"No. Liz come to Mary."

Eventually Liz would totter forward and fall into Mary's welcoming arms saying, "Here I am!"

"Here you are. Safe and sound." Then Mary would repeat the process. Nobody else could persuade Elizabeth to take more than two steps. And because her father whom she had loved could no longer be regarded even with respect, and her mother whom she loved was immured in Kimbolton, and Reginald Pole whom she could have loved was still on the continent, Mary loved Elizabeth.

No sign of that love showed on the days when Anne came to visit her daughter. Most often then the Lady Mary was absent, keeping to her room with a cough, a cold in the head, a stiff neck, a headache, a pain between the shoulders. The little ailments were genuine enough; it was by the grace of God, she thought, that they coincided with the visits of the usurper. When, in a sunless January, they came all together, for apparently no cause at all, and continued, accompanied by high fever and moments of delirium, she took to her bed willing to die rather than face again the torture of indecision, the knowing that every message which Chapuys sent her urged one course of action, the one she longed to take, while Katharine said, "be still," "be deaf."

She had borne for months the conflict of loyalties. Was Fisher to die, and More and Abell and more than two score others while she sat with folded hands? With the whole of the North, and the East, ready to rise and the Emperor willing—so Chapuys said—to come to the aid of any party that declared for the Pope and the Queen. It needed only the word which Katharine, at Kimbolton, was unwilling to give, but which Mary could, and perhaps should.

She saw, quite clearly, where one duty lay, the stemming of heresy; but there again, all was confused. Father had dipped a toe into Lutheran waters, just long enough to justify his defiance of the Pope and to take, with English connivance, permission to make this bigamous marriage. Then he had retreated and taken up the untenable double position of Head of the Church in England *and* Defender of the Faith. Even he could not long hold the balance between the old and the new. And if Anne gave England the needed prince, the slide into heresy would be certain.

Her indisposition offered a respite; she was now unable to do anything but to stay still; too sick to ride northwards and rouse Darcy and Dacre; too weak to be responsible for anything. So she lay in bed sometimes thinking that perhaps this was God's will being made plain to her, and at other times thinking that it was a test of her resolution; sometimes, blessedly, not thinking at all, back at Ludlow, back at Greenwich, or here, at Hatfield, teaching Elizabeth to walk.

Chapuys was assiduous in his inquiries and expressions of sympathy whenever he came into the presence of the King. "I sent my own physician, Dr. Butts, who reports that he can find nothing that would account for the trouble. But she is ill; and I am worried."

He was worried; he still had no son.

"I wonder," Chapuys said, "whether Your Grace would consider calling upon Dr. de La Sa?" He said it gently, almost humbly, but the memory of another conversation hung heavily between them.

"If he can be spared and if his presence would give any reassurance," Henry said, answering the implication rather than the words, "we will send for him."

Chapuys' message to Katharine went by devious ways; the King's order was carried direct, so the first Katharine heard of Mary's illness was a message from Sir Edmund requesting that Dr. de La Sa should leave at once to attend upon the Lady Mary. January days were short; the courier anxious to reach Huntingdon before dark. There was not even time to send a letter, "Give her my love, my dearest love. Tell her to banish troublesome thoughts and think only of recovering her health. And Dr. de La Sa, let me know. I must know. Inform the Spanish Ambassador . . ."

There followed an endless time. Chapuys' letter came at last, but it was the one he had written before Dr. de La Sa was sent for, so it told nothing new and it contained an ominous sentence. "Illness can be of mind as well as of body; indecision can destroy and forced inaction can drive men mad." For her own sake Katharine must be prodded and made to understand—as Chapuys was sure she did not—that Mary's position was worse than her own.

Katharine felt the prod and moved in a direction opposite to the one Chapuys had planned.

"I must write a letter," she said to Maria, and went into the small, cold, north-facing little room. It was a letter which must go openly and fast.

Filipez had brought back from his outing, as well as Chapuys' delayed letter, one of Jennie's goodwill offerings, a tender little pullet which Maria was about to cook over the fire in the big outer room. She had no spit, a string, hung from a nail served. A youth of privation had made her resourceful and lately she had plied every poverty-inspired trick, things she had thought to be done with forever when she embarked at Corunna, one of the ladies of the Princess of Wales. Presumably Concepcion and Manuella had known poverty, too, but of a different brand, a brainless acceptance of circumstance. Maria did not accept, she combatted; she had even solved the business of getting a fairly bright fire. One day, when the daily allowance of logs, most of them damp and green, was delivered, she raised a great fuss because no fuel had come. A second lot, after some commotion, was sent over, and all that day while half the double allowance smouldered and smoked, the other half stood on end, drying out, turned every now and again. Next day, and ever after, the fire was considerably brighter.

The pullet was done to a turn when Katharine came out, a letter in her hand.

"I am going across to the other side. I shall not be long."

Startled—for never once had the Queen set foot in the part of the house where she was not acknowledged—but practical, too, Maria tied a knot in the string so that the fowl would stay warm but cook no more, and said, "It is a cold night, Your Grace. We shall need our shawls."

"It would be better that I go alone."

"You cannot go *there* unattended."

"Those who ask favours must go humbly, Maria."

Those who asked favours were often repulsed and she wanted no witness to her humiliation.

So she went humbly, her head wrapped in a square of grey woollen cloth. A thin cold sleet was falling.

The humiliation, through a boy's mistake, came early.

In the great hall of the other house supper was over and the trestle-tables were being cleared; hounds were crunching bones. Some of the boys, laughing and shouting as they made preparations for the night, had never even seen her, but one recognised her, ceased dousing the candles, came towards her and bowed.

"I wish to see Sir Edmund or Sir Edward. Either would do."

"They are this way." He ran ahead to the door of the little room, similar to her own sanctum, to which the knights had withdrawn. He opened the door with a flourish and said:

"Sir, the Queen!"

He was a local boy and sometimes slipped home to his family where Katharine was regarded as Queen, and once, when he had referred to the Princess Dowager, his mother had said, "Up at the castle you must do as others do. But not here, James. Not here."

She stood in the doorway, a small shawled figure. She had, both knights remembered, rebuffed every well-meant overture.

"Come here, boy," Sir Edmund said. "*Who* is at the door?"

"Sir, the Princess Dowager."

"To help you to remember . . ." Sir Edmund reached out and clouted the boy, a buffet on either side of the head. The eager young face creased, the bright eyes began to water.

She had a weakening thought: Does it matter so much how I am named? Poor little boy! Had I borne such a one none of this would have come about.

By this time Sir Edmund and Sir Edward too were on their feet, bowing, saying "Your Royal Highness," and offering her the chair nearest the fire.

"Thank you; I will not sit. I need not detain you long. I have come to ask a favour. I know that I am allowed no communication, but my daughter, the Princess, is ill, as you know. And I have written to the Spanish Ambassador asking him to ask His Grace to allow her to come here, where I can tend her. Will you despatch the letter?"

Both remembered the snubs which had rankled.

"We have our orders," Sir Edmund said.

"I beg you, disregard them. My daughter is ill, she needs a mother's care. If you will forward this letter I will take the onus upon me. Say that I begged you and that you, out of pity, disregarded orders. Or say that as Queen I ordered you . . . Either way, any way . . ."

"If Your Royal Highness will leave the letter with us, we will deliberate," Sir Edmund said.

"And inform you, shortly," Sir Edward said.

"I thank you," she said, and went away.

"And what do we do with this?" Sir Edmund asked.

"Open it." It was typical of her arrogance that it should be sealed. Anyone with the slightest sense of what was proper would have offered the letter open, inviting them to read what they were asked to despatch. "It may well contain something other than what she said; the Lady Mary's illness might offer just the needed excuse to slip a letter out."

It contained exactly what Katharine had said.

"And do we send it on?"

"I *think* so. The cat may not have taken its last jump. Even the King veers. Sending all this way for that doctor fellow," Sir Edward said thoughtfully.

"Everybody veers. Even the new Pope; one minute promising to look into the business again as though he questioned Clement's ruling; and the next minute making Fisher a Cardinal— and he in the Tower for holding to what Clement said—even before it was said. Things have never been in such a muddle. *And* you heard what the boy called her. A slip of the tongue, but it shows how they think. The country is riddled with it. We'll send the letter."

Chapuys hurried straight to Henry, took the letter from his pouch and offered it. Henry recoiled, recognising the writing at a glance.

"I ordered her," he said angrily, "not to write to me."

"The letter was sent to me, Your Grace; I thought it wise to bring it to you."

"Read it." He had no wish to touch it; those regular letters when he had been away in France! The very news of Flodden had been written in this hand!

"The answer to that is no!" he said angrily. "Of all the impossible things to ask. My daughter's place is either at my Court

or with her sister. And there is this to consider; separately they
are wilful and headstrong beyond bearing; together they would
be worse. And there is another thing too, Messire Chapuys."
The bright blue eyes narrowed and looked dangerous. "I have
heard rumour of a plot to steal my daughter out of my kingdom.
This might be the first step."

"Indeed? No such rumour has reached me. But naturally
Your Grace has sources inaccessible to me." He looked innocent
and between them was the fund of carefully fostered goodwill;
and there was no evidence against him, but Henry's suspicion
was no longer dependent on evidence; it was rapidly becoming
self-sustaining.

"Kimbolton," he said, the stare bearing down, "would be just
the jumping-off place."

"Would it? Your Grace may remember that I have never seen
it."

A reminder that he had been implicitly obedient.

"I have, so far, been lenient," Henry said warningly. "I am
astounded at my own leniency. But those who work against me,
or oppose me will learn . . ." His mind's focus shifted, as it did
so often, to Thomas More, in prison. He had valued More beyond price; so much so that when, offered the Chancellorship
after Wolsey's fall, More had demurred and said, "But, my lord,
you know that I am against you in this great matter," he had
said, "Thomas, I promise you freedom of conscience."

The distasteful truth was that freedom of conscience was a
thing that could only be allowed when things went well.

". . . they will learn. Leo may send Fisher his Cardinal's hat,
but there'll be no head to wear it!"

And yet, if they would only give in, how good he was prepared to be to them. More with any office he cared to name:
Fisher back in his Bishopric; Mary given some resounding title—
if he could make Anne a Marchioness in her own right, he could
make his daughter a Duchess; Katharine, completely free,
properly and even regally attended, could have Greenwich.

If they would give in.

"I do not think," Chapuys said, "that I, in any regard, have opposed Your Grace. My impartiality has become a byword and prevents me, perhaps, from hearing things of interest."

"Your impartiality is such, Messire, that people hesitate to say to you, It is a fine day, lest you should make some qualifying remark." If only you knew some of the things that are said to me!

"Thank you, Your Grace," Chapuys said, as though replying to a compliment. "I trust I shall not be thought partial if I remind you that there is now no physician at Kimbolton. In case of illness or accident . . ."

"The fellow can return . . ." No, that would not look well, to remove the Spaniard as soon as Mary showed signs of improvement. ". . . to Kimbolton, if a house can be found, not too near, suitable for my daughter until she is fully well. They can share a doctor, but have no other communication."

Both the women whom Chapuys wished to influence within short distance of one another and a physician making daily visits!

Concealing his jubilation, the Ambassador said: "Both ladies will find that hard, Sire."

Let them! Why should he be the only one to suffer. They had defied him, and by defying him driven him out on to a lonely, uphill road; and his situation was made worse by the fact that occasionally he could only admire their steadfastness. When Mary refused the oath and sycophants said, "Were she my daughter . . ." and mentioned what they would do, he said nastily, "You are unlikely to sire such a daughter!" And in his own Privy Council, issuing a warning about conspiracy, he said, "The Lady Katharine is a proud, stubborn woman of very high courage. She could quite easily take the field, muster a great army and wage against me a war as fierce as any her mother Isabella ever waged in Spain."

It was a possibility which he had considered and dismissed as improbable, though it did no harm to keep the Council alive to the danger. Katharine would never rebel against him because —Jesu, what irony!—she still considered him her husband, and her duty submission to his will. And anyone else who tried open rebellion would come up against something that would jar their teeth—his personal popularity, so far unshaken. People might grumble and mutter and receive Anne in silence, but he had only to ride out of any palace gate or appear on the river to be greeted with enthusiasm. People who utterly deplored his actions were susceptible to something, a gift almost, as eclectic as water-dowsing. He did not give it much thought, it was something he had been born with and would carry until he died, gross and with death's corruption already upon him. As he had said to Katharine long ago, "They are only people." He thought about it so little that he never realised that therein lay the secret. Elizabeth, taking her first steps, had inherited it; Mary, moving to a house more than twenty miles from Kimbolton and hoping every day that the rule about not seeing her mother might be relaxed, had not. And Henry, counting on his popularity wherever he made contact with people, overlooked the far north and the west; the thousands of people who had never seen him or come into contact with anyone who had seen, spoken to, or brushed shoulders with anyone who had.

Chapuys knew better, taking a wider view.

24

Dr. de La Sa failed, as Dr. Butts had failed, to find any physical reason for Mary's ill health; the head cold had cleared by the time he reached Hatfield, the cough lingered and would not disappear, he thought, until the weather grew warmer. She continued to complain of pain in the head, in the shoulders, and she still suffered short spells of something that was neither genuine swooning nor fever delirium. Whenever she recovered from one of these the pains vanished for a little time; if she slept well under the influence of one of his sedative potions she had no pain for an hour or two after waking, and once when Elizabeth was brought in to see her—at her own insistence, "I want Mary! Where is Mary?"—Dr. de La Sa, coming in to say that he thought the visit had lasted long enough, found his patient out of bed, playing some game which demanded more exertion than he would have believed her capable of making.

From this he deduced that misery of mind lay at the root of the trouble. Released, by sleep, or unconsciousness or distraction, from the melancholy of her thoughts, she was better; and alas, he knew of no cure for melancholy. Yet, unwittingly, he supplied one.

They talked, naturally, a good deal about Katharine and de La Sa described the routine of life at Kimbolton. He was a man who had enjoyed, and still missed, the comforts of life and without fully realising what he was doing, he allowed to slip into his account mention of the privation which Katharine and those with her had lately endured. The indifferent food, the inferior fuel, a shortage of linen. "In fact," he said one day, when the talk had taken this turn, "I hope that when Your Highness is sufficiently recovered to dispense with my services, the King will receive me for a moment. Then I pray God to give me courage to say what I believe—that another year in such conditions will gravely damage the Queen's health." The moment he had said it he regretted it; the worried expression which made the Princess look so much older than her nineteen years, formed itself there, under his watching eye. He said hurriedly, "I shall plead for a removal to some more comfortable place. And if my ministrations have improved Your Highness's condition, His Grace may be grateful enough to listen to me."

"My condition is greatly improved," Mary said.

He had solved her problem for her, reducing the whole muddled matter to something plain and clear, the simple duty of a daughter to save her mother from intolerable and detrimental conditions.

Mary was now so embittered towards her father that she knew that Dr. de La Sa would waste his breath in pleading—it would suit Father only too well if Mother died. He could then go through a mockery of remarriage to the Concubine and the next child—Anne was said to be pregnant again—would be legitimate by any standard.

The sending of Dr. Butts, the calling of Dr. de La Sa from Kimbolton, had not deceived Mary at all. She knew her value to her father, the man with one son, illegitimate, and two daughters, one regarded, if Chapuys was to be believed, by three quarters of the country as his legal offspring, and a woman grown; the other regarded by a quarter of the people as his heir, a mere toddler who, since Mary had taken sanctuary from the world in illness, had almost ceased to toddle.

This was the moment; she had been right to wait. Mother had been right in saying that patience and time sorted all things. God had His own way of doing things; He chose His time and His tools.

"I am quite restored today," she said. The torturing indecision was over. She knew what she had to do.

And then, as though by a miracle, came the order that as soon as the Lady Mary was well enough to travel she was to go to a house, near enough to Kimbolton to allow her to share a physician with her mother, the Dowager Princess.

"I shall be able to ride tomorrow," Mary said. Every omen seemed propitious; she would be in touch with her mother; in or around Kimbolton Chapuys had his secret contacts; Huntingdonshire was nearer the North than Hatfield. All things work together for good for those who love God.

"Now," Henry said, bringing the down-bearing stare to focus upon de La Sa, "understand this. You are the Princess Dowager's personal physician, I thought it wrong to deprive her of your services; you have done something to restore the Lady Mary's health—and for that I give you thanks. But in coming and going between them you are *not* to act as messenger. Inquiries about health may be answered; nothing more."

"Any order that Your Grace gives me shall be observed to the letter," de La Sa said. "But if I might venture to remind Your Grace, the present conditions in Kimbolton are not conducive to health."

"*You* look well enough."

"I am a man," de La Sa said. "And I am kept busy. Even in so small a household . . . and the other side of the house, having no physician of its own, calls upon me from time to time. So I have other things to concern me. For the lady it is different, Your Grace. The bleak conditions, the poor food, the . . . the . . ." he spread his hands in an un-English gesture, "the general atmosphere is unfavourable to health. I do not think she will survive another winter there."

"She has the remedy in her own hands, Dr. de La Sa. A few words and she could be back at Greenwich. Or Richmond. She could have Hampton Court if she chose."

He was no longer wholly comfortable anywhere. Greenwich was peculiarly Katharine's place; there was the lime avenue down which he had walked to meet and claim her, the room where Mary had been born. In Richmond there was the room where an old man had used his last breath to gasp out a few warning words; and the room in which a most precious child had died.

Whitehall and Hampton Court had been Wolsey's and memories hung heavy in both places. What he needed, Henry realised, staring at the Spanish doctor's earnest face, was a brand-new palace. And he knew where. The idea came to him in a flash, as in earlier days his songs and their tunes had come. A manor named Cuddington, on the Kingston road; near enough to the City of London to be accessible, far enough removed to be healthy. He visualised it, not unlike the fairy-tale palace of the Field of the Cloth of Gold. (Wolsey again!)

"She could live where she chose," he said, his inner eye entranced by towers rearing into the sky, such a palace as had never yet been built; and he would call it nonsuch. My Palace of Nonsuch.

De La Sa refrained from making the obvious retort and simply said, "As her doctor, Your Grace, I wish she could be ordered elsewhere."

"That needs thinking over," Henry said, dismissing it from his mind.

The house which had been chosen as a temporary residence for Mary was nearly twenty miles from Kimbolton. To Dr. de La Sa the journey seemed endless—he made it in different directions each alternate day and the spring weather was cold that year—but to Katharine and Mary it seemed so short a distance that the proximity was cruel. The promise which the doctor had made to the King he tried to observe, stretching health to include looks. "The Princess appears to have shed five years," he could say, with truth and without feeling that he was breaking his word. He could say, "The change of air has greatly benefitted her." And since Mary now seemed fully recovered, lively and strong, he felt that she could bear to hear that her mother suffered a good deal of pain, partly from the rheumatism which the winter had exacerbated, partly from some puzzling cause. "High in the chest, Your Highness, and sometimes it strikes into her arm." He demonstrated on his own body the site of the mysterious pain—mysterious because, so far as he could tell, neither heart nor lungs seemed affected.

"Will you tell her that I hope she will be better soon? That I *know* she will be better." De La Sa would carry only messages concerned with health. "I gave my word, Your Highness, hoping thereby to lend weight to my plea that the Queen should be removed from Kimbolton."

"She will be removed; and shortly," Mary said, "I know, Dr. de La Sa, that you are allowed only to speak of my health to her and of her health to me, but this is a word concerning health. Tell her, from me, to be of good cheer and to cherish herself. Better days are coming."

It was incredible, de La Sa thought to himself, comparing in his mind's eye this upright, sturdy, lively girl with the miserable creature to whom he had been called at Hatfield. And he felt at liberty to deliver the message; it concerned health; good cheer and self-care were healthful measures; and the better days, the summer days must come.

Katharine never knew how nearly she missed liberation or by how narrow a margin civil war had been averted. On a comparatively mild day Francisco Filipez rode out and came back with three eggs, a pot of honey and some news. "It is only gossip, Your Grace, but they are saying that the Princess is to be more closely watched, and recalled to London very soon because the King has heard whisper of a plot against him. A rising, Madam, led by the Princess and the Spanish Ambassador. And it is true that four men, spies by the look of them, Jennie said, stopped at her place to drink ale and asked direction to the place where the Princess is."

Let it happen, had been his first thought. Singlehanded he would deal with Sir Edmund and Sir Edward, and glad to. And there were several others, within the walls of Kimbolton who could be counted upon to take the Queen's side or remain neutral.

Everything suddenly fell into place; Mary's sudden improvement in health; "a different person," de La Sa had said. The messages about better days on the way; the doctor's assurances that she would not spend another winter in Kimbolton; and from Chapuys, of late, nothing. The focus of his attention had shifted. To Mary?

He could not persuade me, she thought, he found Mary more malleable. And it must not be!

She said, "Francisco, tomorrow you must make some excuse to ride again. I have a most urgent letter to despatch."

She sat down and wrote to Chapuys so forcibly that the quill spluttered. "I have heard that His Grace has some suspicion of her surety, but I cannot think that he has so little confidence in me. I am determined to die in this kingdom and I offer my own person as surety for my daughter to the end that if any such thing be attempted, the King, my lord, may do justice upon me as the most traitorous woman ever born."

She sent for poor Dr. de La Sa and spoke to him so sternly that it seemed another transformation in a patient had taken place.

"What do you know of the plot in which my daughter appears to be involved?"

"Nothing Your Grace. What plot?" His innocence was manifest.

"I believe you. But think back. Her recovery was sudden. What happened on that day? Was she visited? Try to remember."

"So far as I can recall, Your Grace . . . I gave her, perhaps incautiously, yes, I thought after, it was incautious, some account, moderated because of her condition, of the way in which you were housed and treated. And I said that I hoped that when her condition had improved His Grace would be sufficiently grateful to receive me and give some heed to my plea that you should be removed from here. She then said that her condition was improved; and from that moment she has never looked back. She became, as I have told you, a different person altogether."

"Then I regard you as responsible for all that has happened since."

"Responsible for what, Your Grace? I am sorry. I fail to follow . . ."

"You told her the food was poor? The fire, despite Maria's trick, insufficient, bed linen scarce; and that another winter in Kimbolton would be the end of me? True or not?"

"Your Grace, I mentioned hardships. The advisability of a change of residence . . . The Princess appeared to be concerned but not unduly distressed. And as I said, she immediately announced that she was better. I thought at the time she said so in order to expedite my interview with His Grace; but she *was* better and has remained so."

He was completely puzzled.

"As I thought," Katharine said, still looking at him with disfavour. "You must now undo the harm you did—unwittingly, I grant you, but grave harm which must be undone."

"But, Madam, what harm? How can I undo something that I am ignorant of having done?"

"You must break the promise that you made to His Grace and carry a letter for me to my daughter. And be ready to ride with it within ten minutes." He had only just arrived back in Kimbolton. "Moreover, tomorrow morning you must rise early and come back to me bringing the assurance that the Princess has understood and is prepared to obey my order."

"Perhaps Your Grace will permit me to say that this is precisely the kind of communication which I undertook not to assist in."

"You were to concern yourself with health only. I know. Health is concerned—I shall neither sleep nor eat until I am reassured. The health, indeed the lives, of thousands of people are in danger. Do you wish to see civil war in England, Dr. de La Sa?"

He gaped at her.

"Madam, are you feeling quite well?"

"Quite well, thank you. You can occupy yourself while you wait by making a copy of this letter," she tapped the one she had written to Chapuys. "And in a legible hand, please."

Never, in all the long time he had served her had he seen her like this. Then, when he had glanced through what he was to copy, he felt again that she was suffering from some disturbance of the mind. He said, almost timidly:

"Your Grace . . . Are you fully aware of what this means? The situation is not clear to me, but what is clear is that such a statement might involve grave risk to yourself."

"It was intended to," Katharine said, without looking up.

De La Sa wrote with unaccustomed slowness and clarity, rounding each letter like a child. He still could not see in what respect he had offended.

"Make the best speed you can," Katharine said, handing him both letters, folded together. He had never heard her speak so curtly to the youngest page and he did not realise that the manner was deliberately assumed in order to frighten him into an act of disobedience.

Mary looked stunned when she read the letter and the enclosure and then burst into a passion of weeping more violent than Dr. de La Sa had ever seen, even in a house from which Death had snatched an only child, or a breadwinner. Most women sat down in order to weep; Mary walked up and down, wringing her hands together and drawing harsh noisy breaths that sounded more like the death rattle in the throat of a strong man than the sobs of a woman. Dr. de La Sa, weary—he had ridden forty miles that day—and under some emotional stress himself, was flustered.

"Your Highness; sit down; try to be calm. You will undo all the good . . . you will bring on a headache . . ."

"This ruins all," she said hoarsely, and continued to walk and wring her hands while the tears—not copious, the doctor observed, but slow and difficult—squeezed themselves out and ran down her face which was as pale now as when she lay in bed at Hatfield.

"You must," he said, "Your Highness *must* strive for calm. You will be ill again . . . I beg you, sit down . . . Take a little wine . . ."

"Leave me be. I have to make up my mind." She locked her

fingers together and beat on the air with them as though hammering something.

Then, abruptly, she was calm. She sat in a chair and brushed the last tears away with the tips of her fingers.

"So!" she said. "It is over. I cannot, even her own cause, sacrifice her. There she sits, a prisoner, helpless and without hope. She is ill-housed, ill-fed, ageing, ailing—and she is the most powerful woman in this world, Dr. de La Sa, the most powerful woman in the world."

As she said it she shuddered, a spasm that rattled from her teeth to her heels on the floor.

"A little wine now?" Dr. de La Sa suggested again. Wine heartened and soothed; given enough of it a man could bear the amputation of a limb by a barber surgeon with no more noise and complaint than a man with no wine in him would make at the removal of a splinter or the lancing of a boil.

"Yes. This bitter pill needs something to wash it down; and you have made a double journey. Pour for us both; I should not wish to be seen in this state . . ." She brushed away two more slow running tears.

In this house whose owners were uncertain of their role— host and hostess? unofficial gaolers?—a natural good-heartedness had tipped the balance and Mary had been served with the best. The wine which the doctor poured—his hand a little less steady than usual—was both heartening and soothing.

Mary said, "I am well now. I need you no more. I shall return forthwith to Hatfield or any other place to which the King orders me." All over, the trumpets, the banners, the release of Katharine, Queen of England, the triumphant ride into London, the restoration of Papal authority. Finished, done with. God's will.

"It is a wise decision," de La Sa said—not knowing what it concerned. "Being so near, and not allowed to meet, has imposed strain upon you both." He was still in the dark; he had, he realised, become involved with something outside his sphere; the Queen's strange manner towards him; his own breach of faith; the Princess's behaviour. From his confusion and exhaustion and the effect of a full glass of good wine after more than a year of abstinence, he took refuge in his profession and the Hippocrean oath: "The regimen I adopt shall be for the benefit of my patients according to my ability and judgement and not for their hurt. Whatsoever house I enter I will go there for the benefit of the sick."

He said, "Your Highness, wherever you go, and whatever happens, I advise calm and contentment of mind. Upon such basis all health depends. The Queen, your mother, has survived trials that could have destroyed her had she not maintained a quiet mind, willing to wait upon events."

"And never one event brought her good. I could, I would have saved her. But faced with this . . ." she tapped the papers which she had flung down in the paroxysm of anger and frustration, "I am helpless. A hobbled horse. She waits in Kimbolton for death to release her. For what do *I* wait with this quiet contented mind?"

Bit by bit, helped by the wine, he saw the situation in which he had played his unwitting part, like Justice, blindfold, in the morality plays.

He thought quickly; the King was not his patient; the Princess was.

"I can no more look into the future than any other man— except as a doctor. And this I can say: Men who in their forties grow fat and continue to eat as though they were still young and are of a choleric disposition, seldom make old bones."

Mary said, "Oh," and put her hand to her face.

"Your Highness, that is an observation, not a prognosis."

"But my mother might, despite all, outlive him?"

"It is possible; even likely. With an untroubled mind . . ." He realised his duty to his other patient, and in turn tapped the papers. "This kind of thing is not good for Her Grace."

"There will be no more of it," Mary said. "Tell her that from me. I yield to her will as to the will of God. Tell her I shall not stir, that remembering she is my surety I shall walk most warily and wait. Go now, Dr. de La Sa and give her this assurance."

She added with the good common sense that the doctor recognised as a sign of mental health, "It is almost dusk; but every horse knows the way to his own stable."

Sixty miles in a day!

25

In April Fisher, More, Abell and others taken from Buckden, and a number of Carthusian monks, forty-five people in all, were executed. Fisher took with him to the block all immediate hope of Paul III's making—as he had considered doing—any compromise with Henry. The political situation had seemed to warrant a review of the whole dispute and Paul had thought about making an offer to recognise Henry's present marriage in return for the restitution of Papal authority in England. That was now impossible. Fisher was a Cardinal, a man of learning and of exemplary life and his sole offence was that he had believed in Julius' dispensation, which Clement had confirmed; the olive branch could not readily be extended to the man who had killed him. Also, word came seeping through that the Carthusians, while awaiting trial, had been villainously treated, so shackled that they could neither sit nor lie down and practically starved. The papers for Henry's excommunication were drawn up; but not signed.

More went to death almost gaily; at the scaffold he said, "I pray you, master Lieutenant, see me safe up, and as for my coming down, let me shift for myself." All London mourned him. He had been an honest lawyer, insusceptible to bribery. He took with him the last vestige of Henry's youth. Henry had loved him like a brother, enjoyed his company, revelled in his wit. In allowing him to die Henry had again violated his own nature and he was less resilient now. He refused to admit any sense of guilt or of wrongdoing and took refuge in a vast corrosive self-pity. He was right; those against him were wrong and they would regret it.

Even in the streets of his beloved London he seemed, for a moment, to have lost that personal popularity which meant so much to him. Immediately after the executions he rode out and faced, for the first time in his life, a crowd whose cheers were thin and faint-hearted. He reined in his horse and said in a loud, carrying voice, "I did not know that so many of you were dumb. You have my sympathy."

"You," was the magic word; it was addressed directly to every man, every woman in the crowd, with the mocking I-know-you, you-know-me grin. Had he shown discomfiture at the silence, or merely ignored it, it would have lasted and there would have been other, longer silences. But he had challenged them, and they responded. There he sat, solid, confident, handsome, their King. They proceeded to show him that they were not dumb. It was a gift, like being able to walk a tightrope, this ability to establish intimate contact with people whose names he would never know, whose opinions and feelings he was prepared to disregard if they conflicted with his own. Such moments provided the exact counterbalance to those of self-pity during which he would think: Forty-four this year, and still no son; love for Kate dead, passion for Anne soured into something worse than indifference; the damned heretics battering on the gate that only he, good Catholic, kept barred; and the Pope threatening to excommunicate him. Lonely, too; one daughter a mere prattler, the other a surly, defiant young woman who by rights should be in the Tower.

And Katharine was to blame for it all.

He could no longer bear to be reminded of her existence. When Chapuys began to speak of the advisability of her removal from Kimbolton before another winter set in, Henry said, "Speak of something else, Messire, or withdraw." When Cromwell said, "I have another communication from Sir Edmund Bedingfield . . ." Henry said, "Forget it." He did not wish to hear that the allowance was inadequate, in the face of rising prices, or, presently, that it was not paid at all.

Chapuys had recovered from the failure of what he now

thought of as the Winter Plot which had come to nothing because a woman who could not order herself a proper dinner or a supply of new bed linen, had issued an order which her daughter had obeyed. He was eagerly awaiting the day when Henry should be excommunicated. Excommunication was a curse and it cancelled out all bonds of allegiance. Those who, in January, might have stood by the King or wavered, could turn against an excommunicated man with clear consciences. The Queen would feel differently, too; such a staunch upholder of Papal authority would be bound to take the ban very seriously.

But sentence must be executed before the Concubine quickened again. So just as Chapuys had urged Clement to give his verdict before Henry took matters into his own hands, so now he urged Paul to sign and seal the sentence of damnation before it was too late.

Clement had adopted time-wasting measures in the hope that Henry's infatuation for Anne would wear itself out; Paul delayed from making the final breach in the hope that Katharine would die. In Rome the shock and horror of Fisher's execution had begun to die down. With Katharine dead the way might yet be open to some kind of bargain with the man who held the balance of power between France and Spain.

Paul's delaying tactics made Chapuys anti-Papist for several minutes. It was a letter explaining that the papers of excommunication could not be sealed, signed and delivered because the aggrieved person—Katharine—had not made a formal application for such action to be taken. If she would write to Rome, requesting the King's excommunication, matters could proceed.

Chapuys saw through that all too clearly. The Pope and his officials believed that Katharine, shut away and denied all communication with the outer world, was incapable of making such a demand. And that was where they made a mistake; reckoning without Francisco Filipez and Jennie Turnbull and ten or eleven other people who formed the secret network. Most of all reckoning without Chapuys, the son of a stubborn woman who had once fallen down the cellar stairs of the Annecy house and put her knee out of joint. She had never laid up for a day. She sat in a chair, the injured leg, with the knee hideously swollen, stretched out on a board nailed to the chair seat, and propelled by the sound leg she had hitched herself about the kitchen and cooked for her family and a houseful of guests. Eustache and the younger ones could go to market, fetch water, sweep floors and empty slops, but they could not cook. So she did it, though the pain was so great that when it was necessary to move from the chair, she fainted. This quality of doggedness she had transmitted to her son and it was the thing which he recognised in Katharine.

When Katharine received from Filipez's hand the letter from Chapuys telling her what she must do, she was as much distressed as she had ever been in her life. She was in poor health; the April executions had shattered her; she felt directly responsible and lost—never to fully regain it—that absolute certainty of being *right*. She had so firmly repudiated the idea that any blood should be shed over a purely domestic matter; and now blood had been shed, the most innocent blood, the blood of best and the most faithful. Fasting, she had prayed for the souls of the dead; in the Chapel the Bishop of Llandaff had said Masses for their souls. They were martyrs, he said, reminding her that the blood of martyrs was the seed of the Church. She listened, but could not be wholly comforted. And the pain in her chest came more often, more sharply, sometimes leading to nausea which she tried to conceal from Maria who took such pains over the food.

And now this. This momentous and terrible decision.

It seemed such a horrible thing to do. To ask that Henry should be cut off from every sacrament, cursed, severed from God; in worse case than any animal which, never having known the communion of souls, did not know the lack.

The Henry she remembered was the man so meticulous about his religious observances, making his confessions, doing his penance; "Six Masses and on a hunting day!"

Could she do this to him? She had failed to give him a son,

she had lost his love, by holding to what she thought right she had driven him to defy the Pope who also thought she was right. She had loved him, loved him still, and had been his ruin.

And now she must decide upon this.

She looked at the word *aggrieved*. The aggrieved person. The word was inapt; it held implications of a desire to retaliate. She had been wronged but she had never for one moment felt any desire to be avenged. Never a day, from that terrible one at Greenwich, eight years, eight dragging years ago, when she would not have been ready to go back, with no recrimination, no reserve, to be his wife again.

Thinking was useless; she must pray about this. She went into the Chapel and knelt, said the ritual prayers and laid the whole problem at the feet of God, of Mary, the Mother of God, and of Christ Jesus their Son who had died for the sins of the world.

She prayed for help and for guidance. From time to time she realised that she was no longer praying, but thinking in her limited, human way.

Mary's rights to be considered and protected.

The Concubine may yet bear a son. She reads Lutheran books and on one occasion, at least, begged for leniency for a man who had smuggled such books in. No child of hers—when Henry is dead—would bring England back to Rome, thus denying its own legitimacy. When Henry dies, unless Mary becomes Queen immediately, England will go headlong into heresy. If I write this letter will Henry realise . . .

The thoughts, the questions went round and round in her mind like an old horse turning a mill wheel. From time to time she realised that she was not praying, but trying to reason, and pulled herself up sharply. God help and direct me. Mary, Mother of God, pity me—not meant for such great matters . . .

Time passed.

Maria de Moreto, hovering in the narrow place between the door of the Chapel and that of the large room, was relieved to see Dr. de La Sa come in from the third door which opened on the courtyard where he had been taking his afternoon's exercise.

"Her Grace has been in there," she said, looking towards the Chapel door, "for three hours. I have looked in four times. She might be turned to stone for all the notice she took."

"The letter Filipez brought her this morning disturbed her. I could see that. I am seriously considering asking Sir Edmund to forbid these rides of his. Whether he brings back a letter or mere gossip, she is always disturbed."

"You do that, Dr. de La Sa," Maria said, speaking between her teeth, her eyes narrowed, the very image of her formidable old father, "and you will have no blanket on your bed and no pillow. And I will use every book you have to stoke the fire."

Taken aback, he said, "I meant no harm. It was her welfare I had in mind. Every time Francisco goes out . . ."

"He brings something to eat," Maria said fiercely. "Something *fit* to eat. The smell of autumn is in the air already. How can she go through the winter on such fare as we are given?"

How could any of them, de La Sa wondered. The coarsest, darkest barley bread, pease porridge, a kind of stew, mainly cabbage with little shreds of meat: and even this poor fare none too plentiful.

"I have done what was possible," he said, with hurt dignity. "I went across to the other side and made my protest."

"You might as well have spat in the moat," Maria said, still angered. "Now, get in there and persuade her to come out— for her health's sake."

Dr. de La Sa tiptoed in, bowed to the altar and then, stooping above Katharine, said softly, "Your Grace! I think you should come with me now. It is cold in here. We are concerned for you."

On the hottest day of summer the Chapel was chilly, its thick wall to the north never catching the sun, the southern one shaded by the buildings on the other side.

She ignored him as she had ignored Maria, and for a moment he thought that she might be dead. The immediate result of death was a flaccidity; people keeled over, collapsed into a huddled heap; but with her elbows propped, her head in her hands and her knees already bent, the Queen might have passed that stage. Rigor mortis? The timing was unpredictable; surrounding temperature, the bodily build. The Chapel was cold, and she had wasted since April.

He reached out and touched her hand. Cold as stone, cold as clay. He withdrew his hand and thought a dispassionate doctor's thought: Perhaps, for her, just as well, before the pain which he could neither diagnose or cure, passed the point where the laudanum drops brought no relief—or the apothecary in Huntingdon ceased to give credit.

He was about to investigate more closely when Katharine moved, lifting her head, dropping her hands and attempting to rise. He helped her up.

"I have been trying to pray," she said. "But my thoughts went round and round."

"Your Grace is exhausted, and chilled."

"It is something I have never felt before. As though God were no longer there. Only my own thoughts, turning in emptiness. Is it possible . . . No, the notion is too fantastic." Yet she considered it. Suppose that far away in Rome the Pope had not waited for her request but had signed the papers and excommunicated Henry, and the sentence had fallen upon her, too. Husband and wife were one; no couple had ever been more truly one than she and Henry in the golden days.

"Without God life would be unbearable," she said.

It seemed to be a thing for her confessor to deal with; so de La Sa sent for him. Maria de Moreto fussed about with the little shawl and found a place in the larger room where the westering sun was still warm.

"What troubles you?" Llandaff asked gently, yet with a certain authority.

"Something to be decided. And I cannot. I cannot even pray about it. For the first time in my life, *I could not pray*. I was alone."

Maria and de La Sa made to withdraw, leaving her with her confessor. But Katharine said, "Stay. It is too great for me alone; and God gave me no answer. *You* must help me."

It took only a few minutes to explain what had been going

round and round in her head for three hours. The three looked at one another in silence. Then the doctor said irritably:

"The Spanish Ambassador shows little sense and no consideration. You were better in every way when you had no communication with the world. I should advise you to ignore the request and do nothing at all. A letter whose delivery depends upon the schooling of a baulky horse might never have reached you."

"But it did," Katharine said.

Llandaff also brushed the main question aside. "The feeling that God has withdrawn is a test of faith. Many saints have experienced it. And Our Lord on the Cross cried that God had forsaken Him."

"Have *you* ever felt it?"

"I have never attained sufficient virtue. Only the strongest spirits are called upon to pass through the dark night of the soul. It will pass . . ."

Only Maria had been thinking about the original problem. She hated the King; she wished him to be punished in this world and throughout eternity. Hell was too good for him!

But it would never do to say so. It must be put cunningly. Her ability to make the most of very little, to whip up an omelette from one egg and half a cupful of water must now be employed on a different level.

She said, "I think your prayers for guidance *were* answered, Madam. In the feeling that God was lost to you. So the King must feel when he is excommunicated. And it will bring him to his senses. For eight years he has been in error, and for the last two living in a state of sin; and nothing so far, nothing, has ever been done, or said to bring home to him the perilous state of his soul. This well might."

She saw, and so did the others, the bewilderment and hurt lift and vanish. Katharine made one protest,

"It might also lead to bloodshed."

"Blood has already been shed," Llandaff said. "More's, Fisher's, and the rest. And unless this headlong course is arrested, more blood will flow."

"Not in battle," de La Sa said, contributing his mite, anxious only for the matter to be settled and his patient's mind at rest. "For who would fight for an excommunicated man?"

She had her answer. Conveyed by human voices, but direct from God who chose His instruments.

Writing the formal demand for Henry's excommunication she felt like a mother, chastising a child for its own good; my dear one, my darling, I slap you to teach you that fire is not a thing to play with . . .

When she had written she went back to the Chapel and prayed that the curse might be the instrument of Henry's salvation. And this time God was there; in a physical sense at the altar in the wafer and the wine which were His flesh and blood; and in the space which had been dark and empty, a terrifying void; now occupied again by all the unspeakable glory . . .

The days shortened; the weather worsened; the waiting time dragged itself out. Nothing happened.

"That request which cost me so dear to write," Katharine said to Maria, "might have been dropped down the well for all the good it did. I sometimes think that I shall die as I lived, waiting."

"Your Grace, do not speak of dying." How could I bear to go on living? And what will happen to me? To us all?

26

"I fear, Your Grace, that I must insist," Chapuys said. So soon as he had mentioned Dr. de La Sa's name the King's face had darkened and he had made a dismissing gesture with his hand. "It is the last time that I shall be obliged to trouble you, on this subject . . . but now I must, and immediately. Five minutes will suffice."

"If you tell me the gist of the letter and do not read it word by word. It is still Christmas, Messire Chapuys, Christmas, and out there they await me."

"The gist of the letter, Your Grace," Chapuys said, pushing the rejected missive back into his sleeve, "is that the Princess Dowager is dying and has expressed a deathbed wish to see me and her daughter."

"Dying?" The word jolted, though he had known her to be ailing, been warned that another winter in Kimbolton would kill her.

"So her doctor says. And sorry as I am to disturb the festivities, I must ask Your Grace's permission to go to Kimbolton and to take the Lady Mary with me."

Kate dying. He had pushed her away, out of sight, out of mind, refused to listen to any plea on her behalf. Let her suffer, he thought without any very clear idea of what she was suffering, because he had never in his lifetime sat down at a table that was not well spread or slept in an ill-furnished bed. When he thought of her he thought of a stubborn, proud woman who had kept him and Anne apart through several good breeding years and ruined their whole relationship by the uncertainty and the distrust and suspicion which even bedding together could not wipe out. It was a long time now since Katharine had seemed anything to him except an obstacle and nuisance. Now, for a second the past revived, and with it the knowledge that she was only fifty, this very month. Me too? One day.

He said defensively, "She was never a strong woman."

For once Chapuys forgot to be mindful of his tongue. He said with asperity, "Her circumstances of late have not been conducive to good health!" What was he saying? Provoke Henry now and he would not obtain the necessary permission. He added quickly, "She has, I understand, voluntarily confined herself to a few rooms and refused what company was available."

"All her troubles have been of her own making. Except her poor health. Her experiences in childbed prove that she was never strong."

"She has been very unfortunate," Chapuys agreed. It seemed to him that the byword about fortune favouring the brave was without truth; those who bore one trouble bravely had others heaped upon them.

"You may go to her when you like," Henry said, with the magnanimous air of one conferring a great favour. Katharine's death would be timely, he thought, recovering from the jolt. Anne was pregnant. That news had been the best of Christmas gifts. It must be a boy this time; and if Katharine died the boy would not be born to a man with two wives. If Anne gave him a son he would send her into dignified retirement, possibly at The More; give her whatever in the way of worldly goods she cared to ask for, and never see her again. If she bore another girl he would take more drastic steps to be rid of her . . . He had recovered some of his old buoyancy; the year was ending, the sentence of excommunication had not fallen upon him, and if by the end of the coming summer he was the father of a prince all England, all the world would see that he had been right.

Chapuys, prepared to take a prompt leave, was thinking much the same thing. But if he could reach Kimbolton before Katharine breathed her last, and could get her and Mary in one room together, there was still a chance. People often had moments of enlightenment on their deathbeds, looked back over their lives and saw where they had made mistakes. And in any case Katharine's promise—or threat—to hold herself as surety for Mary, would have no more validity now.

Henry was also thinking of deathbed scenes. He remembered that room at Richmond, smelling of death on a sweet April afternoon; the gasped-out warning which he had disregarded. Mary was more dutiful. Whatever Katharine said to her at such a moment would be held sacred. And what might Katharine not say?

"*You* may go, Messire; but I cannot entertain the thought of the Lady Mary travelling so far in such weather, and—if she ever reached Kimbolton—witnessing a distressing scene. She is not a strong woman, either."

"Your Grace, it is a deathbed request. The Lady Mary is a good horsewoman, and I promise to see that she is not over-tired. Or, if you thought it wise, she could travel in a litter."

A litter would delay them; a litter until they were out of London, perhaps.

"Messire, I have expressed my opinion."

There was nothing more to be said, except, "Has Your Grace any message you wish me to convey?"

Idiot! One kind word now, and something of a kindly nature was plainly expected—and back it would come, borne on the wind to Anne who must not, must *not*, be upset in any way, by anything, from now until July. August?

"Tell her I commend her to God."

Hatred of him flared in Chapuys' unemotional mind.

I shall ask to be recalled. I will *not* remain in a position where I must be civil to the brute. If she dies without giving her daughter permission to lead a rising against him, there is nothing more for me to do here and I cannot force myself any longer to say smooth things to her murderer. And I will not take another diplomatic post. The Emperor will give me a pension, which I will turn over to the family, and I will retire, perhaps to Louvain and spend the rest of my days in quiet study. I have had enough of this.

Then Henry said the words which were to twist Chapuys' life in another direction. "And, Messire Chapuys, when it is . . . over; I commission you to break the news to my daughter. She is at odds with me at the moment and there is none about her who would do it . . . kindly."

What a mass of contradictions the man was!

"I will do that, Your Grace. And now, if you have no further instructions . . ."

Both men, as they parted, looked past Katharine's death and misread every sign. Henry looked ahead and saw the birth of a prince reconciling even the most stubborn Papists to the new régime. Chapuys saw himself cloistered from this troublesome, disappointing world, with only fellow scholars and books for company.

And before a month was out Henry was to be unhorsed in the tiltyard at Greenwich, lie unconscious and get up with a wound in the leg which was never to heal: Anne, told by her stupid uncle, Norfolk, that the King was dead, was to miscarry. And Chapuys, going to tell Mary of her mother's death, was to transfer to that tough, tender, passionate, controlled young woman all that he had felt for Katharine, and was to stay on in England for the next ten years, watching her interests and furthering her cause.

All unknowing Henry went to join the Christmas revels and Chapuys crossed the courtyard where a thin sleet was falling, to collect his pass for Kimbolton from the office where the Duke of Suffolk presided.

Suffolk remembered Buckden. Handing the pass to the Ambassador, he said cheerfully, "When she is dead, Messire, there will be no barrier between my master, the King and your master, the Emperor." Suffolk had reason to feel and speak cheerfully; Katharine's death would solve for him a very troublesome problem. He had recently married again, and his mother-in-law, a truly fearsome old woman, before allowing him to marry her daughter had extracted from him a promise, the thought of the need to keep it enough to make him sweat in the night, even lying beside his bride. He would be free now.

Chapuys thought: You are hateful, too: it is a living woman you thus dismiss as though saying that when the mist clears the day will be fine.

He said politely, "It will not be an enviable journey. North of Bedford is a harsh country, as your lordship knows!"

In another December, north of Bedford, in Buckden, Suffolk, hero of the battlefield and the tiltyard, victor of many a bed-chamber, had been defeated, outmanoeuvred by a headstrong woman and a group of peasants. It had been the joke of London for a month and any mention of it could still make him writhe.

The wind blew from the northeast, the sleet fell down, the mud splashed up. Chapuys could stay nowhere long enough to have his clothes properly dried out and brushed; mud layer caked upon mud layer until they were as stiff as armour, and in the morning just as cold. And because he was travelling at speed he could not turn aside to rest for the night in any comfortable manor, but must hold to the road and lodge at inns where in such weather, with the Twelve Days of Christmas still being kept, chance travellers were not expected or welcomed.

He reached Kimbolton late in the afternoon of the second day in the year 1536. The place looked dead. He had brought two men with him, for even on such an urgent, hasty errand a man of his rank could not travel unaccompanied, and it took the full force of their united voices to provoke any stir of life. When, from the inner side of the leaden moat, the shouts were answered, "Who are you? What do you want?" Chapuys had reached the point of recklessness that enabled him to answer, "The Emperor's Ambassador, come with the King's permission to wait upon the Queen."

"It will be," Katharine said in the weak voice, so unlike her own, "my last public appearance. Prop me high. My collar, where is it? And the headdress I wore . . . at Blackfriars? Maria, this shawl is cosy, but it is peasant wear. The skirt of my purple gown; drape it over me, bedgown and all." The Spanish Ambassador was going to be correctly received: she had already sent Llandaff to command the presence of Sir Edmund and Sir Edward, and Manuella to search for, if necessary borrow, some extra candles.

Filipez conducted Chapuys to a comfortless room and hurried away to fetch water, saying simply, "It will not be hot, sir. Since Her Grace has kept to her bed the only fire has been in her chamber."

Chapuys had known that there was a lack of comfort, but he had not visualised a shortage of fuel. Gloomily he washed in water so cold that it seemed to burn, and changed his muddied riding clothes for others, much creased. There was no glass in the room, so he tidied his hair and beard by sense of touch alone and waited, growing more chilled every moment, until Filipez returned to say formally, "Sir, the Queen is ready to receive you." Filipez had discarded the nameless garment, a kind of knitted shroud, which Jennie had made for him after he had confided to her that he felt the cold in the Castle more than the lack of palatable food, and had dressed himself in the rose and white tunic and hose designed for wear in places which, if high and draughty, had heaped hearths and the heat of many bodies to warm them.

At the door of the room where Katharine lay he announced the Spanish Ambassador in proper fashion and then slipped to take his place with Maria, Llandaff, de La Sa, Concepcion and Manuella, on the right-hand side of the bed. The two knights stood on the left. The Queen of England was receiving the Emperor's Ambassador with all the style and formality that could be mounted at a few minutes' notice and with such slender resources.

Between the low bow at the door and the dropping to his knees beside the bed, Chapuys noticed all that there was to see. A macabre scene; the Queen so bleached and emaciated, propped upon pillows frayed, mended, frayed again; the hangings of the bed were faded and tattered; some of the candles mustered on a table at the foot of the bed were not candles at all, they were rushdips, the lights of the poor. Chapuys had made thousands of them in his time, in Annecy, a thousand years ago.

He seemed to notice nothing; to walk straight towards her. He knelt; she extended her hand.

"Messire Chapuys, you have come. I thank you for coming. I feared that I might be left to die, like a beast in a field."

"Your Grace, you must not speak of dying. The King and the whole country are anxious for your recovery. The Princess is not with me, but that is because His Grace was averse to the idea of her travelling so far in such foul weather."

For a long time he had dealt in half-truths; never the lie that could be nailed down, but now he was reckless. She shall die happy, if I can contrive it, he thought.

"I have many messages to convey to Your Grace. The King is concerned for your health and well-being . . ." The lies rattled out; a move to a more comfortable place; an increased allowance, more company. On the right-hand side of the bed the waiting woman who looked as if she had been crying for a week, choked and put her hand to her face; on the left-hand side the two knights shuffled their feet. And midway between them, propped in bed, Katharine's ravaged face wore a look of incredulity and of understanding. Chapuys had time to think: That is their strength, these honest ones; they never attempt to deceive and they can tell the false from the true in others. But he was sorry that she had not believed and been cheered by his lies.

She asked a few questions of general interest and then said:

"I would like a few words with you, Messire Chapuys. I will not keep you long. You must be very weary."

When the others had gone she said, "Tell me about my daughter. How is she?"

"I have not seen the Princess for a long time. But I have reports, from a reliable source, with fair regularity. Her health continues good, her spirits variable, but that is understandable."

"I have messages for her; but they can wait." She slipped down against the pillows and the headdress tilted. She lifted her hand to remove it and drop it on the floor beside the bed, and the movement allowed Chapuys to catch a glimpse of the shawl under the purple silk that she wore as a cape. His heart burned and his stomach knotted: Poor, foolish woman, had she only listened to reason, taken up arms, allowed Mary to take up arms . . . too late now. She was dying in less comfort than any merchant's wife. The hearth in the room was wide, but the fire was small and dull.

"I understand," she said, "that the Concubine is with child."

Who had been foolish, or brutal enough to report that? In fact, Katharine had heard Maria telling Llandaff in the outer room; Maria was crying as she spoke and the words carried.

"That has been said before," Chapuys said cautiously. "And with little truth. It was said in September. Nothing came of it. I sometimes think that the tale is put about to retain the King's interest."

"There are times when I pity her," Katharine said, knowing what the loss of Henry's interest meant. "Tell me truly, did he send me any message at all?"

"Yes. He said: Tell her, I commend her to God."

It had been a grudging message and it was grudgingly repeated; but her sunken eyes brightened.

"What better message could he send?"

"Time was very short. I was anxious to set out and the King was awaited elsewhere."

"I think I could sleep now. I have not slept well of late. Your coming has brought me great comfort. You have always been my truest friend . . . This is a disordered household and I apologise for it; but if you would send Maria to me—and tell Filipez to look after you well . . ."

He thought: Sleep, poor weary soul, and God grant the last merciful gift, a drifting from sleep into death, out of the world that has been so cruel.

Chapuys, Llandaff, de La Sa and Maria sat down to supper and Filipez served them with a dish of doves, freshly cooked and sent across from the other side of the house wrapped in woollen so that it was hot.

Maria de Moreto, her face swollen and in places almost transparent from weeping, said wildly:

"Have I not said, time upon time, that they could have done better by us had they willed? These doves did not fly in on the wind. They are from the dovecot in the garden. And while she *could* eat did she ever see one? She did not. And now that she cannot even sip broth . . ."

She turned away from the offered dish and bent her head over her hands, crying again. "God will punish him," she said; and everyone knew whom she meant.

The three very different men, the diplomat, the priest and the doctor, looked at her with a curiously similar expression of misery, distaste and resentment. They were all distressed, but they were also hungry and they had the male ability to dissociate emotional state from physical need. Maria's outburst had ruined appetite and they ate almost guiltily.

Afterwards Chapuys talked with Dr. de La Sa.

"There is no symptom of any mortal disease that I can recognise," the doctor said. "For the pain, once sporadic, lately constant, I cannot account at all. Nor indeed for the nausea. And she is certainly not being poisoned." It was necessary to say this, for within a few days he, like the others, would be looking for new employment; and who would want a doctor whose last patient had died of poison? "As a rule, we all eat the same food—and very poor. And even when Filipez smuggles in some little offering from a kind woman whom he visits and Maria de Moreto cooks it, she is most careful and invariably eats herself, first. She has never been even mildly indisposed. I am positive, sir, that there is no question of poison. I think . . ."

"Yes?" Chapuys said.

"I think it began with her removal to The More. She has never been quite the same. It was an uprooting and neither Buckden nor this place—as I have said before—were suitable residences. And there is more to it . . ." Dr. de La Sa became for a moment heroic; for when he was unemployed the favour and patronage of the Spanish Ambassador would be his best hope. "Your communications have disturbed her . . . I have observed the effect. Only once has Her Grace taken me into her confidence in this regard and that was over the question of whether she should or should not make the request for the King to be excommunicated . . . That decision, which I think she should never have been called upon to make, did her great damage . . ."

"It was for her own good. Everything I have done, Dr. de La Sa, has been for her good, from my wish to see her vindicated and reinstated."

"And everything *I* have done . . . though as a doctor *my* concern has been with her physical welfare. You may not have noticed, sir, but even when you were formally received, I did not wear my doctor's robe. I sold it, and other things, all I had of value, to help to pay the apothecary's dues. It did not suffice and his reckoning against us is heavy now. If she lives the week out even the doses that deaden pain . . ."

"I will guarantee," Chapuys said. "If she can be kept alive . . ." The Emperor's resources were infinite. Let go the great wide issues, politics, religion, military alliances and concentrate on fuel for the fire, linen for the bed and an apothecary's bill . . . It was many years since his mind had been called upon to operate at such a level, but his experience of penury in youth was useful now. "I will give you a warrant, Dr. de La Sa. And for Sir Edmund also . . . And believe me, if necessary I will go to the Emperor, to the Pope and explain how ill she has been used. I had no idea. Nobody has any idea . . ."

He slept badly on the thin hard mattress in the unheated room, broke his fast on a bit of dark barley bread and a cup of the sourest ale he had ever tasted. Sir Edmund and Sir Edward had heard his promise to Katharine of better conditions pending and they had sent across the courtyard a better, an edible supper dish. Then, over their own, they had discussed the

situation and decided that it would be inexpedient to send
Chapuys away under a false impression.

"If we feed him well it will deny the truth of the letters and
the petitions," Sir Edmund said sensibly. "We said, and it was
true, that we were in sore straits. He will stay until she recovers,
or dies and in either case let him know what it is to live without
means. How say you?"

"I say wait. If his promises have any worth, supplies will be
ordered and the payment for them guaranteed. Boy, I will have
some more ham."

Katharine had slept better than usual and Maria coaxed her
to take a little broth; but soon afterwards, while Concepcion
was about to wipe her face and hands with a dampened cloth
and Maria stood by with the comb ready, pain and nausea returned.

"The worst yet," she said feebly; and Maria who had dared
to hope a little, began to cry once more.

It was drawing on to midday, but hardly light, the sky was
so low and dark, before Chapuys was admitted to her room,
with Maria whispering at the door, "Do not tire her. Agree to
whatever she says."

He greeted her and said he was glad that she was better—
meaning better than she had been earlier in the morning.

"I am dying, Messire Chapuys, and I know it. I do not grieve.
I hope no one else will. I know that we must bear what we are
called upon to bear, but the pain is fierce . . . However the
drops are beginning to take effect. What is necessary for
writing is on that table. I must make my will—though I have
little to leave but debts."

A married woman could not make a will without her husband's consent, Chapuys remembered; but, as law in England
now ran, she was not married; she was the widowed Princess
of Wales. And that brought him straightaway into difficulty.

He said, "We will begin in the usual way—In the name of
God, Amen. The other formalities we will leave to be put in
later." That dispensed with the writing of "I, Katharine, Queen

of England," which would invalidate the document, and with "I, Katharine, Dowager Princess of Wales," which must inevitably offend her. "If you would just tell me your wishes . . ."

"I want Mary, my daughter, to have my gold collar, my prie-dieu, and my books." Most of her books had been wantonly destroyed by the looters at Buckden. "And my furs. They are somewhat worn, but while the Concubine rules she will get no better . . ." So little to bequeath, really; less than any yeoman's wife would leave. That extortionate dowry, half never paid, but what had been paid was substantial; the revenues due to her if she were, as Henry claimed, Arthur's widow; all gone. "No, my friend, make an exception of my sable cloak, that to Maria de Moreto, with the rest of my clothes. And all else that is mine to be equally divided between Concepcion and Manuella." Nothing, not even a memento to Llandaff, de La Sa and Filipez. "Write down that I commend my servants to His Grace and beg that they be given pensions and that he will discharge my debts and bury me with some respect. If not as Queen, the title he bestowed on me and then denied, then as one who regarded herself as his wife, and was always faithful, and chaste. Do I go too fast?"

"I have it all here," Chapuys said, forcing the words through the iron stranglehold in his throat. "Now, if you could sign . . ."

She signed, and, handing back the pen, said, "So that is done with. I thank you." She lay limp against the pillows and closed her eyes. In the silence the green logs, still damp despite Maria's management, hissed a little.

Then Katharine opened her eyes and in a voice of more vigour and less certitude said, "My message for Mary. More important than my poor leavings . . . And more difficult. I should have written, but it needed thought and I put it off until, as you see, it is as much as I can do to sign my name. So, first give her my love, my dearest love. You know, Messire Chapuys, it was for Mary's sake that I took my stand. Had my marriage been truly childless I should have agreed to be put away, though still regarding myself as lawfully married." She stopped and brooded. "As you know, I eschewed violence and urged her to. I believed, I still believe that God would recognise her rights. So tell her, from me to be patient, and steadfast, and to obey her father to the limit of conscience, as she has done hereto. But say this also . . ." Something flashed in the dull eyes and changed the ravaged face. "If when *he* is dead any child of the Concubine's, male or female, makes a bid for the throne . . . and if there is no possible alternative, then she will go into battle with my blessing . . ." She looked back over a lifetime of failure and knew that she had failed again, too weak now to pass on to Mary what she knew about waging war, things no woman brought up as Mary had been, could possibly know. The value of surprise, of doing the unexpected, apparently impossible thing, the importance of a strong rear, the worth of personal leadership and a sharing of hardship. It was too late, now. She must lie still and gather strength in order to issue her last order to Chapuys.

Chapuys looked ahead and foresaw a pretty tangle. The London he had left had been sibilant with whispers. If Anne bore a prince it might be her son who would one day challenge the Princess Mary's rights. Another girl would seal her fate. It could very well not be her child at all who would push Mary aside . . . But such speculation was no subject for deathbed talk.

"And now, my friend, I want you to leave at once. Now, as soon as your horses are ready. When Mary hears of my death I wish her to have someone she can trust close at hand. I want her to have my message before some ill-advised person can use my death to provoke her into ill-advised action. It will snow later, but if you leave now you may just be ahead of it—moving southwards."

The suggestion distressed him. He had intended to use his influence to gain her more comfort. He hated the idea of riding away and leaving her, dying, in this demoralised household. Maria de Moreto had broken down with the thoroughness of which only strong-minded women were capable, the girls were poor helpless creatures, and though both the doctor and the priest would do their duty in this room, they were men, so accustomed to discomfort that they hardly noticed the cold or the fact that the bed itself needed fresh linen.

"If that is your wish," he said. "Though I am reluctant to leave you."

"It is the last thing you can do for me. For all you have done and for all you have tried to do, I thank you from my heart . . . Let us have no long leavetaking. I wish you God-speed. I pray God guard and bless you to the end of your days."

He could not speak at all. He could only kneel again and kiss her hand, with reverence and love.

27

By the time that he was in his cheerless room Chapuys was
practical again. Pulling on his riding clothes and boots—still
insufficiently dried, and stiff and cold—Chapuys was thinking:
If I could wish one wish it would be for some good sensible
woman to come and be with her till the last. Somebody not too
grief-stricken; but kind. He must snatch a minute before he
left to speak to Sir Edmund.

Over the courtyard the sky sagged, purplish, and the wind
which yesterday had driven the sleet in his face had dropped,
giving way to an unnatural hush, sure sign that the snowfall
would not be long delayed.

Sir Edmund and Sir Edward, alerted by the bustle, saw that
his horses were being made ready. The Spanish Ambassador,
after the shortest possible visit, was leaving. He had brought
no money, issued no definite order; his promises of yesterday
afternoon were mere empty words. They were glad that they
had not provided him with a good breakfast, and sorry about
the dish of doves.

"A woman of that kind," Sir Edmund said, when Chapuys
had made his request, "would be impossible to provide. The
Princess Dowager would not welcome the ministrations of anyone who will not call her Queen, and anyone who *would* cannot
be admitted to Kimbolton—as you must see, Messire."

"She needs other things too, bed linen, fuel, delicate food.
It is in my mind, sirs, that neglect has played no small part in
her decline."

"Not ours," Sir Edmund said firmly and with some justification. "You, of all men, should know. The allowance was never

enough and for the last six months it has not been paid at all. We have not been paid. But for the fact that we had some small means of our own . . ."

"I know, I know," Chapuys said placatingly. "I left London hurriedly, with only just enough money for my journey. But I do assure you, sirs, that my master, the Emperor, will be responsible, will pay all debts, reimburse any expenditure—if the King fails. As I think he will not. He, no more than I, realised the true state of affairs. But he will know, so soon as I am back in London."

"What is that?" Sir Edward asked, cocking his head.

It was a voice; the loud, confident, carrying voice of an Englishwoman of rank, accustomed to issuing orders in spacious places and to having those orders obeyed.

"Fetch your master, fool. Don't stand there arguing with me."

The two knights and Chapuys ran to the archway from which the moat and the drawbridge were visible. The men who were preparing to lower it for Chapuys' exit, stood staring across the moat's width, at a woman on the farther side. She held a horse by the bridle.

Chapuys recognised her and turned so dizzy that he almost fell down. An answer to prayer, and he had not even prayed; he had simply thought that if he could wish one wish . . . And there she stood, the Dowager Countess of Willoughby, who had once been Maria de Salinas. One of the secret friends . . .

Sir Edmund went forward a few paces and before he could speak the voice bellowed,

"Are you in charge here? Order that bridge let down and let me in."

"I can admit no one who does not carry a pass."

"I have no pass. I have a lame horse. Am I to be benighted? In the snow?"

Chapuys said, "It is the Countess of Willoughby. Her daughter recently married the Duke of Suffolk." He then turned away, back to the courtyard where his servants and the horses waited.

"Lower away," Sir Edmund said. The moment the moat was

spanned, the Countess was on the bridge, her voluminous skirts bunched in one hand, the other tugging at the limping horse. Chapuys, waiting on the inner side to allow her passage, gave her the mere, formal salutation that any well-bred man would give a lady in such circumstances. He bowed from the saddle, doffed his cap; but when she was dead level with him, he said, "Thank God you are here!" Then, followed by his servants, he clattered across and took the road to London, just one hour ahead of the snow.

Filipez, as usual, had come out to see what was afoot. The Countess's dark eyes, undimmed by the years, saw him. She left the horse, tremulous and with broken knees where he stood, and said to Filipez "Take me to her."

Maria de Moreto sat by Katharine's bed with a bowl of broth growing cool between her hands. She had said, "Just a sip, to please me," and Katharine had said, "I would do anything to please you, Maria. But it sickened me this morning and the very smell of it sickens me now." So there they were, quiet and waiting, when Filipez opened the door and said, "Your Grace, the Countess of Willoughby."

The other Maria; the fortunate one. Maria de Salinas over whose dowry the Queen had taken such trouble—all wasted, for the Englishman was so infatuated that he would have taken the girl in her shift. And off she'd gone to a great house, two great houses, in the country, coming back to Court now and then, Lady Willoughby, more English than any native. She had sent gifts and messages at New Year and on the Queen's name day. Until trouble came. She had made one visit to The More. After that nothing.

"You!" Maria de Moreto said in a voice that held everything, the old jealousy, the envy, the accusation of faithlessness. "Her Grace is asleep." She made a silencing gesture.

Katharine was not asleep; she had closed her eyes to avoid any more pestering with the broth. Dr. de La Sa's latest dose of drops had dulled the sharpest edge of the pain and she had lain neither sleeping nor waking, drifting, the Alhambra and

Joanna, Ludlow and Arthur, Henry and Greenwich all one, all muddled. When, with a great effort, she opened her eyes and saw Maria de Salinas—the other Maria, the high-spirited one, she was no more real, for a moment, than the phantoms. But she was real; here in the room, the daylight dying, no candles yet, we must be sparing with candles; and a poor sulky fire. I was on my way . . . now I am called back. There is something different, an outdoor smell . . .

"It was good of you to come, Maria. I am glad to see you." Even though your coming pulled me back. "How did you get in?"

"I shouted," Maria de Salinas said simply. She had learned, so long ago, that if you shouted loudly enough and in the right tone of voice you got what you wanted that the ease with which she had gained entry had not surprised her. "I should have been here earlier, but my horse fell. I walked the last six miles."

"Can you stay?"

"I shall stay until Your Grace is better."

Dimly, aware of being dragged back, farther and farther into the pain, the need to think, Katharine remembered the old enmity between the two Marias.

"That will be good," she said. "My other Maria has watched tirelessly and is worn out. You can relieve her."

"I need no relief. Or at least . . . it would relieve me if Your Grace would take just a spoonful . . ."

The Countess looked into the bowl and then into Maria de Moreto's face and her expression was eloquent: Is this the best that you can tempt her with?

"Could you take a little manchet bread, sopped in wine?"

"Maria, explain," Katharine said.

"Her Grace has seen no wine for more than a year. As for manchet bread, we have forgotten what it looks like." While you, uncaring, full-fleshed, not a wrinkle, not a grey hair, nothing but the sagging jowls to show that you are of our age, you have fed full every day! We have shared her hardships and her exile.

The Countess's sharp eye had taken it all in; the shabby bed, the poor fire, the other Maria's air of hopelessness and defeat. It was plain to her that there was some more shouting to be done.

She said, "If Your Grace will excuse me for a moment . . ."

"And a fine pair of rogues you are," she said to the knights. "Guzzling and stuffing your own bellies while the poor Queen dies of neglect. Your fire half way up the chimney and hers worse than a tinker's. You will rue this. I will make it my business to see that you are properly punished."

For the second time in an hour they tried to explain.

"So!" she shouted. "What are you drinking? Well water? I need wine for her."

They admitted that they had a little, a very little wine; and she was welcome to it. But when she mentioned manchet bread they said, truthfully, that there was not a crumb of it in Kimbolton.

"Get somebody to make a batch then. And the linen on her bed is a disgrace."

"She brought very little," Sir Edward said, not without spite. "Most of her stuff was looted from Buckden." And who was responsible for that? The man who was now this termagant's son-in-law. "And I would inform your ladyship that Sir Edmund and I have made repeated requests. . . ."

"Words on paper. Filed away and forgotten. Did either one of you think of going to London and *asking*? Well, I am asking now. I want fresh linen and some logs that will burn, and bread made of flour sieved three times and mixed with milk. And do not tell me that you have no milk. I heard a cow. Are you keeping it for a pet?"

It was not until she had gone, carrying the jug of wine snatched from their own table that they remembered that she had no right here at all.

"You should have come sooner, my Lady Willoughby," Maria said in a soft, very vicious voice.

"So it seems. And so I should, had I known half. It was not

until I was at Bedford to attend a wedding that I heard that she was sick, not likely to live long. Even so I had no idea that she was living in such discomfort and squalor."

The words cut Maria de Moreto who had tried so hard and managed so well on so little.

"Things have changed since you last saw her—at The More, was it not? Three years ago."

The Countess was not prepared to explain to the other Maria what lay behind this seeming neglect and indifference. When the Queen rallied—as she must, now that things were taken in hand—she would explain to *her*, and she would understand that some causes were best served in secret. She said:

"You know full well that after The More visitors were not allowed. But you should have known that if *I* had been informed of how things were here I should have sent such a plentitude of what was needed that even when those vultures over there had eaten their fill, *she* would have had enough. Why did you never think to let me know?"

"How could I? *I* have shared her imprisonment."

"People go in and out every day," the Countess said scornfully. "Any woman with a tongue in her head can find some man to carry a message for her, if she has a mind to."

"And why," Maria de Moreto asked, "should I think of appealing to you? *You* who married your daughter to the lout who robbed us at Buckden?"

That bolt found its mark and the fact that it was fired in ignorance did not lessen the blow. Perhaps the poor Queen had also looked upon what had been a shrewdly diplomatic move as a sign of disloyalty. Yet there had been no shadow of reproach in her greeting.

"What he did at Buckden cannot be blamed on me; and he is already sorry for it. He will be sorrier still, that I promise you," Lady Willoughby said. "Now what you need is a sound night's sleep. Go to your bed and leave watching to me."

"I have one mistress here and it is not you. I shall watch as I have done."

"As you wish. I see no sense in it."

It was an echo of the past when they had bickered contin-
uously and energetically, mostly about trivialities. Both looked
back for a moment and thought, mistakenly, that the sun had
always shone then and the future had seemed long, full of
promise. What the future had brought to them was very different and had worked superficial changes on them both, but in
a way, obscure and perverse, the discovery that something, even
an enmity, had survived intact, rejuvenated them.

Katharine, under the influence of Dr. de La Sa's soothing
drops, slept in fresh linen. Each Maria took a chair, one on each
side of the bright fire. Presently Maria de Moreto's tired mind
accepted the lessening of responsibility, communicated the fact
that another person shared it to her will, and from her will the
message passed to her exhausted body. She slumped in her
chair, slipping downwards and forwards until her head sagged
against the chair's unaccommodating back and her body seemed
about to slip over the edge of the seat.

Maria Willoughby rose to her feet and moving softly, put
a stool under the other Maria's legs, waited, and then, assured
that Maria de Moreto had fallen into a sleep from which she
would not easily be awakened, folded a shawl and wadded it
between her head and the back of the chair. Nothing but her
sense of good management activated her and when Maria de
Moreto, made more comfortable, sinking deeper into the re-
storative sleep, began to snore, she thought: Yes, I remember;
you always slept like a pig! She mended the fire and sat down
again.

Katharine woke to pain. The syrup, in doses large enough to
induce sleep, brought dreams too, very strange dreams, quite
unlike those in ordinary sleep which, however unlikely and
fantastic, had some relationship to this world and could be described. Each time as the pain lessened and she drifted into
sleep and crossed the boundary of the other world her last conscious thought was that she was dying, very easily and with a
sense of happy anticipation. Wakened by pain she thought,

still here and still in misery, and then lay, adjusting herself to this world again.

Tonight the adjustment took longer than usual because when she opened her eyes the room seemed so bright, the bed felt different, and she could not see Maria. Only the pain was familiar and for a moment she knew real panic; *not here and still in pain;* was pain to be her companion through all eternity? Then her confused mind cleared and she saw that the unusual quality of the light was due to the fact that the fire burned brightly and that a real candle had replaced the dim rushlight; that Maria de Moreto was asleep in a chair and the other Maria sat bolt upright on the other side of the hearth. She said softly, "Maria."

"I am here, Your Grace. Maria de Salinas."

"I know. I think God sent you. To do me a service I could not ask of anyone else around me."

And small wonder; handless, spiritless lot, letting things drift into such a state. God sent me to save you. You are just my age, fifty, nothing! Look at me! I dragged a lame horse six miles—and, at the end of a long ride, I ground Sir Edward and Sir Edmund into the dust where they belong. I have strength, I have power, I will save you yet. . . .

"Could you prop me a little," Katharine asked. "Sometimes a change of position eases my pain."

This Maria's arms, in the tight sleeves of her riding habit, were strong and well-padded, lifting effortlessly.

"Is that better, Your Grace?"

"Yes. Yes, thank you."

"Wine helps," Maria de Salinas said. "I had an abscess once, in my breast. Wine deadened the worst pain. Will Your Grace take a sip or two?"

"Dear girl, we have no wine here."

"We have now. You took a little. And kept it down." That had been a triumph and it had encouraged the Countess. Tomorrow, if she knew her way about, there would be a bowl of good veal broth. Wherever there was a cow in milk there was a calf not far away. Of course the gluttonous scoundrels on the other side might have eaten it, in which case they could send out into the countryside to find another. Inch by inch, with a sip of wine, a spoonful of good broth, a slice of manchet bread, a slice of boiled fowl, with comfort and cossetting and with *hope*, she would drag Katharine back from the brink of the grave. Only fifty, she thought again, just my age and ailing nothing that anyone can put a name to . . . but I have always eaten well!

Katharine took the wine. There was a slight, too slight to be acknowledged, link between this bright, warm world in the heart of the night and the world into which she slipped away when the dose worked. The quality of the light, Maria de Salinas, suddenly back and moving about so cautiously, not to wake the other Maria. And the wine running down, easing the pain a little. Once she had seen a man, dead drunk, have his arm cut off . . . This was a halfway world, not completely real, not completely fantasy, a stopping place on the road to death. She must make the best use of it.

"Come and sit near me, Maria. There is so much to say . . ."

"I have something of importance to say to Your Grace," Lady Willoughby said earnestly.

"About my daughter? Do you see her?"

"No. Of late I have avoided London, and the Court. It is about that that I wish to speak. She . . ." she jerked her head at the sleeping Maria, "considers me disloyal because I allowed my daughter, Catharine, to marry the Duke of Suffolk; and because I have not embroiled myself by asking permission to visit. Visits have not been allowed and to ask would be to draw attention to myself. Some causes are best served in the dark."

"Until I was known to be dying no visitors, not even the Emperor's Ambassador was allowed to see me. That you should be here now is miraculous. You must not mind Maria; hardship has soured her. And if your Catharine wished to marry the Duke . . ." Maria de Salinas' own marriage had been a love match, she would probably have sympathy with her daughter's choice.

"She wanted to be a Duchess," the Countess said cryptically. "And, being so young, she was flattered by the attentions of so experienced a womaniser. But she did not *love* him and that gave strength to my hand. I talked to her very straightly." Maria's voice rose a little as she remembered that straight talk and its result. Katharine made a warning sound and looked at the sleeper. In an incongruous whisper the tale went on. "I said to her, 'Do you wish, in ten years' time to be put away as his second wife was, or to live in loneliness and neglect as his third did—and she once a Queen?' The child said, 'No,' of course. 'Then,' I said, 'you must establish supremacy over him *now*; what is lightly come by is lightly regarded and what is lightly regarded is easily discarded.' She is a dutiful girl, well brought up and she heeds me. She asked what she must do, and I told her: 'You must say to him,' I said, 'and hold to it, that you will not marry him unless he agrees to your mother's condition.' And that she did. Perhaps it will surprise Your Grace to know what that condition was. It was,"—the voice hardened again—"that when the time came for the people to rise in your cause, against the King, my lord of Suffolk would not take arms against you. That promise I extracted from one of the King's closest friends and one of his best soldiers! I have not been idle!"

And Suffolk had dared to call *her* a traitor! What a muddled, corrupt, horrible world! Who would not be glad to be done with it?

"There must be no rising, Maria. I repudiated that idea years ago. I have instructed Mary to repudiate it when I am dead."

"There is no other way to right the ills of this country, Your Grace. You have been locked away so long you have no knowledge of what is going on in the world. Things go from bad to worse."

"Civil war would not improve them."

"There would be no civil war. A rising, to restore you and bring back the old ways. Who would fight for him and his trollop? Do you realise what force you can command? In various places, discreetly prepared, I alone have two hundred men ready to ride at short notice. Well armed, too. There are hundreds like me. A word from you would be enough . . ."

"Maria, I am sure you mean well. You and all the others. But I have had this out with my conscience . . . I may have been wrong. But it is too late now. For my errors, as for my sins, I must soon answer to God."

"Not yet," the Countess said, again trying to put force into a whisper. "Not yet. With a little care and comfort and proper feeding, you will be restored and if . . ." with some reluctance she turned away from the dream of riding at the head of her two hundred men under the banners of Spain and the Wounds of Christ, "if Your Grace is truly averse to taking up arms, I will still get you out of here. My son-in-law shall himself beg for your removal. Catharine and I have him well-bridled now."

Katharine turned her head away from this Maria's persuasions as she had turned away from the other Maria's broth.

"I tire easily, my dear. And there is something yet to do. Maria, did you love your lord?"

"So much that when he died the sun went out for me." Even to her own ears the statement sounded somewhat extreme; but she thought: Yes, that is how I felt, at the time; but the years pass and there was always so much to see to.

"Then *you* will understand, as *she* could not. As no man could. That is why I think God sent you. To write a letter for me . . . I delayed . . . every day thinking that tomorrow I should be better. This extreme weakness took me unawares. But before I die . . . a letter to *my* lord. Maria, all my friends look upon him as an enemy. He was, he *is*, my husband, in the sight of God; and in my heart."

Maria de Salinas had certainly loved the English lord who had been willing to marry her without a dowry, who had given her wealth, title and status, and being by nature kind and peaceable, had accepted her competent, mildly bullying role. But by Christ's Holy Wounds, had he ever so much as looked at another woman, he would have had something to reckon with; she would have spat in his face, torn out his beard, hit him over the head, cut his clothes to shreds, set fire to his house. He would have learned that Spanish blood running hot in love, could be equally hot in hatred.

Thinking these things, actually far less understanding of Katharine's attitude than poor, withered Maria Moreto with her unrequited love for her worthless cousin who when she had a little money had borrowed it shamelessly and when she was penurious had never offered her a penny, Maria Willoughby went to the side table and came back with all that was necessary for the writing of a letter.

She tried the quill experimentally on her thumb, and as she suspected, it shared the general decrepitude of the household; it splayed out like a goat's foot.

"Begin then," Katharine said. "My most dear lord, King and husband . . ." The Countess thought: A fine lord, repudiating the lady he had chosen, an admirable King who had denied his subject a just trial, a splendid husband who had made a bigamous marriage. But she wrote and as Katharine paused said, "Yes, I have that. My hand is fast, if not elegant."

The temporary relief of the wine was weakening, the amnesty wasted by Maria's talk, the pain drove in its fangs and tore and gnawed. But God was good; He had spared her until this letter was written.

She said, "The hour of my death now drawing on, the tender love I owe you, my case being such, forceth me to commend myself to you and to put you in remembrance with a few words of the health and safeguard of your soul . . ." She had done with his body, except in memory, she was still concerned for his soul.

"Do I go too fast, Maria?"

"No," Lady Willoughby said, scowling at the sputtering, flat-footed quill. "I have it."

". . . which you ought to prefer before all worldly matters and before the care and pampering of your body, for the which you have cast me into many calamities and yourself into many troubles."

She paused again and Lady Willoughby thought: No truer word was ever spoken. She seems to be so saintly, so remote, but she knows the urgencies of the flesh and to what, unreined, they lead. *His* body and its hungers must be to blame for everything that has happened in the last nine years and if even a half of what I hear, remote from London as I am nowadays, it is through his body that he will be punished. He is a man who would sooner have faced an armed rising than the hint of physical lack which the word "cuckold" implies. No woman, the Countess thought, curling her lip into a sneer, ever went out to buy a slice of bacon when a whole flitch hung from her own kitchen beam. Anne was said to have five lovers—her own brother one of them.

Katharine said, "For my part, I forgive you everything, and wish to devoutly pray God that He will pardon you also . . ." She paused once more and said, "Maria, that is true. From the first he was misguided . . . Sometimes I think this, running the whole thing through my mind, misguided in marrying me, lawful though our marriage was and made by the dispensation granted by the Pope; and made in love . . . as it was, Maria. He loved me . . . once. But I can see that for a King who needs an heir. . . ." This was difficult to put exactly, even to Maria, even in the middle of the night. "There are family trends, a colouring of eye, of hair, of disposition . . . And Maria, strange as this sounds, it is not in opposition, but in accord with the will of God who made everything after its kind, the blackbird black, the wren brown. In *my* family girls live, boys die. My mother was Queen in her own right; and my sister. And so, God willing, will my daughter be. So I am sorry for Henry and find it easy to forgive him. He wanted a son; he should have passed me over and married some Princess with two or three thriving brothers."

Unable to make the one retort that occurred to her: Nonsense! the Countess was silent.

Katharine said, almost apologetically, "It is such thoughts; and the knowledge that he has always been ill-advised that makes it impossible for me to be angry with him. Now, to continue . . . For the rest I commend unto you our daughter, Mary, beseeching you to be a good father unto her. I entreat you also, on behalf of my maids, to give them marriage portions."

Maria Willoughby wrote, lifted her head and looked at the other Maria and wondered derisively just how large a marriage portion would be needed to bribe a man to marry her. And the serving wenches were little younger.

"For all my other servants I solicit the wages due to them, and a year more, lest they be unprovided for."

Even so, the Countess reflected, the future was not very bright for them. She might herself find a place for Filipez with his knowledge of horses. The chaplain and the doctor she considered not worth their salt to have let things get into such a state.

"Maria, there is only one thing to add. Write—and lastly, I make this vow, that mine eyes desire you above all things."

That was the sentence which nobody could be expected to understand, except a woman who had known love.

The Countess wrote that extraordinary sentence, of which her mind disapproved and then blinked her eyes several times. She was *not* weeping. It was the strain of writing with a bad pen, by the light of a single candle and the fluctuating gleam from the fire that was affecting her eyes.

A log burned through and fell inwards. Maria de Moreto, half roused by the noise, stirred and muttered. Katharine signed to the Countess to push the letter and all concerned with its writing under the bed. "Her feelings would be hurt." They waited, rather like children almost caught in some forbidden activity. Maria settled to sleep again. Somewhere a cock crowed, greeting the false dawn.

"I will sign it now."

Dipping the pen, the Countess said, "It is the worst I ever handled."

"It will serve," Katharine said, taking it with fingers limp as wilting candles. She wrote *Katharine*, and then when Maria would have removed letter and pen, shook her head and with a last gesture in support of the belief she still held, added, *The Queene*.

"You will see to its safe delivery?"

"When needs be," the Countess said in a voice that sounded as though her throat was stuffed with flannel.

"Thank you, Maria. It was on my mind. I shall rest now."

Die, perhaps, the last duty done, the last effort made. But the pain was lively, gnawing away and though she tried to think of it as a friend, loosening the last bonds of flesh that held her to this finished life, presently she was driven to ask had Dr. de La Sa left drops. He had, but so few, so meanly measured out that the Countess thought that here was another thing she must speak about and organise tomorrow.

The dose was insufficient to ensure Katharine's entry into that indescribable other world, but it deadened the sharpest edge of the pain so that she lay in comparative comfort, with scenes from the past drifting through her mind, muddled in time and mixed in nature. The midwife at Richmond held a child by the heels and said, Thanks be to God a boy! In Granada Isabella spoke of the world's betrayal. At Windsor Joanna cried that Philip was her disease. At Buckden a door slammed and the pain started.

It had snowed during the night, a heavy fall and she was glad that she sent Chapuys away when she did; he might reach London ahead of it. Maria de Moreto woke and declared that she had not slept at all; she had merely closed her eyes to rest them. Lady Willoughby, having splashed cold water on her face, resumed her organisation of the household. There was the business of the comb. The Countess took it up and Maria said, "Give that to me, my Lady Willoughby. I always dress her hair these days."

"Go get your breakfast. Nobody can do anything properly on an empty stomach!"

"Some of us have learned to ignore our stomachs."

Silly jealous girls. She saw them so; two lustrous-eyed, nubile young creatures who had sailed with her from Corunna. Always bickering.

"Give me the comb," she said. "I can make shift to dress my hair myself."

"Now look what you have done," the Countess said angrily.

"Look what *you* have done," Maria retorted. Using her right hand only because to move her left arm provoked the pain,

Katharine combed her hair. "I would you were better friends," she said.

But at some point in that timeless day she was roused again by a sibilant exchange.

"Let me offer it? I have fed her, spoonful by spoonful, this last week," Maria de Moreto said.

"And a fine job you made of it," said the other Maria who had organised that crowing cock into the stewpot, with onions and oatmeal and some dried herbs wrested from the store room on the other side of the courtyard. "Take it then. But try not to cry into it. It is salted already!"

"I weep because I love her and she is dying."

"Not if I can prevent it."

Katharine said, "If you persist in this squabbling, you will both go back to Spain, forthwith. And with no dowries and no word of recommendation." She had made this threat several times in the past. She added, "And whatever it is, it will only sicken me. In my condition." Pregnant again; God in Thy infinite mercy a boy this time. . . .

With the clouds which had shed their load sailing away in a brisk wind the day brightened and the sun, peering out with the January promise, shone on every whitened surface. Katharine said, "A bright moon." It linked with other times of cold, clear light. Moonlight on the minarets of Moorish cities, on the fairytale palace of the Val d'Or, on Windsor's solid walls and oaks, on the Thames, near Thomas More's garden steps at Chelsea.

"I spend a great deal of time with the dead," she said petulantly, returning to full consciousness and to the two Marias, urging a sip of this, a sip of that, "to please me, Your Grace."

"For the love of Christ," Lady Willoughby said as Dr. de La Sa measured out the two doses, one to be taken immediately, the other held in reserve for later in the night, "give her *enough* this time!" Behind her bold front and the bustling she was now as despairing as the other Maria. Unless food could be taken, and kept down there could be no hope. That the end should be without pain was all she could ask.

The doctor looked at her coldly. She was a great lady now, and she had improved conditions for them all: but he was a physician and not to be dictated to in his own sphere.

"A larger dose would defeat its own object, my lady."

"In what way?"

"It would cause vomiting and that would increase the pain."

"How can you know, never having tried?"

"By rule; and by experience," he said with a certainty he did not feel. He could not even be sure that the apothecary, unpaid and resentful, had sent of his best.

"She suffers," the Countess said fiercely. "She writhes in pain. A woman of less courage would be screaming."

"I know," he said dolefully. "But this is the maximum dose that can be given in safety."

"Safety!" she spat the word at him and flounced away. He thought of the many ways apothecaries knew of adulterating drugs and then, since she was not watching, added a careful couple of drops to each dose.

Exasperated by this defeat at the end of a long day of defeats, Lady Willoughby turned upon Maria de Moreto and said:

"Go to your bed. You do no good sitting in a chair, snoring!"

Maria said, "You are the one who needs sleep. Running about all day like a hen with its head off!" But, settling down to watch, she avoided the chair and sat on a stool near the foot of the bed. Lady Willoughby, not to be outdone, pulled up another stool on the opposite side.

Katharine slept, granted swifter entry than usual to that world where nothing was recognisable and all senses were one, music something to be tasted, fragrance a thing to be held between the hands, colour a sound in the ear. The apothecary in Huntingdon, though he could not go on forever supplying drugs without payment, was honest in those he did supply and divorced from her pain, Katharine moved about in the opium-created world.

At the foot of the bed one Maria and then the other abandoned the bolt-upright position, put elbows on to the bed, heads on propped chins, weakened, sagged forward, slept. The candle guttered and presently the fire sank down, unmended; a mere heap of ash but still capable of sending a warm, rosy glow on to the opposite wall.

When Katharine woke it was not to pain. No pain at all. It had gnawed itself free and set her free too. Dear God, I thank you; all my life I have valued dignity and I did so fear that if the pain went on, increasing as it has of late, I might cry out. As I never did . . . miscarriages, dead children, living children, I bit upon my thumb; and through this later agony, longer and with no hopeful end, I bit upon my thumb. And I am blessed that now, too weak to lift my arm—a marked decline, this morning, or was it yesterday?, I combed my hair—I am blessed that now there is no need to bring my thumb to my mouth.

The pain is dead, and I am dying . . . She said, "Maria!" and there was no answer. But one of them would have stayed. One had never left her; the other had come back. Neither would have left her to die alone. She gathered what strength was left to her and said, "Maria!" Two sleep-heavy heads lifted, two sleep-blurred voices said:

"I am here, Your Grace."

Katharine said, "I am about to die. My confessor . . . please . . ."

"I know my way," Maria de Moreto said. She snatched up the candle and blundered away. The Countess of Willoughby, left standing by the bed and with no light except the rosy, diffused glow from the fire, reckoned that she could make her way to the table where the meagre second dose stood.

"And if it is not sufficient," she said, making her way to it, "I will have him out of bed, by his ears!"

"I have no need of it, Maria. The pain is gone."

The Countess swung round. "Gone? Is it true? Then you are better. You will live. I knew . . . I said . . ." She found Katharine's flaccid hands and held them in her own. Hold on to me; hold on; I am strong. Even now, some strength must flow. . . .

Maria de Moreto roused Llandaff roughly, taking him by the shoulder and saying, "Wake up. Get up. She is dying. And asking for you."

"The end?" He knew that she was dying. Dr. de La Sa had said so when he wrote to the Spanish Ambassador. But the doctor had also said that Katharine would suffer a long, slow decline; and death had seemed still at a distance when she received Messire Chapuys: and Lady Willoughby, coming in from the outer world, bringing a fresh eye to bear, had said with assurance that with good nursing and good food the Queen would recover . . . live for years. Now this.

"I will come," he said. Maria looked about for a candle to light from the one she held. She failed to find it. Did he go to bed in the dark? She set hers down and went out and stood in the pitch dark while he dressed, which did not take long since in this cold room, in this poor bed he slept in all but his outer clothes.

"I must go to the Chapel," he said. There was only the one candle. Without its light she could not fumble her way back to the Queen's room, nor could he, without it, go downstairs to the Chapel. So she followed him and again stood in the dark, waiting by the window of the corridor. She was unfit to enter the Chapel because her soul was in a state of rebellion against God who, in the last years, had assumed, little by little, a terrible resemblance to the heartless, unreasonable old man who had been her father; the images were now inseparable. A parallel transformation had overtaken the Blessed Virgin, no longer a willing advocate, a useful go-between, but like her mother a pretty, spiritless, powerless appendage. And now that the Queen was about to die deprivation would be total, loneliness complete.

She stared into the blackness of the courtyard and it was no darker than the future she faced, alone and without hope, heresy, or worse, in her heart. She saw no symbolism in the light which appeared suddenly and made a slow, bobbing course around the open space. It was only the old watchman making his midnight round.

Even in this isolated place where time meant little, it must still be measured by various means; Sir Edmund's mechanical device, the sun dial, the marked candles and the sandglass. This ancient man sat in his tiny lodge from dark till dawn, turning the glass about and making notches on a stick; at midnight he emerged to see that all was well in byre and stable, that no seemingly dead fire had flared.

When Llandaff emerged she took the candle from him and said:

"Now, listen to me! It is only midnight. I know the canonical hours. But she is *dying*. God will forgive you . . ." The words emerged smoothly from long habit, but remembering her father she thought: When did *he* ever forgive anybody? She hurried on, "Or if not, on me be the blame. I will do penance for the rest of my days, never eat meat, or even fish again, sleep on the floor. But for her, the last Sacrament, even at midnight . . ."

Llandaff looked at this Maria much as the doctor had looked at the other and said, "You may safely leave the decision to me." Once inside Katharine's room, however, being a meticulous man, he felt it his duty to inform her of the hour.

"I thought it was morning," she said. She was now too weak to point or even move her head; but straight in front of her eyes, behind her chaplain's form was the rosy glow on the wall, the first sign of the dawn. She had watched it many times.

"Your Grace, that is only the reflection of the fire," he said gently. She thought: Yes, the fire is mended later now, and burns more clearly; I was deceived.

"Then I will wait."

"I will put forward the hour," he offered.

"No. I can wait." She thought, without self-pity, with a wry, secret amusement: That is the one thing that life has taught me: to wait. Waiting to come to England, waiting for Arthur to grow older, waiting for my future to be decided upon, waiting to be pregnant, waiting to give birth, waiting for the Pope to give verdict. I can *wait*.

"You can pray with me," she said. "And the girls can rest."

They protested; they needed no rest. She gathered energy to

say, with gentle authority, "Do as I say. Leave me with my confessor." Lady Willoughby mended the fire, Maria lighted a fresh candle and they went out together.

They did not go far, only into the little anteroom just beyond the door. It had no hearth and was very chilly. The chest which held Katharine's shabby furs stood along one wall, there was a table, a bench and a stool. It had formerly been kept very neat, the table bearing only Katharine's jug and ewer, soap and towel. Now, as an annexe to the sick room, it seemed cluttered. A pile of fresh linen lay on the top of the chest and the table held the evidence of Maria Willoughby's activities and failures; the bread, not real manchet, but white enough; the bowl of chicken broth, so good that as it cooled it had set into a firm jelly, a syllabub in a stemmed glass, a sage poultice, so hopefully tried but quite ineffective, a jug of wine.

Maria de Moreto saw only the smooth, fresh linen; she thought: There will be no bed-making tomorrow! From some still undepleted source, fresh tears gushed. She set the candle down on the table, so near the edge that it was in danger of tilting over, sat down on the bench and wept. Lady Willoughby moved the candle into safety and looked about at what the table held; one clean wine cup. She tipped the syllabub into the bowl of broth and then poured wine for them both. She pushed the cup nearer to Maria de Moreto's bowed head and said, "Drink that. It will fortify you."

Maria said ungratefully, in a tear-sodden voice, "Drink it yourself!" She wished to be alone in her misery. Still without raising her head she said, "My room is there. Have my bed and be welcome." The offer reeked of hostility—*you* can sleep!

The Countess lifted the syllabub glass and drank deeply. The cream which had been the basis of the syllabub had left traces which affected the flavour, not unpleasantly, Sir Edmund's wine being somewhat harsh.

She said roughly, "You think that I do not know how you feel. I know it all. You wish to die and you imagine that by refusing food, drink and sleep, you will bring death upon yourself. Be assured by me, *it never works that way*. I know. I have buried a husband."

Not worth answering. *She* would, at this moment, choose to remind me that she had a husband. And surely his life must have been so wretched that he was glad to die. In any case, what is it to me, who, when the Queen dies, will have lost everything, even God and the Virgin. Because if God were just, or merciful, He would not allow *her*, so brave, so faithful, to die defeated.

"When my husband died . . ." Lady Willoughby began.

"God in Glory," the other Maria said, "I am well aware that you married and I did not. Is this a time to remind me? What is it to me? Go busy yourself elsewhere!"

"I pined," the Countess said. "I refused to eat or drink. I was determined to die, too. But I did not. One day I half swooned and my daughter, my Catharine, a loving child, still young, poured wine and offered it—to make me better she said . . . I drank it, to please her. And it restored me. For the next two years, whenever misery threatened to take the upper hand, I drank; and I survived. I can therefore commend wine to you. Drink and feel better . . ."

Maria de Moreto did not even look up. Lady Willoughby, somewhat astonished at herself, tried another tack.

"And is Her Grace to go to her burying with only one of the ladies she brought from Spain in attendance?"

Maria de Moreto's head came up. "You mean you will not follow her?"

"I shall. You will not, unless you are able to walk. And you will not be able to walk unless you pull yourself together . . . And there is another thing that we should speak of, but I will not, until you have calmed yourself . . . and drunk your wine."

Maria de Moreto lifted the cup and in a defiant gesture, drained it. Wine might have comforted the frivolous, heartless Maria de Salinas against the loss of a mere husband; it would not comfort Maria de Moreto against the loss of the Queen who had been everything, husband, child, friend. . . . I will show her, she thought, how false and hollow her refuge from grief was.

But it was a long time since she had tasted wine; she had not eaten properly, or slept. She drained the cup, set it down, and waited for a sensation she had never known before to subside. When it did not she thought angrily: So much for her remedies! I feel worse rather than better. She was, however, no longer crying.

"What was this other thing?" She asked.

"I wondered whether you had considered what is to become of you, after . . ."

Trust her, always the tactless one, to mention such a matter at such a moment.

"I have brothers and sisters in Spain."

"And you wish to go to them?" the Countess asked relentlessly.

As a penniless dependent? An aging spinster aunt, grand aunt to children she had never seen? She saw in clearest detail what her life would be; endlessly put upon, earning her keep by helping with the very young, the very old, the sick, acting as a buffer between the servants and those they served, and despite all these services, regarded as an object of charity. A prospect to appal. Yet, but for the curious almost lightheaded feeling induced by the wine, her pride was such that she would have said, Yes, and they will be happy to have me! As it was she said:

"No. I have lived in England so long, my family seem strangers to me now." She thought: And what am I about, talking of myself and my future when she, who has been my family all these years lies dying? And what am I about, opening my heart to *her*? She made a sound, half-sob, half-hiccup. "But there is no reason for you to be concerned for me. I shall manage."

The Countess was also a managing woman. Life had treated them differently, but they were made of the same stuff. Their enmity was rooted in their similarity.

The syllabub glass had been emptied four times, but Lady Willoughby was accustomed to better wine than this and knew what she was doing.

"You could come home with me," she said.

"You are *inviting* me?"

"So I thought," the Countess said dryly. She knew she was doing a crazy thing: high and wide as her house was there would not be room enough for them both under one roof; they would provoke one another twenty times a day. Even had they been amiably disposed to one another the situation, with one dispensing, the other accepting charity, would be fraught with difficulties. But she was a woman who, once having conceived an idea, did not easily relinquish it. "With my daughter married," she said, "I am often lonely; and shall be more so as the years mount." I am making, she told herself, a fine rod for my own back; when we quarrel, as we must, she will turn upon me and say: You begged me to come.

Maria de Moreto looked across the cluttered table and saw this old enemy as altogether more vulnerable than a sister or sister-in-law forced to be charitable. *Lonely*. Maria de Salinas, disarming herself in a single word. When the day came, as come it must, and the battle between them was resumed, she could always say: You begged me to come to you; you said you were lonely!

She said, rather cautiously, "If you wish my company . . ."

"I do," the Countess said recklessly. "And I think it would please *her* to know . . ." now, mind your tongue, Maria de Salinas! Put it prettily. ". . . that we were company and comfort to one another."

Maria de Moreto, momentarily lost to God, had grace enough left to think: In her place I should not have put it so well; nor would I have admitted to loneliness. Under all the bustle and bluster, she is gentler than I! But even as she thought it the other Maria wiped that impression away. She said, "Francisco Filipez, I can find a place for him. The doctor's manner I dislike—and to take as chaplain one known to be of the old opinion would be unwise. The village priest, who has his ear to the ground, serves me well enough. And the maids are slovens."

Slovens! Under *my* supervision! It would not be seemly to wrangle here, on the threshold of the death chamber, but across the table two pairs of eyes threw their challenge. You accuse me of allowing slovenliness? Slovens I said, and slovens I mean. There and then began the wrangling which was to continue until one of them died. And both lived to be old, for friction produced its own energy and interest; and when one ailed, the other nursed her assiduously, eager to prove her own superiority.

Dawn came at last, with no rosy glow upon the wall, a slow, sullen lifting of darkness as another January day broke. Llandaff administered the Sacrament for the last time. "This is My body . . ." Lutherans might deny the miracle of transsubstantiation, but for those who believed the words had the validity of their first utterance.

Then on her eyes, the touch of the blessed oil. "By this holy anointing and with His most loving mercy, may the Lord forgive you whatever wrong you have done by the use of your sight. Amen." Ears, nose, mouth, hands and feet. And even as the solemn ritual was performed, she drifted again into the past, not this time with the dead, but with Henry; she had loved him lawfully, but perhaps overmuch. Her hands had been so eager to caress him, her feet had danced to his measure; her nose had been greedy for the smell of him—leather, clean linen, horseflesh, the sweat of desire, the scent of love's culmination; her ears had been attuned to every tone of his voice and her mouth, under his kisses forgetful even of God. As for her eyes . . . Llandaff moved on to the Viaticum: "May the angels lead thee to Paradise. At thy coming may the martyrs receive thee." She lay so supine that she seemed already dead, but still clenched in a body, fifty years old, wasted with disease, and knew that of all the wonders that Heaven might offer what she most desired was the sight of Henry, young and eager, coming towards her under the green leaves at Greenwich. For a moment it seemed to be so and the people who stood by the bed considered the transfiguration of her face as a sign of her passing. But even for death she must wait; held back by a troubling sense of something left undone, unsaid. It took some time to find and longer still for her to muster strength for the words.

"Maria . . . de Salinas."

"I am here, Your Grace."

"Care for them all."

"I will. I will. I promise."

"All," Katharine said, and although her voice was too weak to be insistent, the Countess understood.

"She shall be as my sister. I have her hand in mine now."

She reached out and took the hand of the other Maria in case, as sometimes happened, the dying eyes should open for a last look upon the world. It was a wasted gesture. Katharine's eyes remained closed as she thought: All done now. I can go.

As she plunged into the abyss she had such a feeling of liberation that the fall was no more than a bird's swooping flight; a seagull's flashing curve, over Dover, Tilbury, Corunna . . .